THE AVENGERS

WRITER
BRIAN MICHAEL BENDIS
PENCILER
WALTER SIMONSON
INKER
SCOTT HANNA
COLORIST
JASON KEITH
COVER ART
DANIEL ACUÑA (#25),
WALTER SIMONSON & PAUL MOUNTS (#26-28),
MIKE DEODATO & RAIN BEREDO (#29)
AND **LEINIL FRANCIS YU & SUNNY GHO** (#30)
LETTERER
VC'S CORY PETIT
ASSOCIATE EDITOR
LAUREN SANKOVITCH
EDITOR
TOM BREVOORT

Collection Editor: JENNIFER GRÜNWALD • Assistant Editors: ALEX STARBUCK & NELSON RIBEIRO
Editor, Special Projects: MARK D. BEAZLEY • Senior Editor, Special Projects: JEFF YOUNGQUIST
Senior Vice President of Sales: DAVID GABRIEL • SVP of Brand Planning & Communications: MICHAEL PASCIULLO

Editor in Chief: AXEL ALONSO • Chief Creative Officer: JOE QUESADA • Publisher: DAN BUCKLEY • Executive Producer: ALAN FINE

AVENGERS BY BRIAN MICHAEL BENDIS VOL. 4. Contains material originally published in magazine form as AVENGERS #25-30. First printing 2012. Hardcover ISBN# 978-0-7851-6079-3. Softcover ISBN# 978-0-7851-
. Published by MARVEL WORLDWIDE, INC., a subsidiary of MARVEL ENTERTAINMENT, LLC. OFFICE OF PUBLICATION: 135 West 50th Street, New York, NY 10020. Copyright © 2012 and 2013 Marvel Characters, Inc.
ts reserved. Hardcover: $24.99 per copy in the U.S. and $27.99 in Canada (GST #R127032852). Softcover: $19.99 per copy in the U.S. and $21.99 in Canada (GST #R127032852). Canadian Agreement #40668537.
acters featured in this issue and the distinctive names and likenesses thereof, and all related indicia are trademarks of Marvel Characters, Inc. No similarity between any of the names, characters, persons, and/or
ons in this magazine with those of any living or dead person or institution is intended, and any such similarity which may exist is purely coincidental. Printed in the U.S.A. ALAN FINE, EVP - Office of the President, Marvel
ide, Inc. and EVP & CMO Marvel Characters B.V.; DAN BUCKLEY, Publisher & President - Print, Animation & Digital Divisions; JOE QUESADA, Chief Creative Officer; TOM BREVOORT, SVP of Publishing; DAVID BOGART, SVP
ations & Procurement, Publishing; RUWAN JAYATILLEKE, SVP & Associate Publisher, Publishing; C.B. CEBULSKI, SVP of Creator & Content Development; DAVID GABRIEL, SVP of Publishing Sales & Circulation; MICHAEL
LLO, SVP of Brand Planning & Communications; JIM O'KEEFE, VP of Operations & Logistics; DAN CARR, Executive Director of Publishing Technology; SUSAN CRESPI, Editorial Operations Manager; ALEX MORALES;
ing Operations Manager; STAN LEE, Chairman Emeritus. For information regarding advertising in Marvel Comics or on Marvel.com, please contact Niza Disla, Director of Marvel Partnerships, at ndisla@marvel.com.
vel subscription inquiries, please call 800-217-9158. Manufactured between 10/22/2012 and 12/3/2012 (hardcover), and 10/22/2012 and 6/3/2013 (softcover), by R.R. DONNELLEY, INC., SALEM, VA, USA.

7 6 5 4 3 2 1

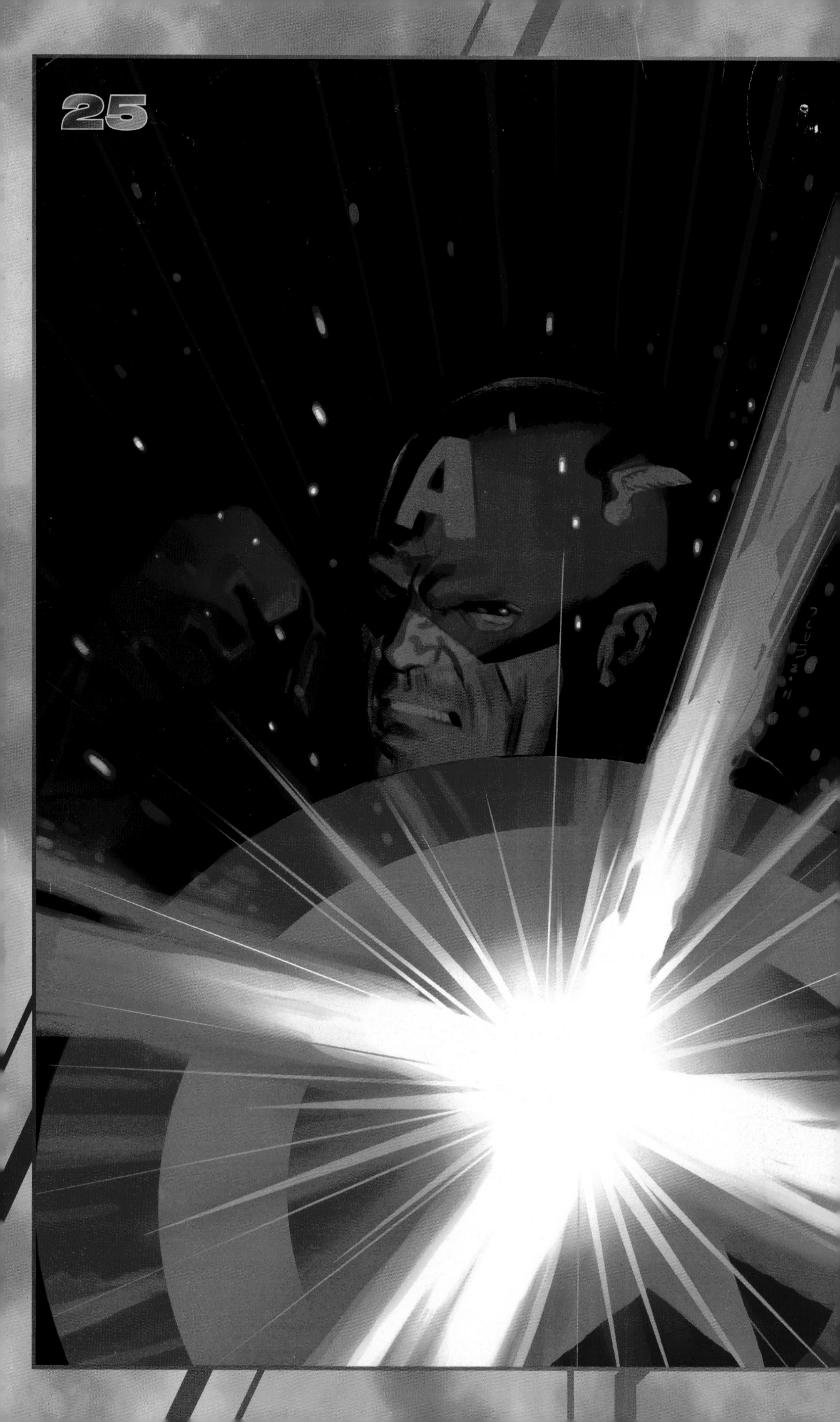
25

EARTH'S
MIGHTIEST
HEROES, UNITED
GAINST A COMMON
THREAT! ON THAT
AY THE AVENGERS
RE BORN, TO FIGHT
ES THAT NO SINGLE
HERO COULD
WITHSTAND!

THE AVENGERS

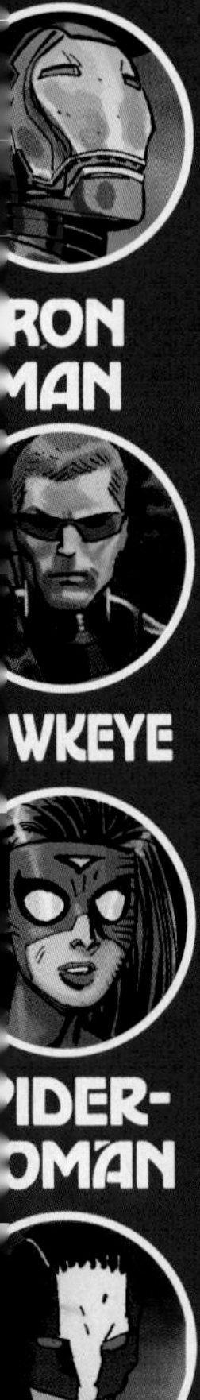

RON
MAN

WKEYE

PIDER-
OMAN

THE
OTECTOR

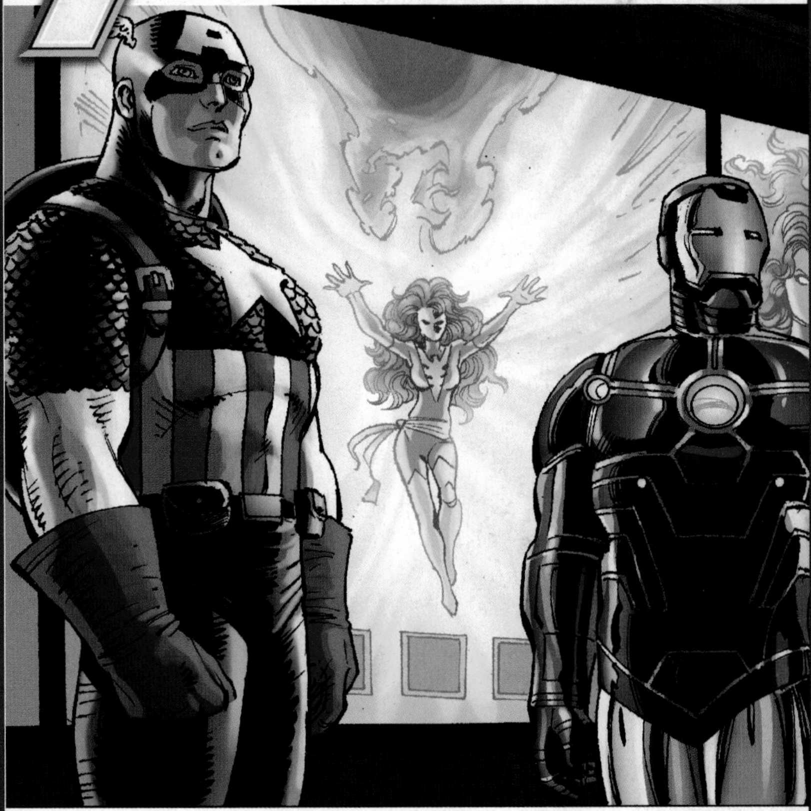

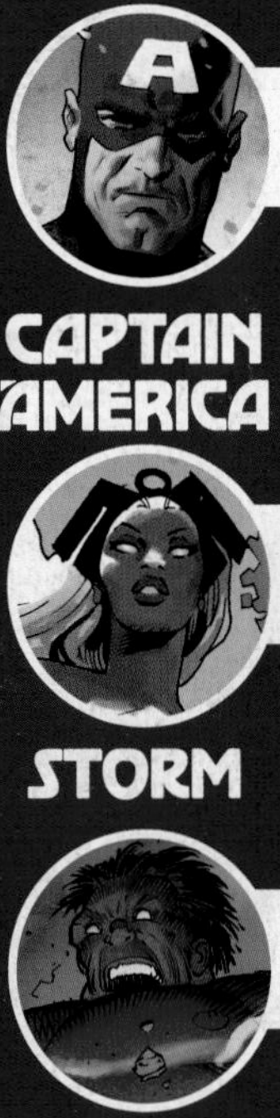

CAPTAIN
AMERICA

STORM

THE RED
HULK

PREVIOUSLY IN AVENGERS:
THE AVENGERS HAVE BEEN HARD AT WORK SAVING THE WORLD. BUT THE PUBLIC IS NOT HAPPY. ALL THEY SEE IS ONE CHAOTIC NEAR DISASTER AFTER ANOTHER.

CAPTAIN AMERICA IS THE HEAD OF THE AVENGERS AND MANY IN THE MEDIA BLAME HIM FOR THE STATE OF THINGS.

PREVIOUSLY IN AVENGERS VS X-MEN:
THE PHOENIX FORCE IS HEADED TOWARDS EARTH. THE AVENGERS BELIEVE THAT IT IS A DESTRUCTIVE FORCE THAT WILL LAY WASTE TO THE EARTH WHILE THE X-MEN BELIEVE IT TO BE A FORCE OF REBIRTH THAT COULD REIGNITE THE MUTANT RACE.

THE AVENGERS AND THE X-MEN BOTH BELIEVE IT WILL USE YOUNG MUTANT HOPE SUMMERS AS ITS AVATAR.

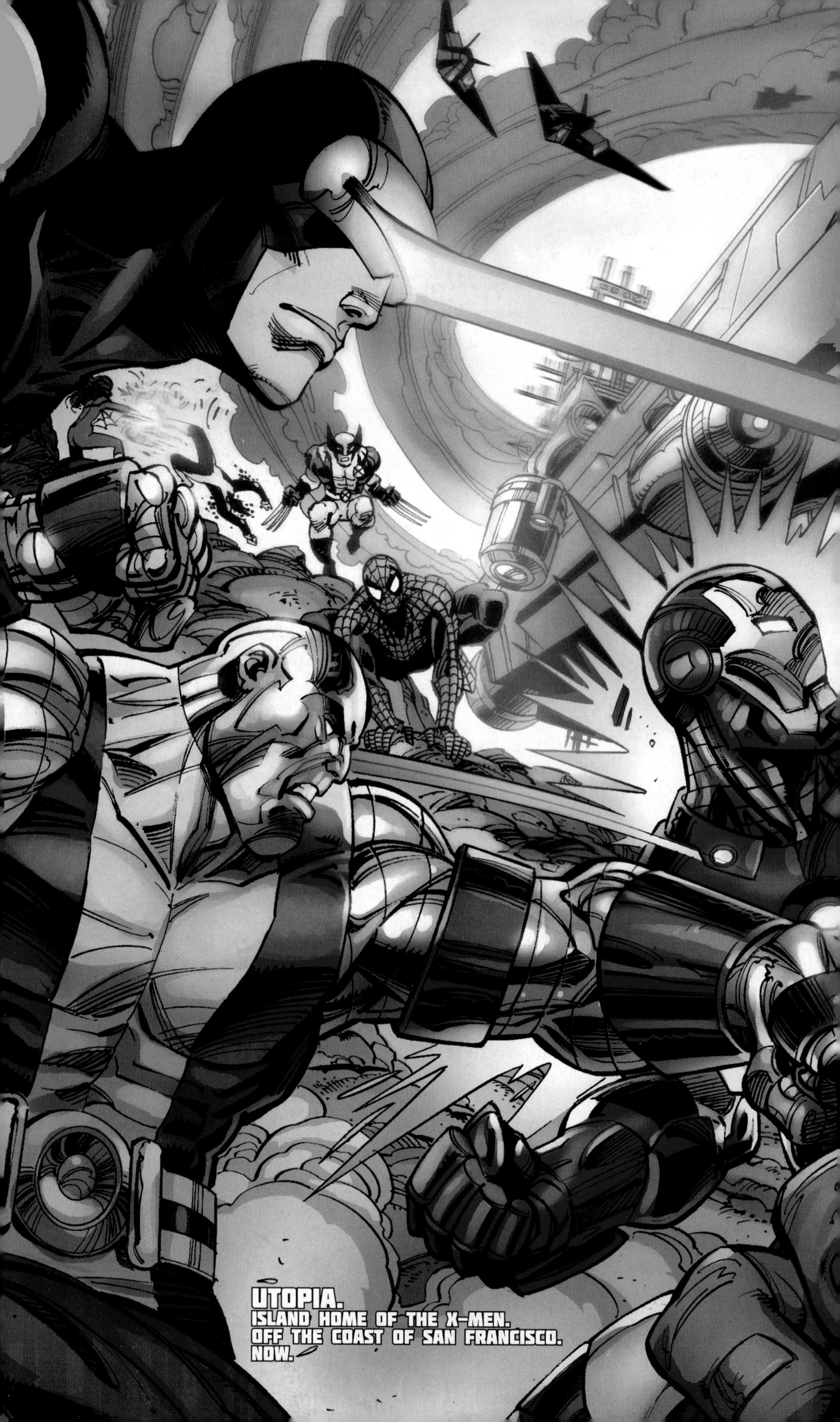
UTOPIA.
ISLAND HOME OF THE X-MEN.
OFF THE COAST OF SAN FRANCISCO.
NOW.

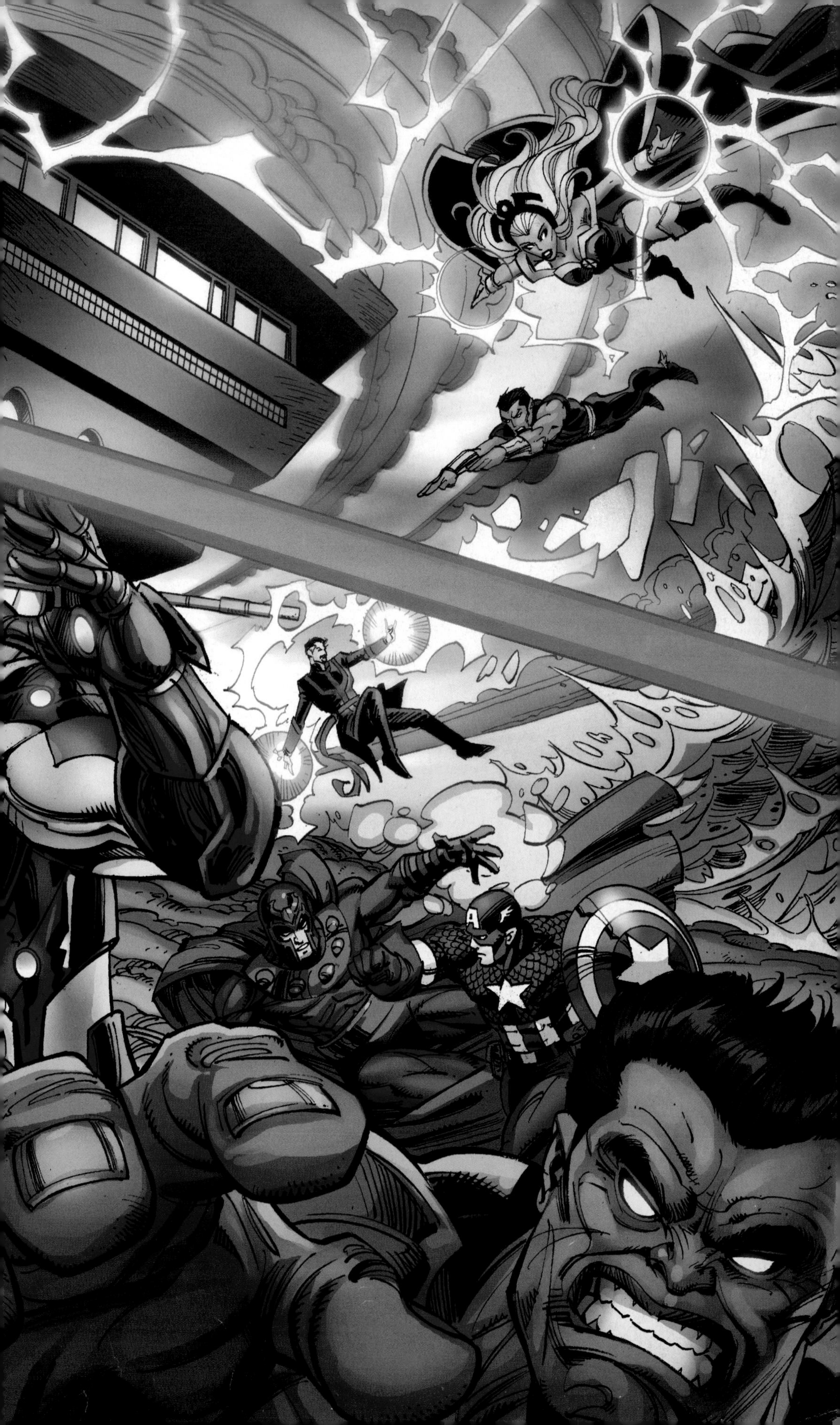

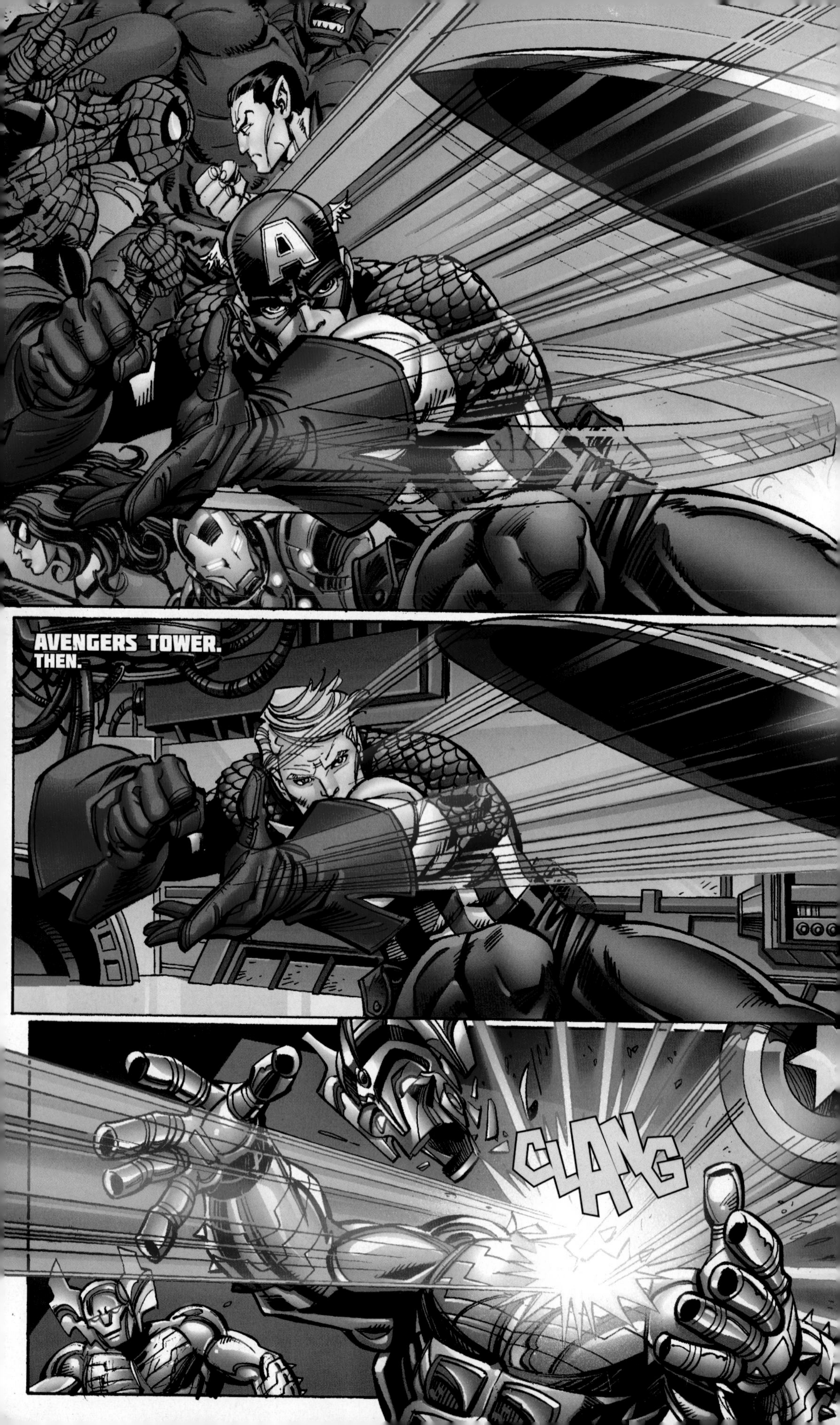
AVENGERS TOWER.
THEN.
CLANG

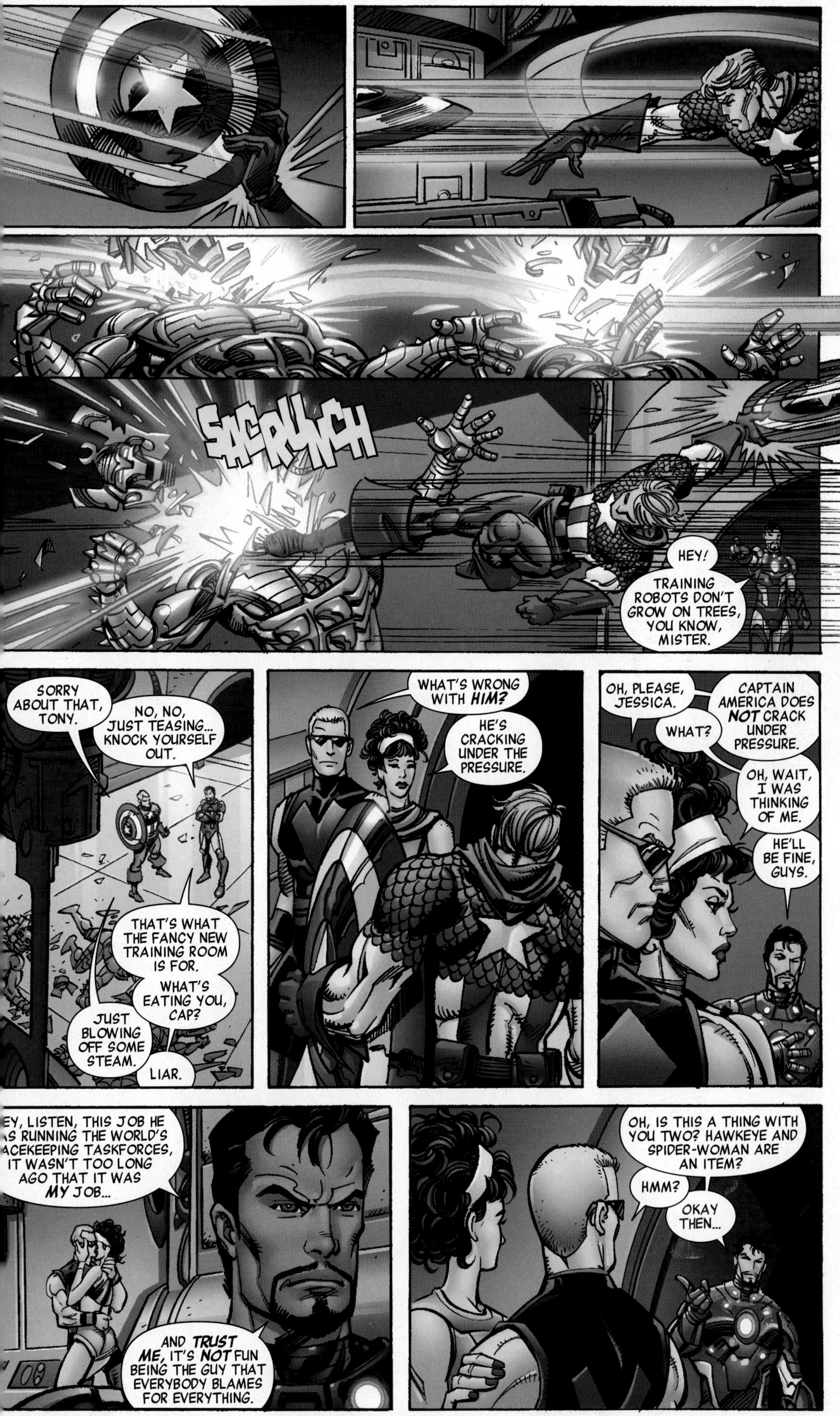

SKRUNCH
HEY!
TRAINING ROBOTS DON'T GROW ON TREES, YOU KNOW, MISTER.
SORRY ABOUT THAT, TONY.
NO, NO, JUST TEASING... KNOCK YOURSELF OUT.
THAT'S WHAT THE FANCY NEW TRAINING ROOM IS FOR.
WHAT'S EATING YOU, CAP?
JUST BLOWING OFF SOME STEAM.
LIAR.
WHAT'S WRONG WITH HIM?
HE'S CRACKING UNDER THE PRESSURE.
OH, PLEASE, JESSICA.
CAPTAIN AMERICA DOES NOT CRACK UNDER PRESSURE.
WHAT?
OH, WAIT, I WAS THINKING OF ME.
HE'LL BE FINE, GUYS.
EY, LISTEN, THIS JOB HE AS RUNNING THE WORLD'S ACEKEEPING TASKFORCES, IT WASN'T TOO LONG AGO THAT IT WAS MY JOB...
AND TRUST ME, IT'S NOT FUN BEING THE GUY THAT EVERYBODY BLAMES FOR EVERYTHING.
OH, IS THIS A THING WITH YOU TWO? HAWKEYE AND SPIDER-WOMAN ARE AN ITEM?
HMM?
OKAY THEN...

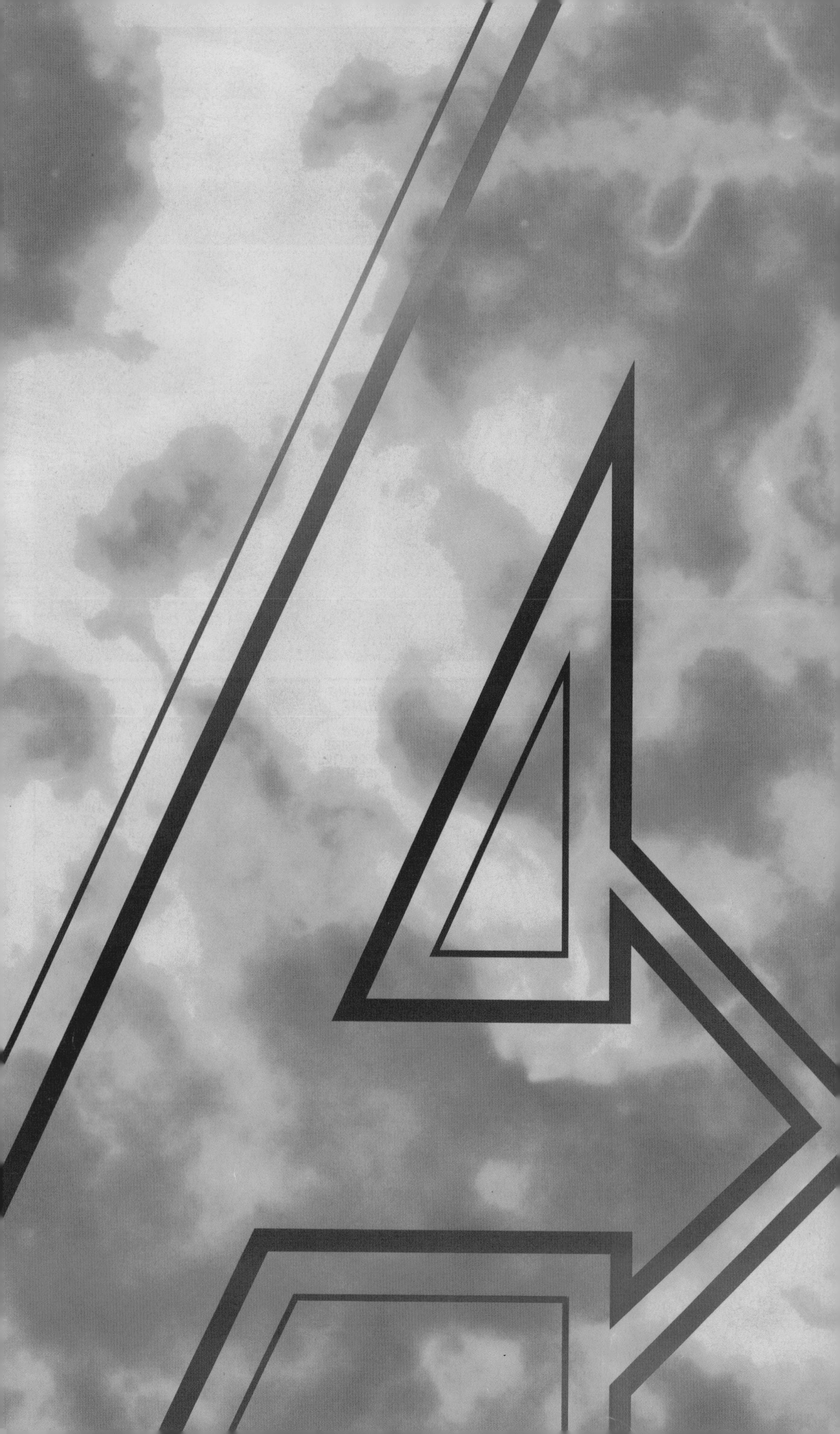

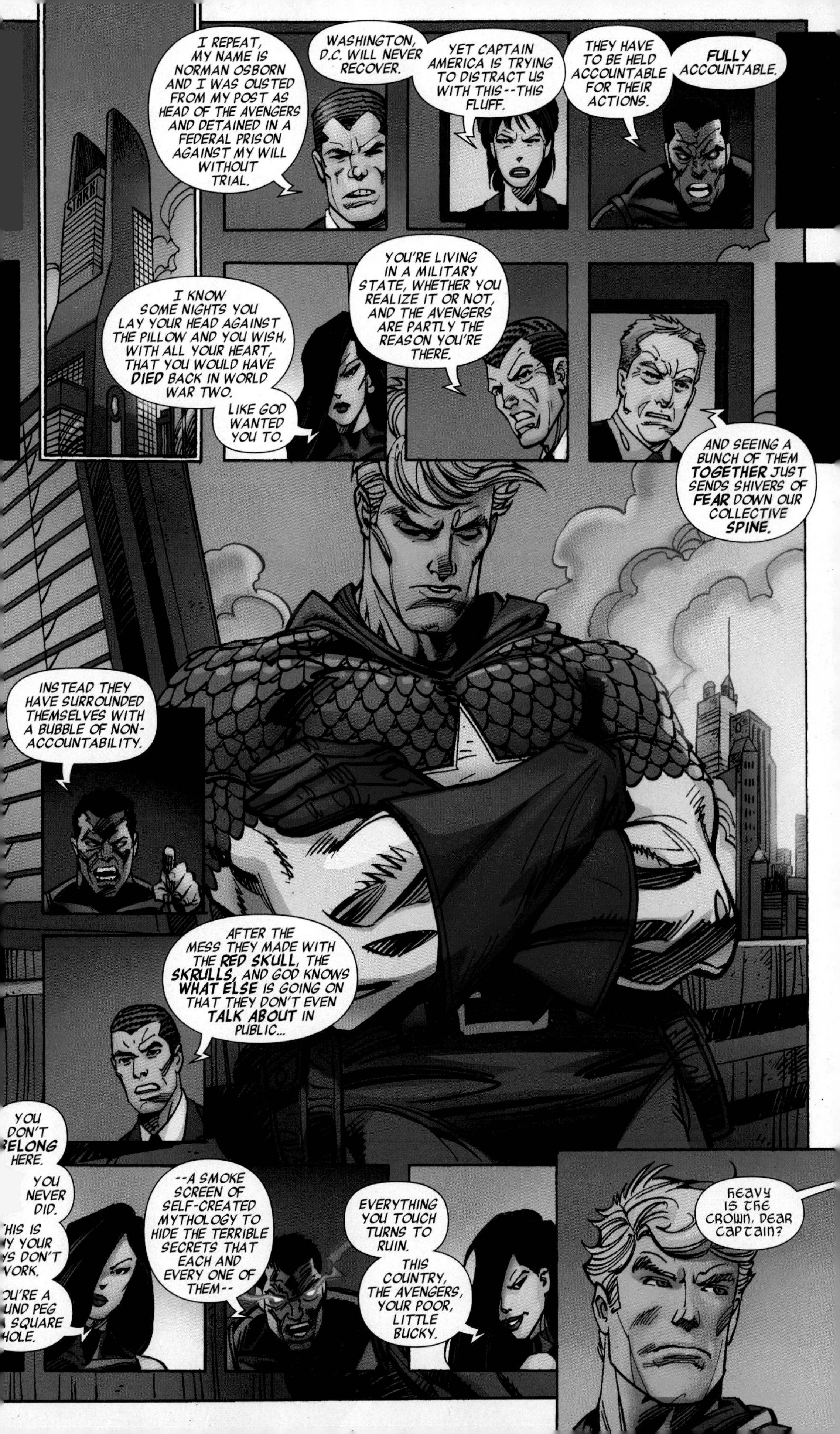
I REPEAT, MY NAME IS NORMAN OSBORN AND I WAS OUSTED FROM MY POST AS HEAD OF THE AVENGERS AND DETAINED IN A FEDERAL PRISON AGAINST MY WILL WITHOUT TRIAL.
WASHINGTON, D.C. WILL NEVER RECOVER.
YET CAPTAIN AMERICA IS TRYING TO DISTRACT US WITH THIS--THIS FLUFF.
THEY HAVE TO BE HELD ACCOUNTABLE FOR THEIR ACTIONS.
FULLY ACCOUNTABLE.
I KNOW SOME NIGHTS YOU LAY YOUR HEAD AGAINST THE PILLOW AND YOU WISH, WITH ALL YOUR HEART, THAT YOU WOULD HAVE DIED BACK IN WORLD WAR TWO.
LIKE GOD WANTED YOU TO.
YOU'RE LIVING IN A MILITARY STATE, WHETHER YOU REALIZE IT OR NOT, AND THE AVENGERS ARE PARTLY THE REASON YOU'RE THERE.
AND SEEING A BUNCH OF THEM TOGETHER JUST SENDS SHIVERS OF FEAR DOWN OUR COLLECTIVE SPINE.
INSTEAD THEY HAVE SURROUNDED THEMSELVES WITH A BUBBLE OF NON-ACCOUNTABILITY.
AFTER THE MESS THEY MADE WITH THE RED SKULL, THE SKRULLS, AND GOD KNOWS WHAT ELSE IS GOING ON THAT THEY DON'T EVEN TALK ABOUT IN PUBLIC...
YOU DON'T BELONG HERE.
YOU NEVER DID.
--A SMOKE SCREEN OF SELF-CREATED MYTHOLOGY TO HIDE THE TERRIBLE SECRETS THAT EACH AND EVERY ONE OF THEM--
EVERYTHING YOU TOUCH TURNS TO RUIN.
THIS COUNTRY, THE AVENGERS, YOUR POOR, LITTLE BUCKY.
HEAVY IS THE CROWN, DEAR CAPTAIN?

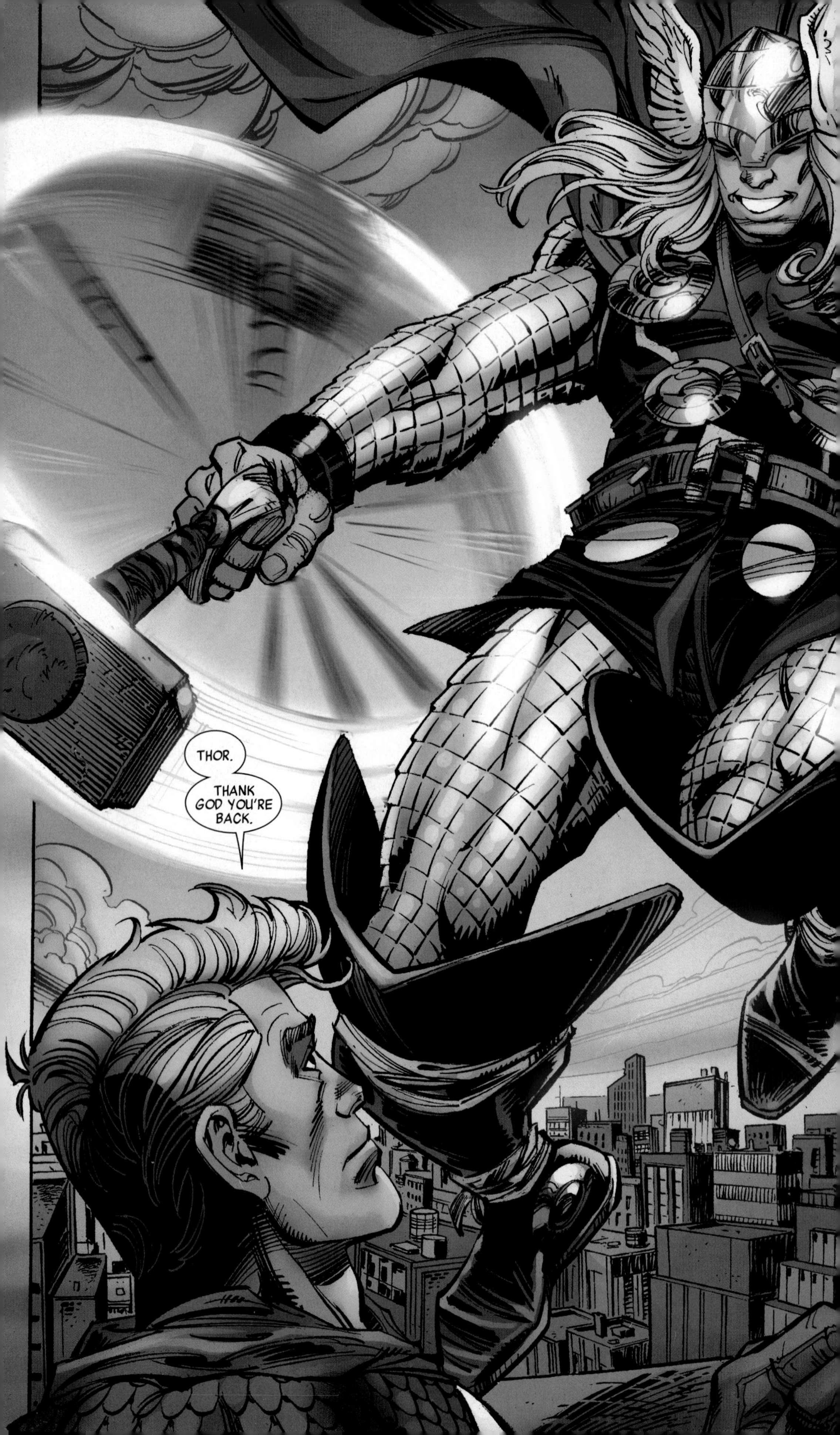
THOR.
THANK GOD YOU'RE BACK.

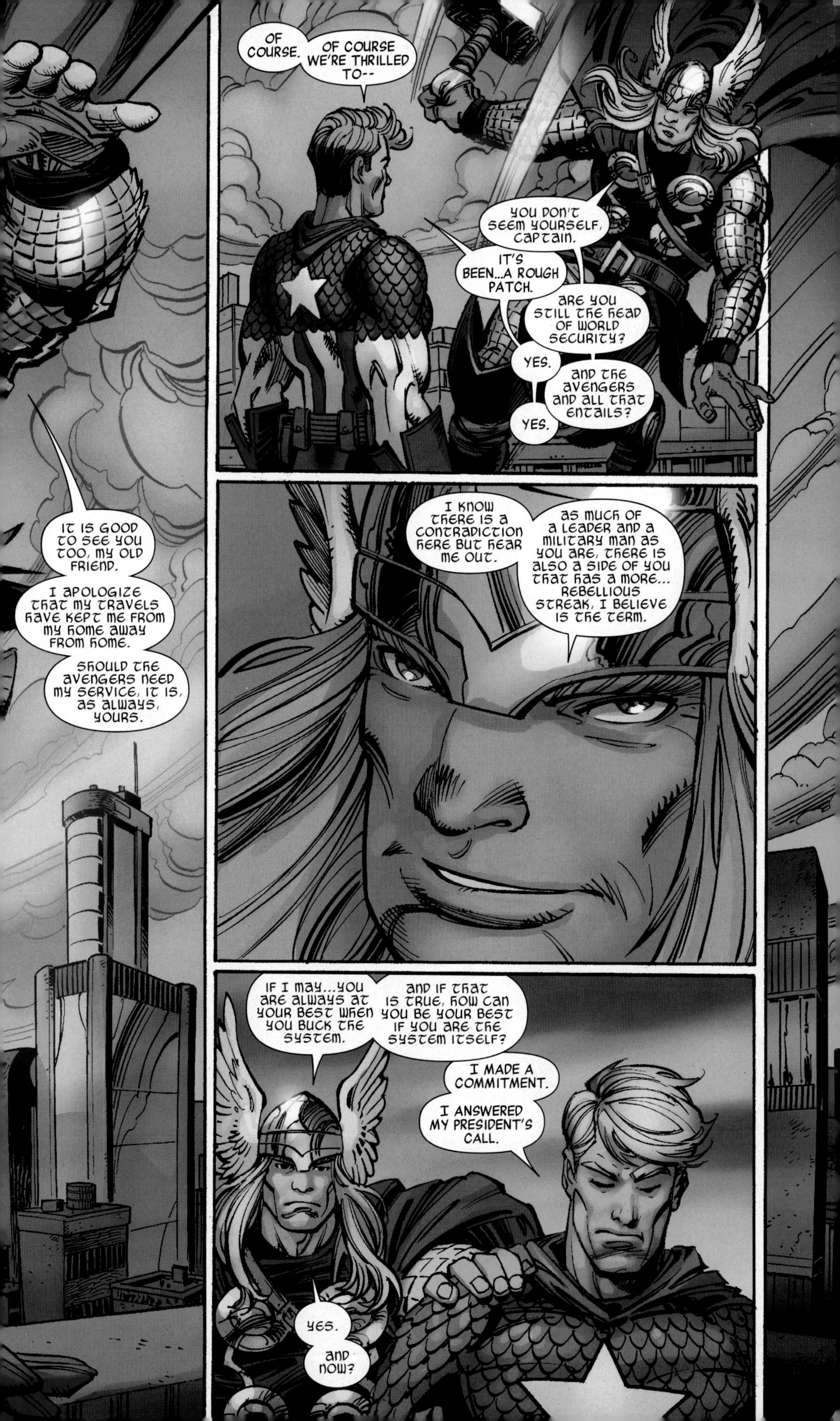
OF COURSE.
OF COURSE WE'RE THRILLED TO--
YOU DON'T SEEM YOURSELF, CAPTAIN.
IT'S BEEN...A ROUGH PATCH.
ARE YOU STILL THE HEAD OF WORLD SECURITY?
YES.
AND THE AVENGERS AND ALL THAT ENTAILS?
YES.
IT IS GOOD TO SEE YOU TOO, MY OLD FRIEND.
I APOLOGIZE THAT MY TRAVELS HAVE KEPT ME FROM MY HOME AWAY FROM HOME.
SHOULD THE AVENGERS NEED MY SERVICE, IT IS, AS ALWAYS, YOURS.
I KNOW THERE IS A CONTRADICTION HERE BUT HEAR ME OUT.
AS MUCH OF A LEADER AND A MILITARY MAN AS YOU ARE, THERE IS ALSO A SIDE OF YOU THAT HAS A MORE... REBELLIOUS STREAK, I BELIEVE IS THE TERM.
IF I MAY...YOU ARE ALWAYS AT YOUR BEST WHEN YOU BUCK THE SYSTEM.
AND IF THAT IS TRUE, HOW CAN YOU BE YOUR BEST IF YOU ARE THE SYSTEM ITSELF?
I MADE A COMMITMENT.
I ANSWERED MY PRESIDENT'S CALL.
YES.
AND NOW?

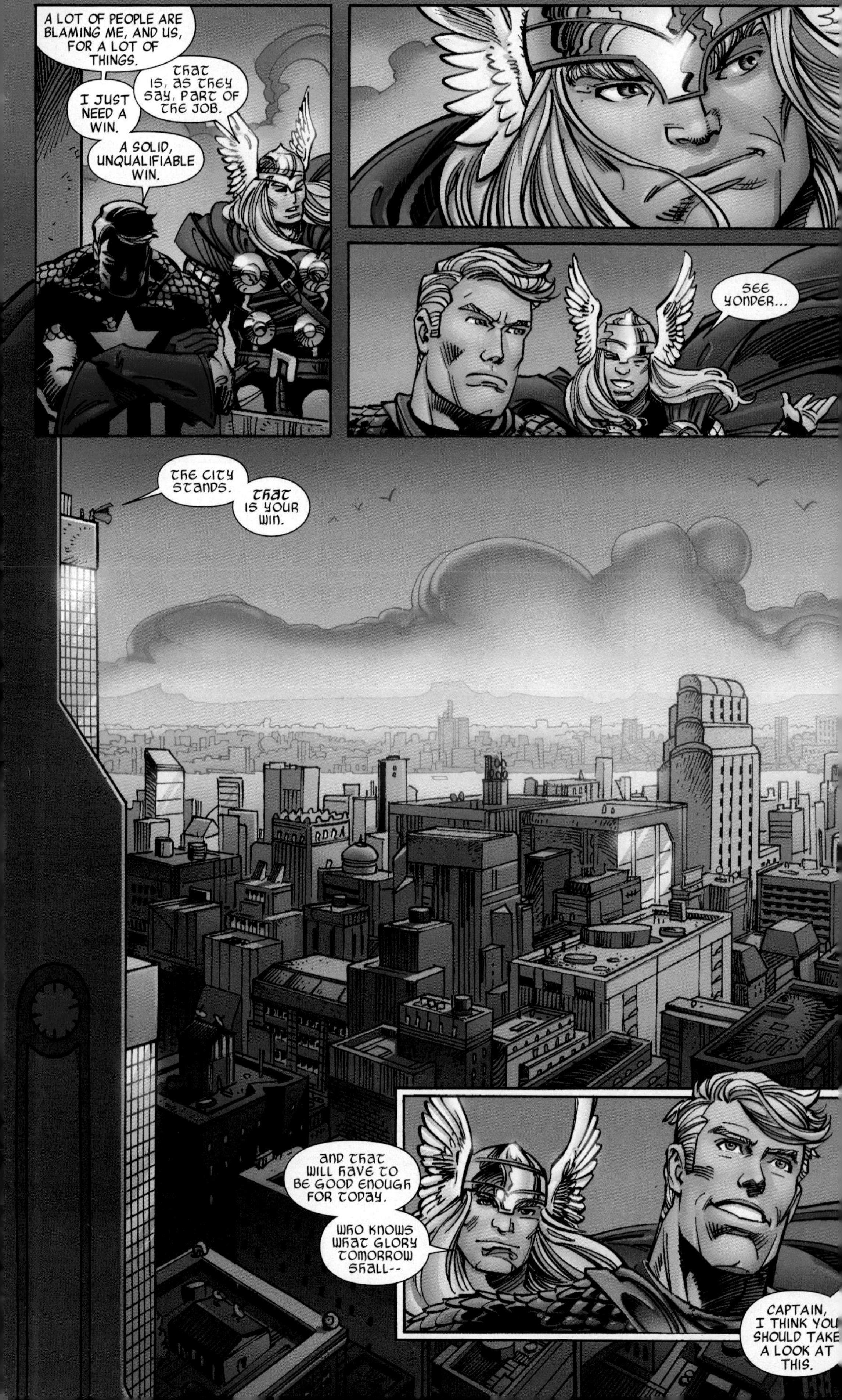
A LOT OF PEOPLE ARE BLAMING ME, AND US, FOR A LOT OF THINGS.
I JUST NEED A WIN.
A SOLID, UNQUALIFIABLE WIN.
THAT IS, AS THEY SAY, PART OF THE JOB.
SEE YONDER...
THE CITY STANDS.
THAT IS YOUR WIN.
AND THAT WILL HAVE TO BE GOOD ENOUGH FOR TODAY.
WHO KNOWS WHAT GLORY TOMORROW SHALL--
CAPTAIN, I THINK YOU SHOULD TAKE A LOOK AT THIS.

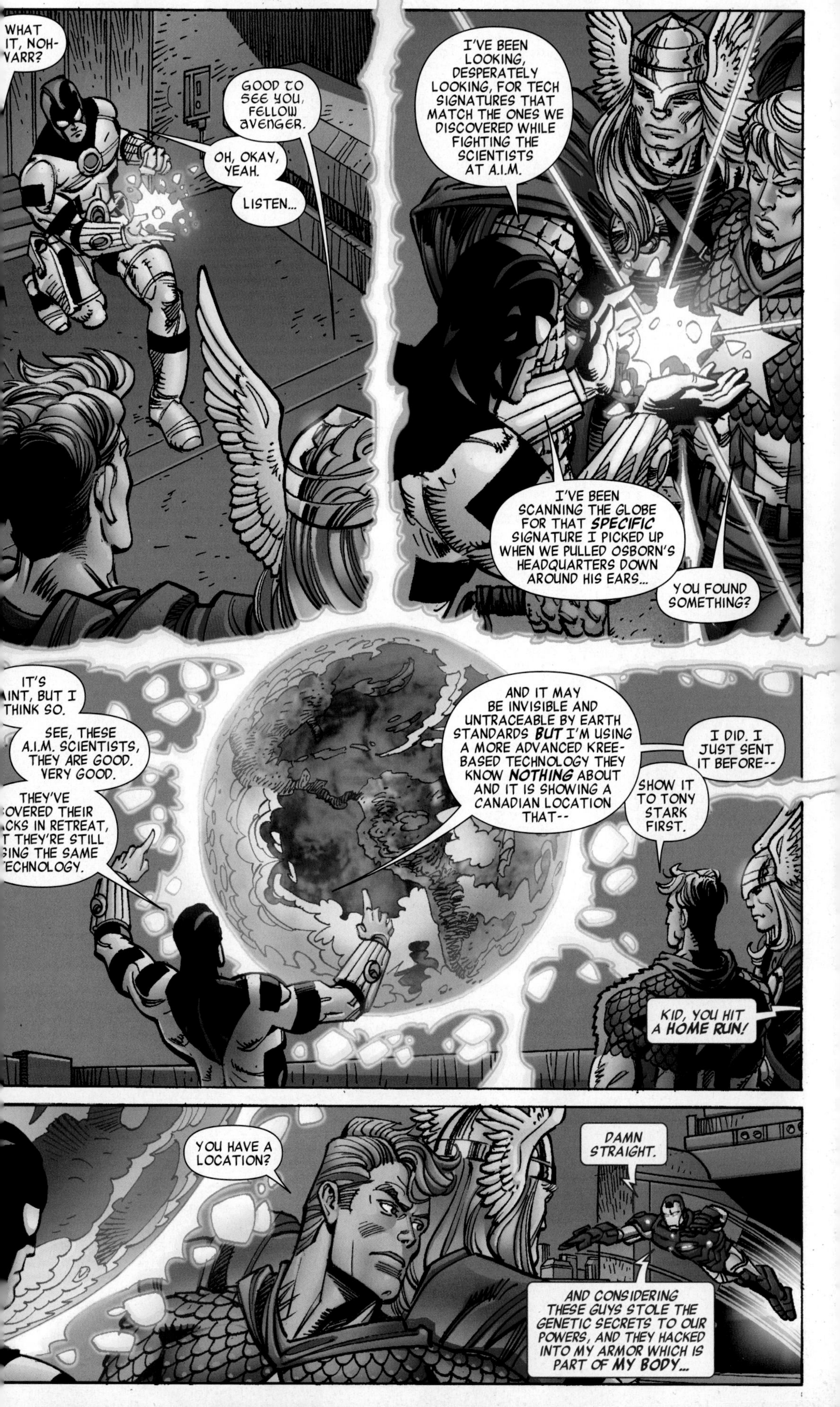
WHAT IT, NOH-VARR?
GOOD TO SEE YOU, FELLOW AVENGER.
OH, OKAY, YEAH.
LISTEN...
I'VE BEEN LOOKING, DESPERATELY LOOKING, FOR TECH SIGNATURES THAT MATCH THE ONES WE DISCOVERED WHILE FIGHTING THE SCIENTISTS AT A.I.M.
I'VE BEEN SCANNING THE GLOBE FOR THAT SPECIFIC SIGNATURE I PICKED UP WHEN WE PULLED OSBORN'S HEADQUARTERS DOWN AROUND HIS EARS...
YOU FOUND SOMETHING?
IT'S AINT, BUT I THINK SO.
SEE, THESE A.I.M. SCIENTISTS, THEY ARE GOOD. VERY GOOD.
THEY'VE OVERED THEIR CKS IN RETREAT, T THEY'RE STILL ING THE SAME TECHNOLOGY.
AND IT MAY BE INVISIBLE AND UNTRACEABLE BY EARTH STANDARDS BUT I'M USING A MORE ADVANCED KREE-BASED TECHNOLOGY THEY KNOW NOTHING ABOUT AND IT IS SHOWING A CANADIAN LOCATION THAT--
I DID. I JUST SENT IT BEFORE--
SHOW IT TO TONY STARK FIRST.
KID, YOU HIT A HOME RUN!
YOU HAVE A LOCATION?
DAMN STRAIGHT.
AND CONSIDERING THESE GUYS STOLE THE GENETIC SECRETS TO OUR POWERS, AND THEY HACKED INTO MY ARMOR WHICH IS PART OF MY BODY...

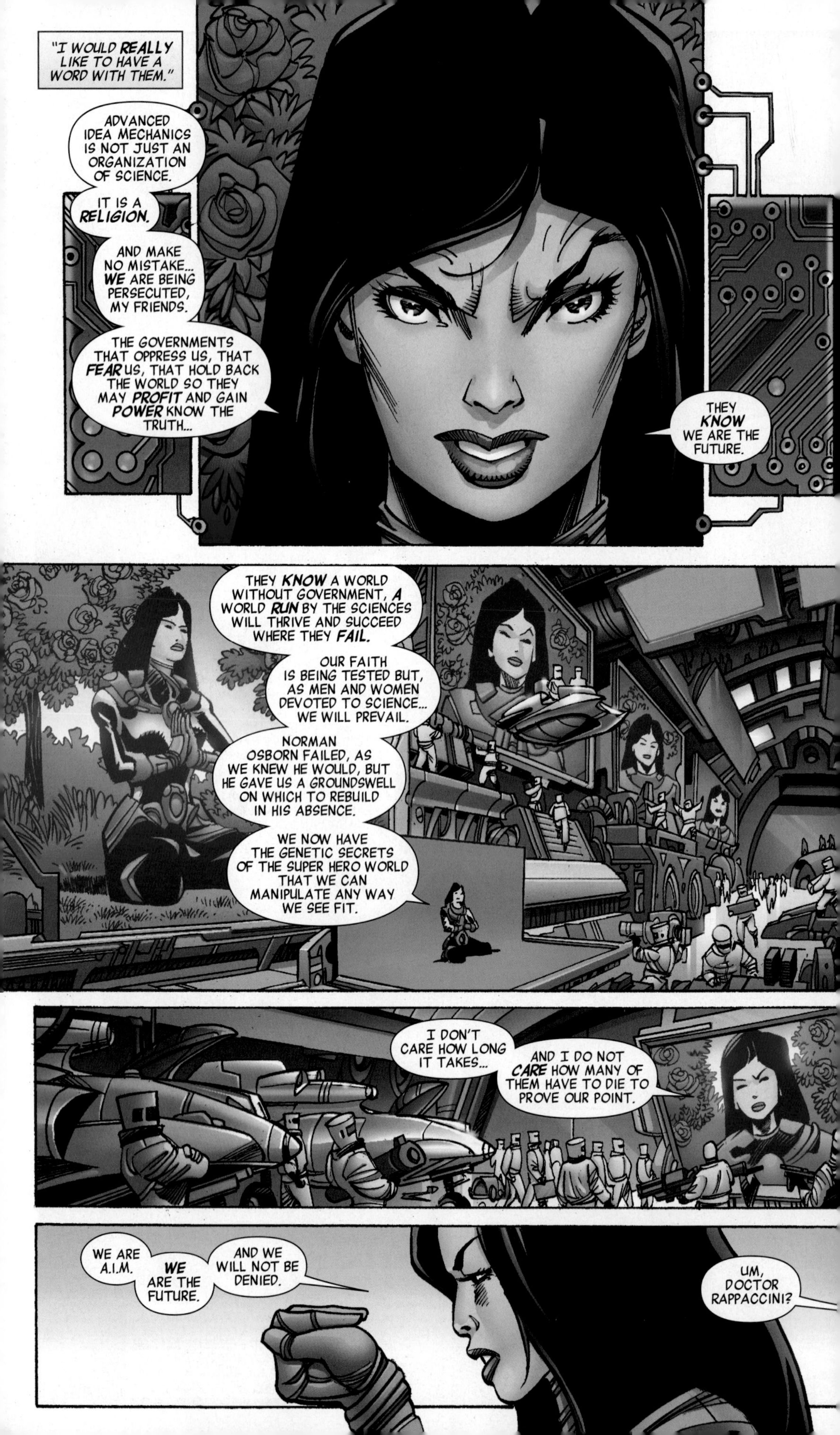
"I WOULD REALLY LIKE TO HAVE A WORD WITH THEM."
ADVANCED IDEA MECHANICS IS NOT JUST AN ORGANIZATION OF SCIENCE.
IT IS A RELIGION.
AND MAKE NO MISTAKE... WE ARE BEING PERSECUTED, MY FRIENDS.
THE GOVERNMENTS THAT OPPRESS US, THAT FEAR US, THAT HOLD BACK THE WORLD SO THEY MAY PROFIT AND GAIN POWER KNOW THE TRUTH...
THEY KNOW WE ARE THE FUTURE.
THEY KNOW A WORLD WITHOUT GOVERNMENT, A WORLD RUN BY THE SCIENCES WILL THRIVE AND SUCCEED WHERE THEY FAIL.
OUR FAITH IS BEING TESTED BUT, AS MEN AND WOMEN DEVOTED TO SCIENCE... WE WILL PREVAIL.
NORMAN OSBORN FAILED, AS WE KNEW HE WOULD, BUT HE GAVE US A GROUNDSWELL ON WHICH TO REBUILD IN HIS ABSENCE.
WE NOW HAVE THE GENETIC SECRETS OF THE SUPER HERO WORLD THAT WE CAN MANIPULATE ANY WAY WE SEE FIT.
I DON'T CARE HOW LONG IT TAKES...
AND I DO NOT CARE HOW MANY OF THEM HAVE TO DIE TO PROVE OUR POINT.
WE ARE A.I.M.
WE ARE THE FUTURE.
AND WE WILL NOT BE DENIED.
UM, DOCTOR RAPPACCINI?

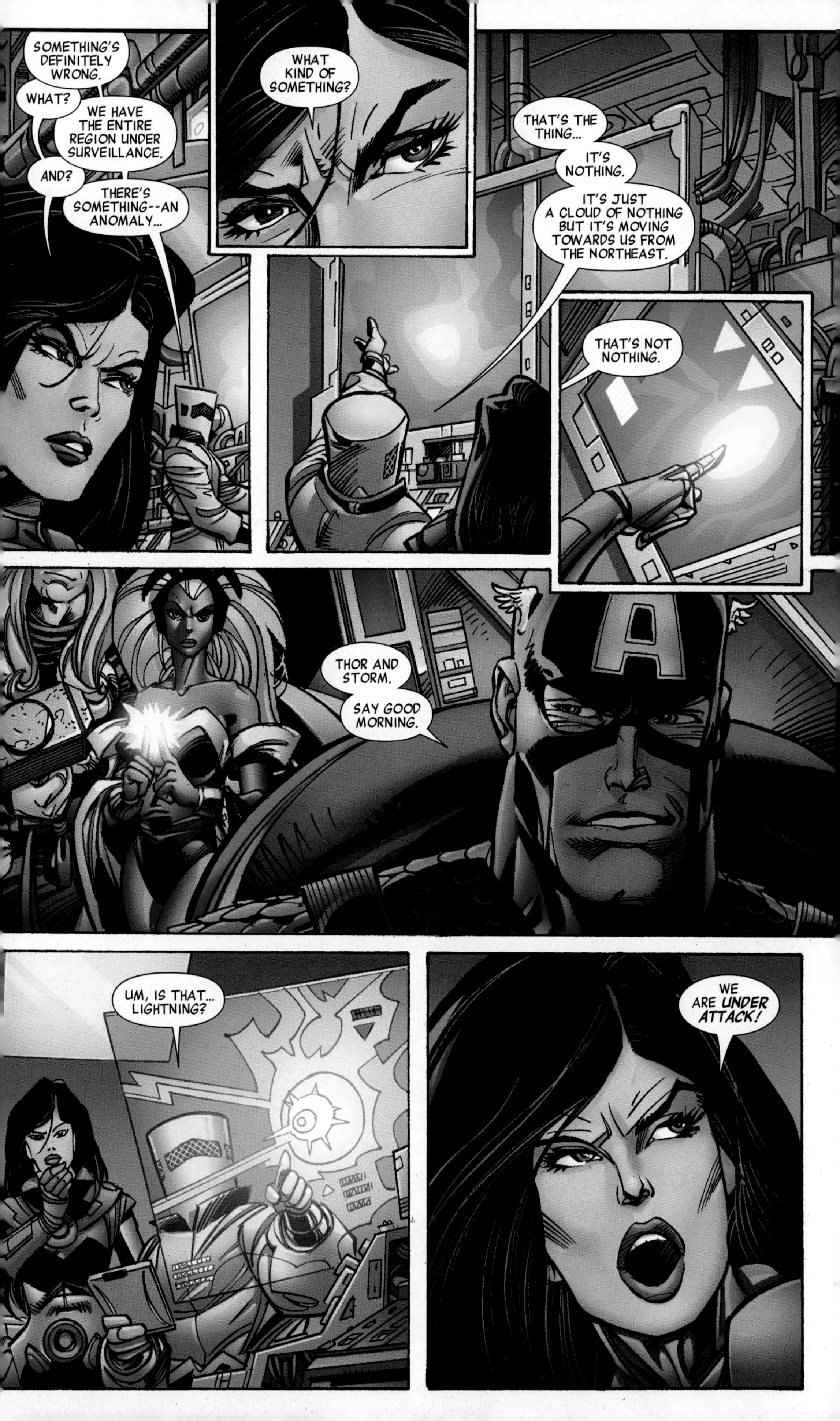
SOMETHING'S DEFINITELY WRONG.
WHAT?
WE HAVE THE ENTIRE REGION UNDER SURVEILLANCE.
AND?
THERE'S SOMETHING--AN ANOMALY...
WHAT KIND OF SOMETHING?
THAT'S THE THING...
IT'S NOTHING.
IT'S JUST A CLOUD OF NOTHING BUT IT'S MOVING TOWARDS US FROM THE NORTHEAST.
THAT'S NOT NOTHING.
THOR AND STORM.
SAY GOOD MORNING.
UM, IS THAT... LIGHTNING?
WE ARE UNDER ATTACK!

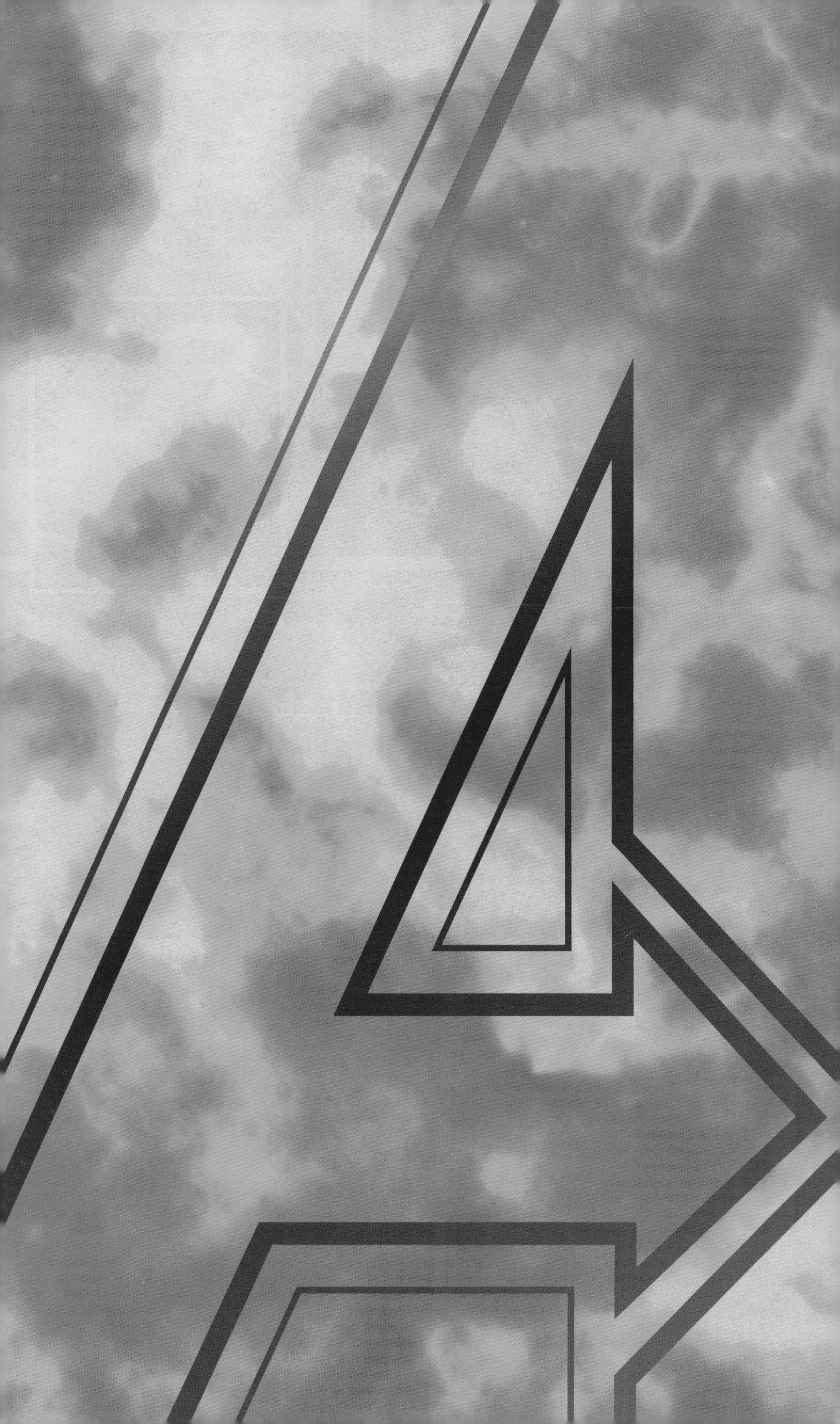

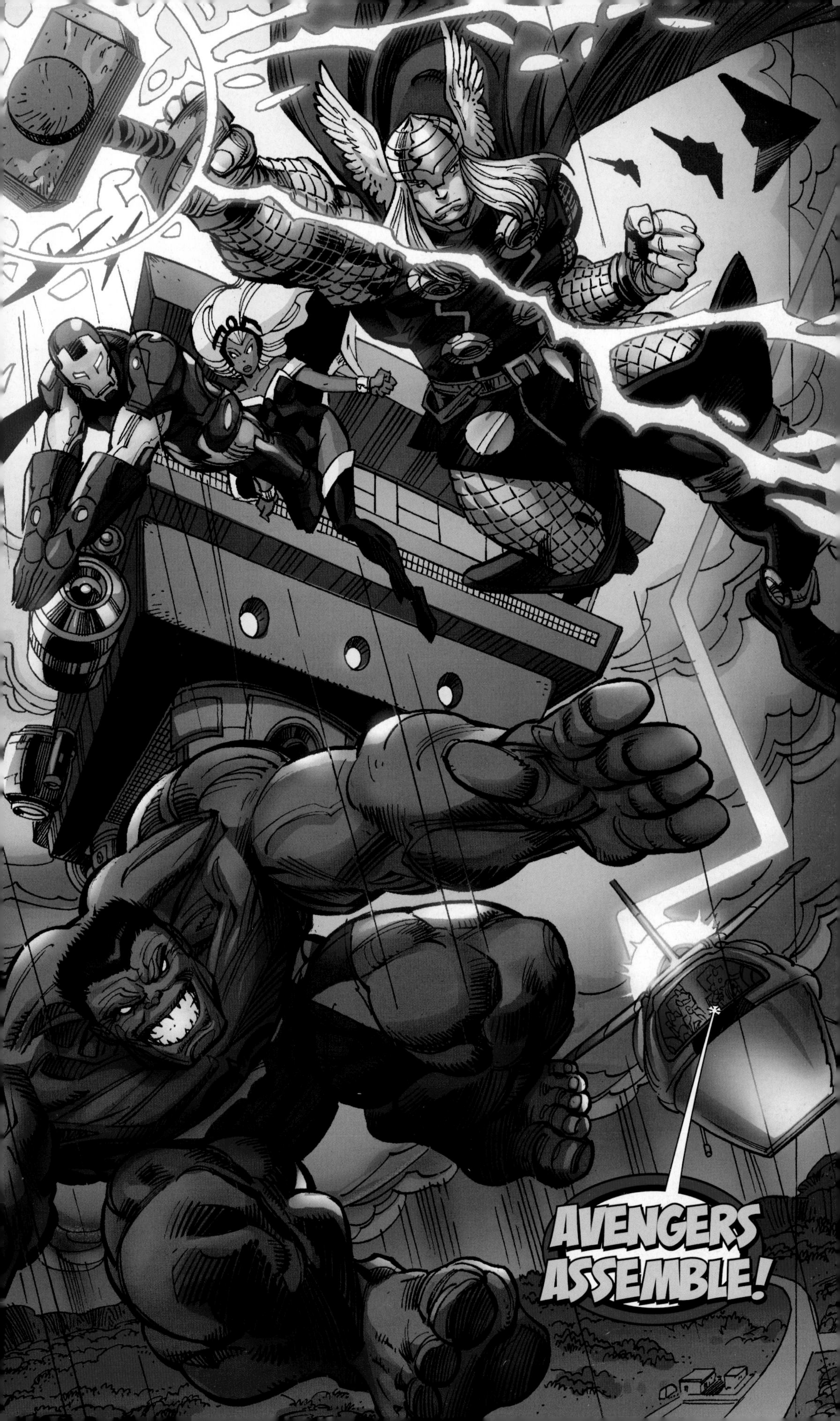
AVENGERS ASSEMBLE!

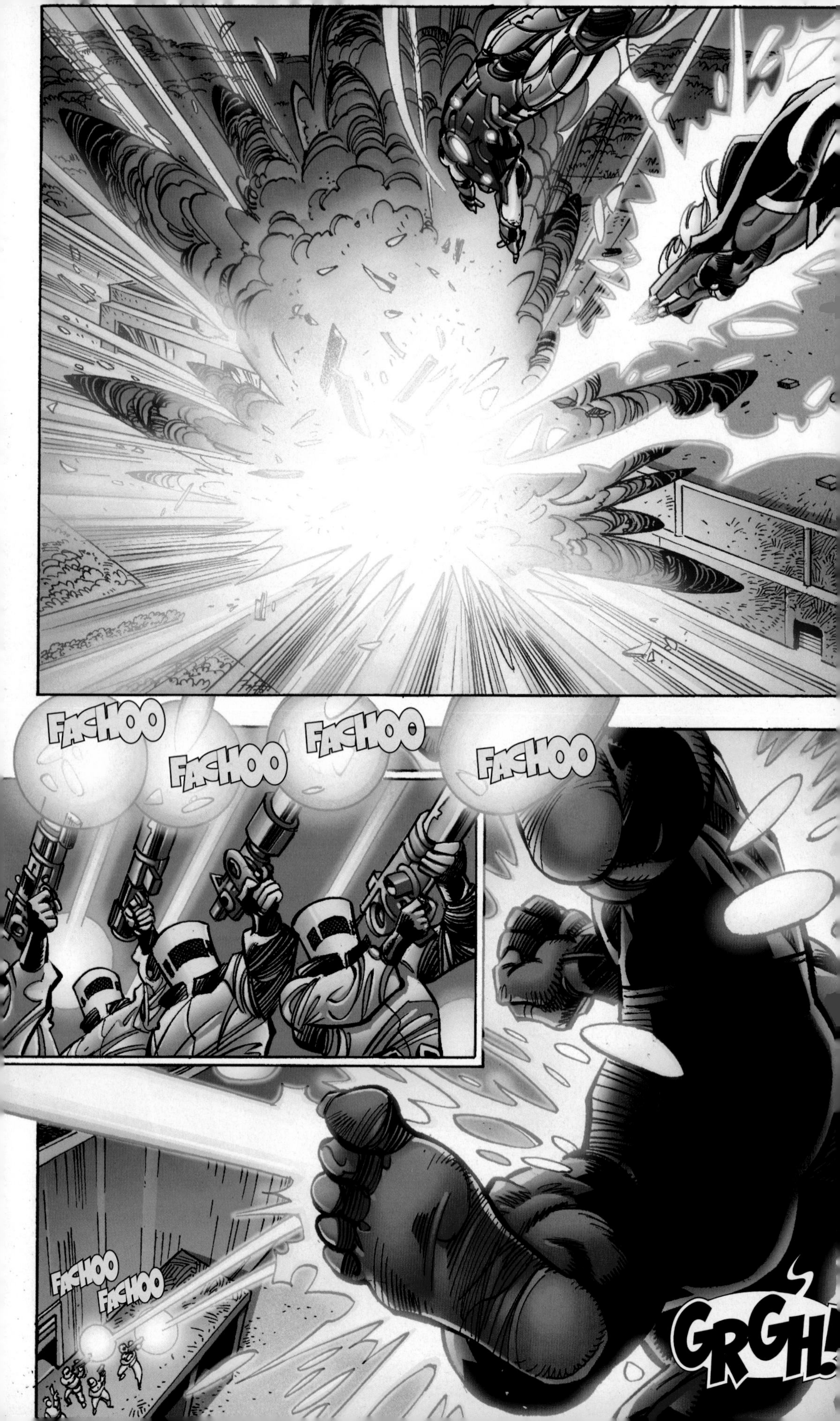
FACHOO
FACHOO
FACHOO
FACHOO
FACHOO
FACHOO
GRGH!

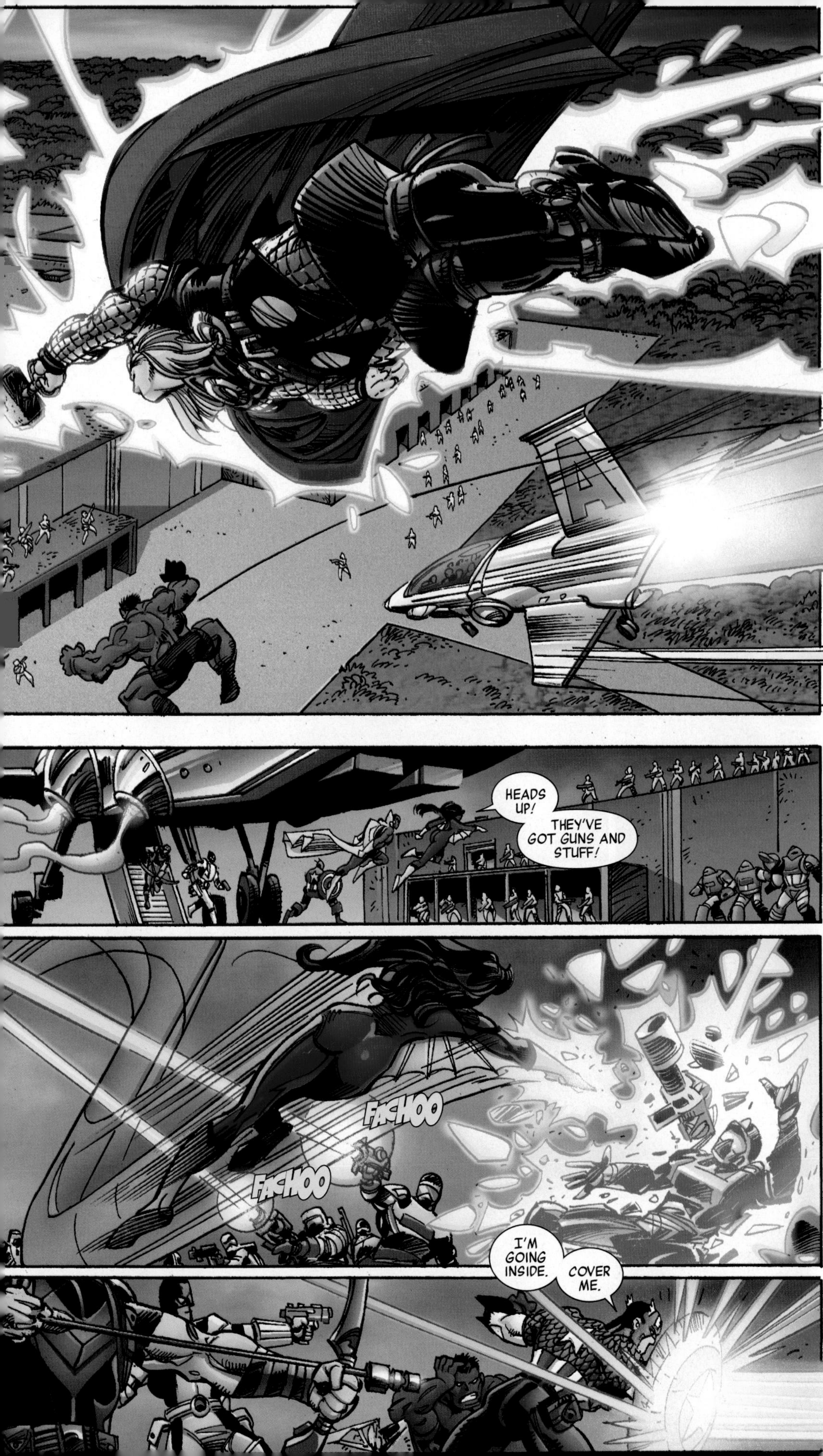
HEADS UP!
THEY'VE GOT GUNS AND STUFF!
FACHOO
FACHOO
I'M GOING INSIDE.
COVER ME.

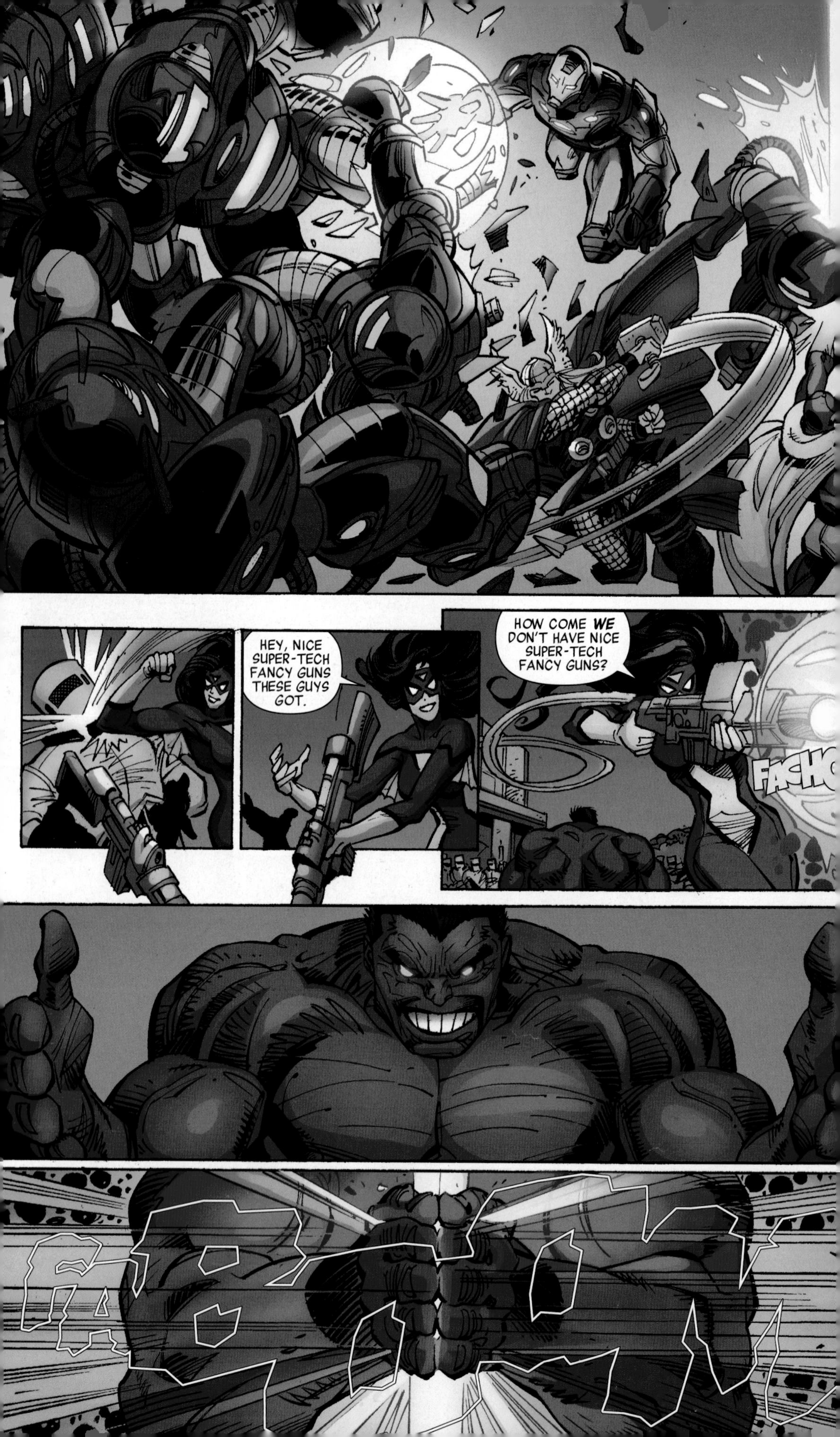
HEY, NICE SUPER-TECH FANCY GUNS THESE GUYS GOT.
HOW COME **WE** DON'T HAVE NICE SUPER-TECH FANCY GUNS?
FACHO

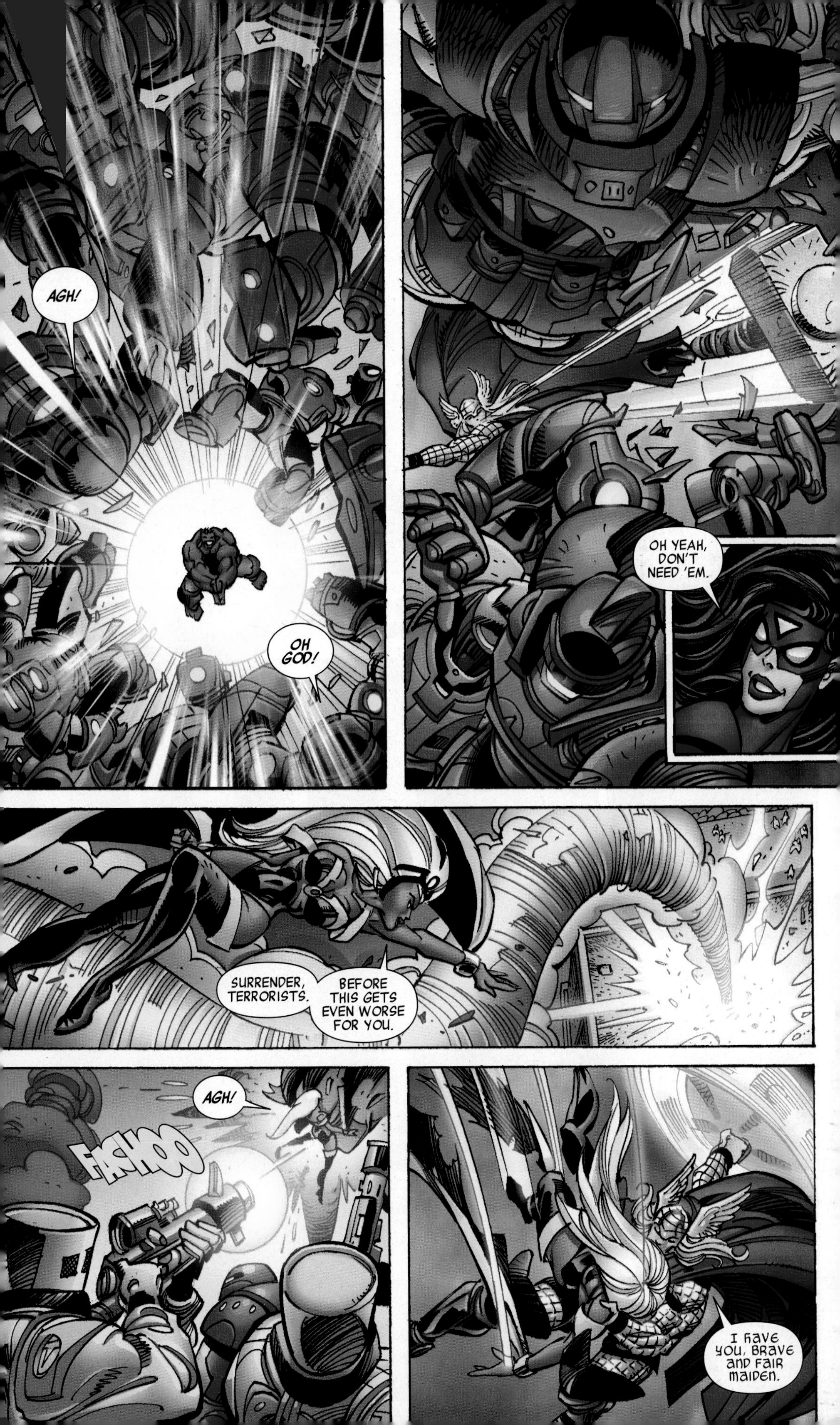
AGH!
OH GOD!
OH YEAH, DON'T NEED 'EM.
SURRENDER, TERRORISTS.
BEFORE THIS GETS EVEN WORSE FOR YOU.
AGH!
FACHOO
I HAVE YOU, BRAVE AND FAIR MAIDEN.

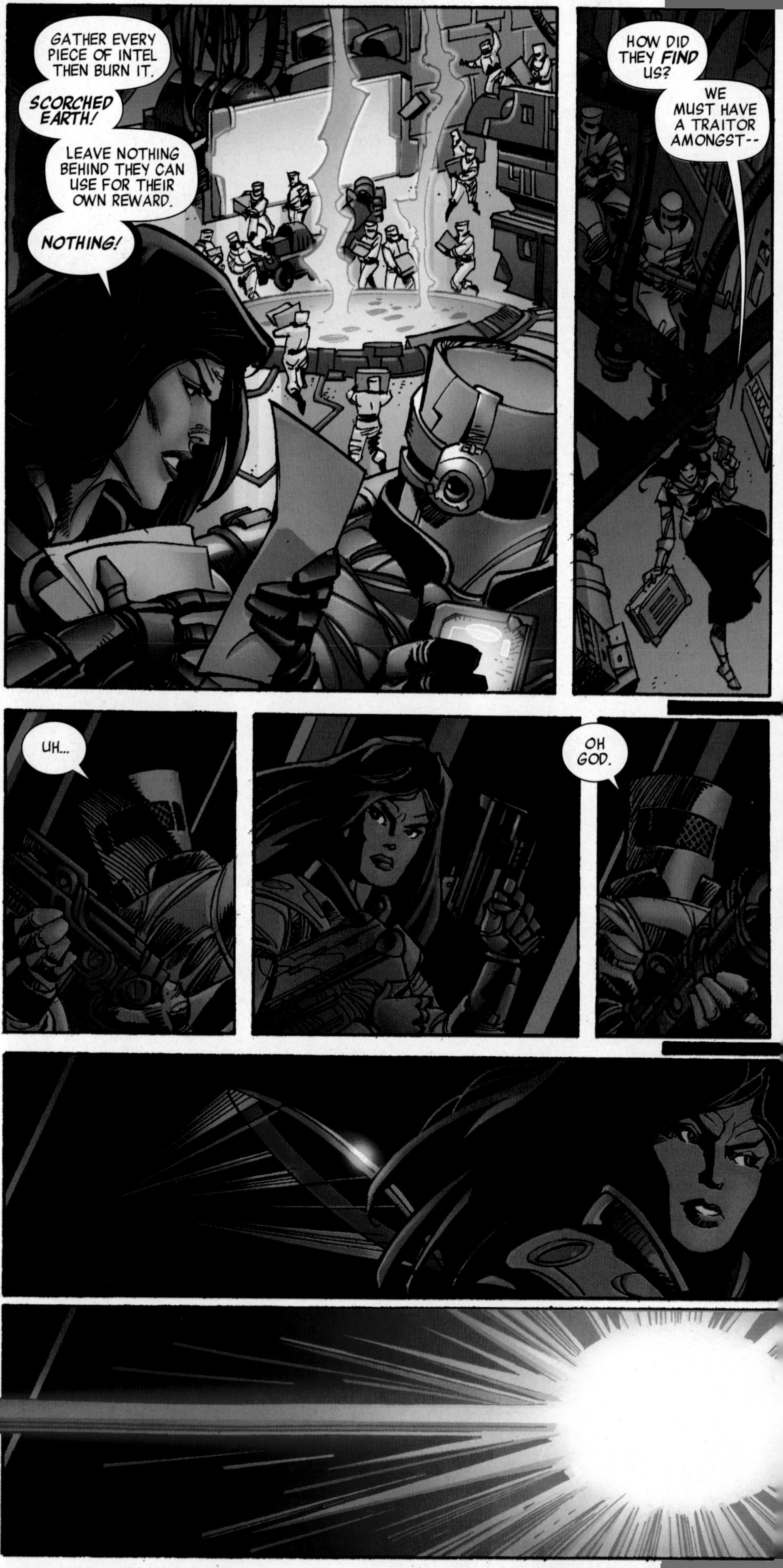
GATHER EVERY PIECE OF INTEL THEN BURN IT.
SCORCHED EARTH!
LEAVE NOTHING BEHIND THEY CAN USE FOR THEIR OWN REWARD.
NOTHING!
HOW DID THEY FIND US?
WE MUST HAVE A TRAITOR AMONGST--
UH...
OH GOD.

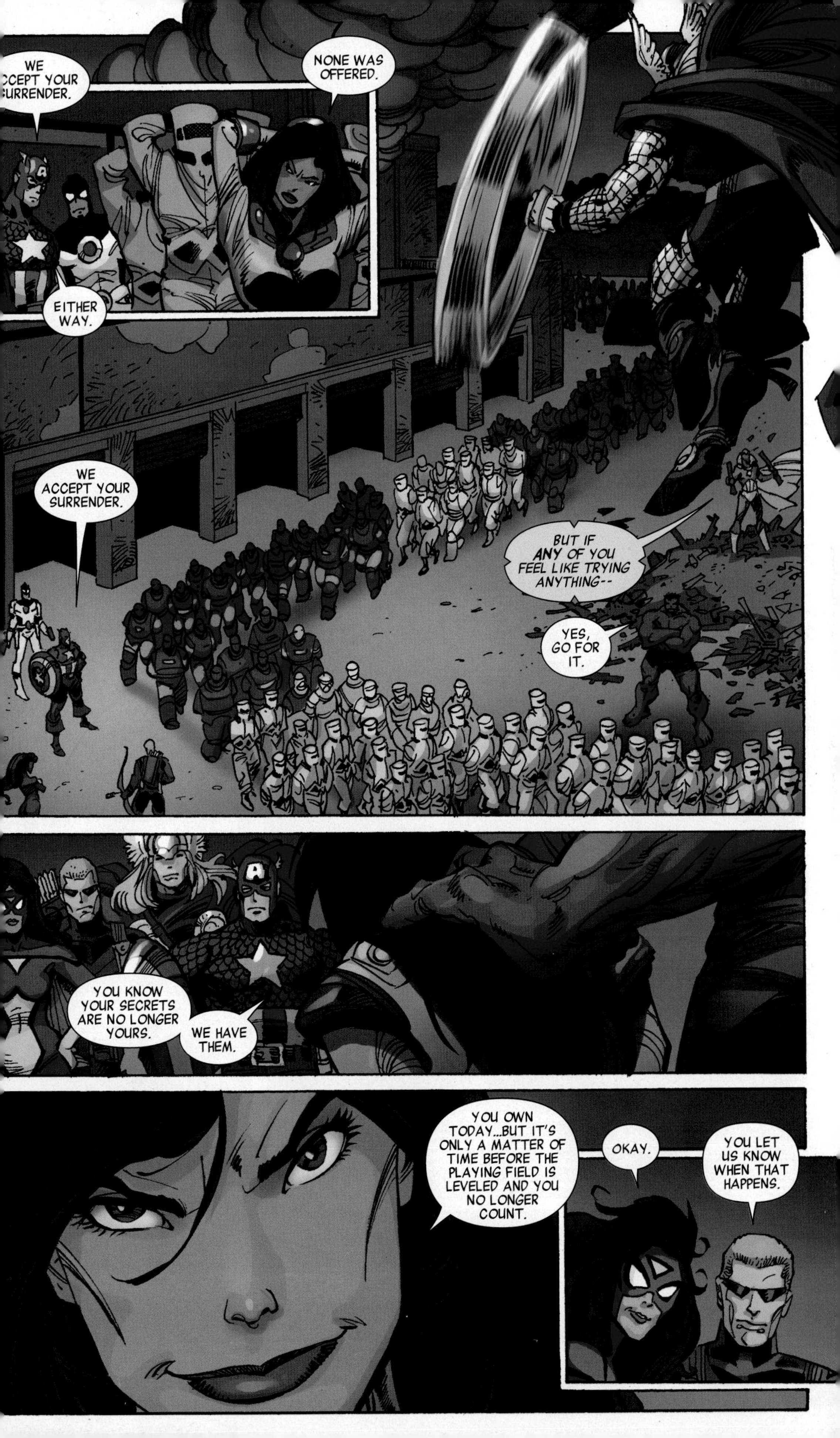
WE ACCEPT YOUR SURRENDER.
NONE WAS OFFERED.
EITHER WAY.
WE ACCEPT YOUR SURRENDER.
BUT IF ANY OF YOU FEEL LIKE TRYING ANYTHING--
YES, GO FOR IT.
YOU KNOW YOUR SECRETS ARE NO LONGER YOURS.
WE HAVE THEM.
YOU OWN TODAY...BUT IT'S ONLY A MATTER OF TIME BEFORE THE PLAYING FIELD IS LEVELED AND YOU NO LONGER COUNT.
OKAY.
YOU LET US KNOW WHEN THAT HAPPENS.

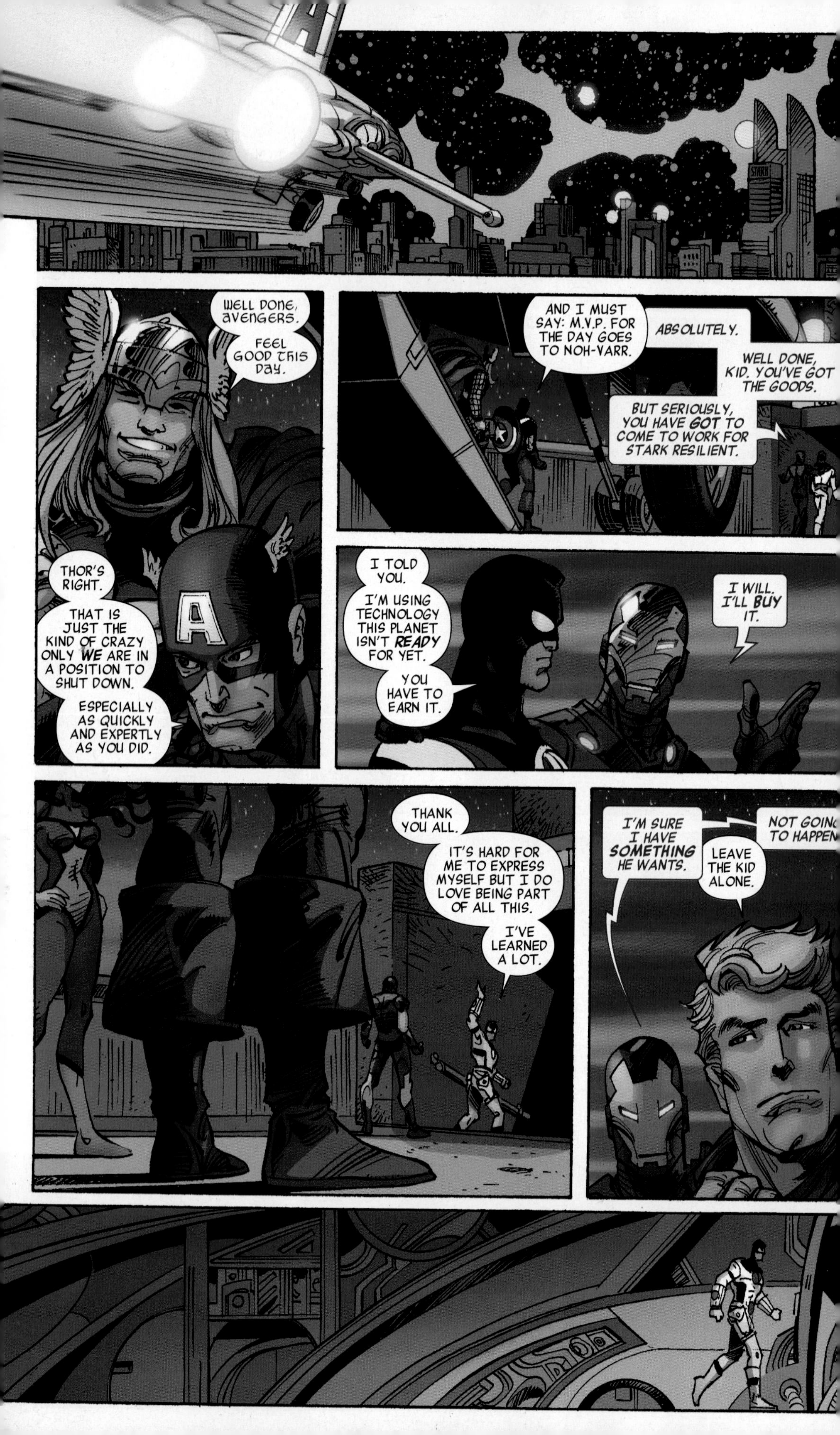
STARK
WELL DONE, AVENGERS.
FEEL GOOD THIS DAY.
AND I MUST SAY: M.V.P. FOR THE DAY GOES TO NOH-VARR.
ABSOLUTELY.
WELL DONE, KID. YOU'VE GOT THE GOODS.
BUT SERIOUSLY, YOU HAVE GOT TO COME TO WORK FOR STARK RESILIENT.
THOR'S RIGHT.
THAT IS JUST THE KIND OF CRAZY ONLY WE ARE IN A POSITION TO SHUT DOWN.
ESPECIALLY AS QUICKLY AND EXPERTLY AS YOU DID.
I TOLD YOU.
I'M USING TECHNOLOGY THIS PLANET ISN'T READY FOR YET.
YOU HAVE TO EARN IT.
I WILL. I'LL BUY IT.
THANK YOU ALL.
IT'S HARD FOR ME TO EXPRESS MYSELF BUT I DO LOVE BEING PART OF ALL THIS.
I'VE LEARNED A LOT.
I'M SURE I HAVE SOMETHING HE WANTS.
NOT GOING TO HAPPEN
LEAVE THE KID ALONE.

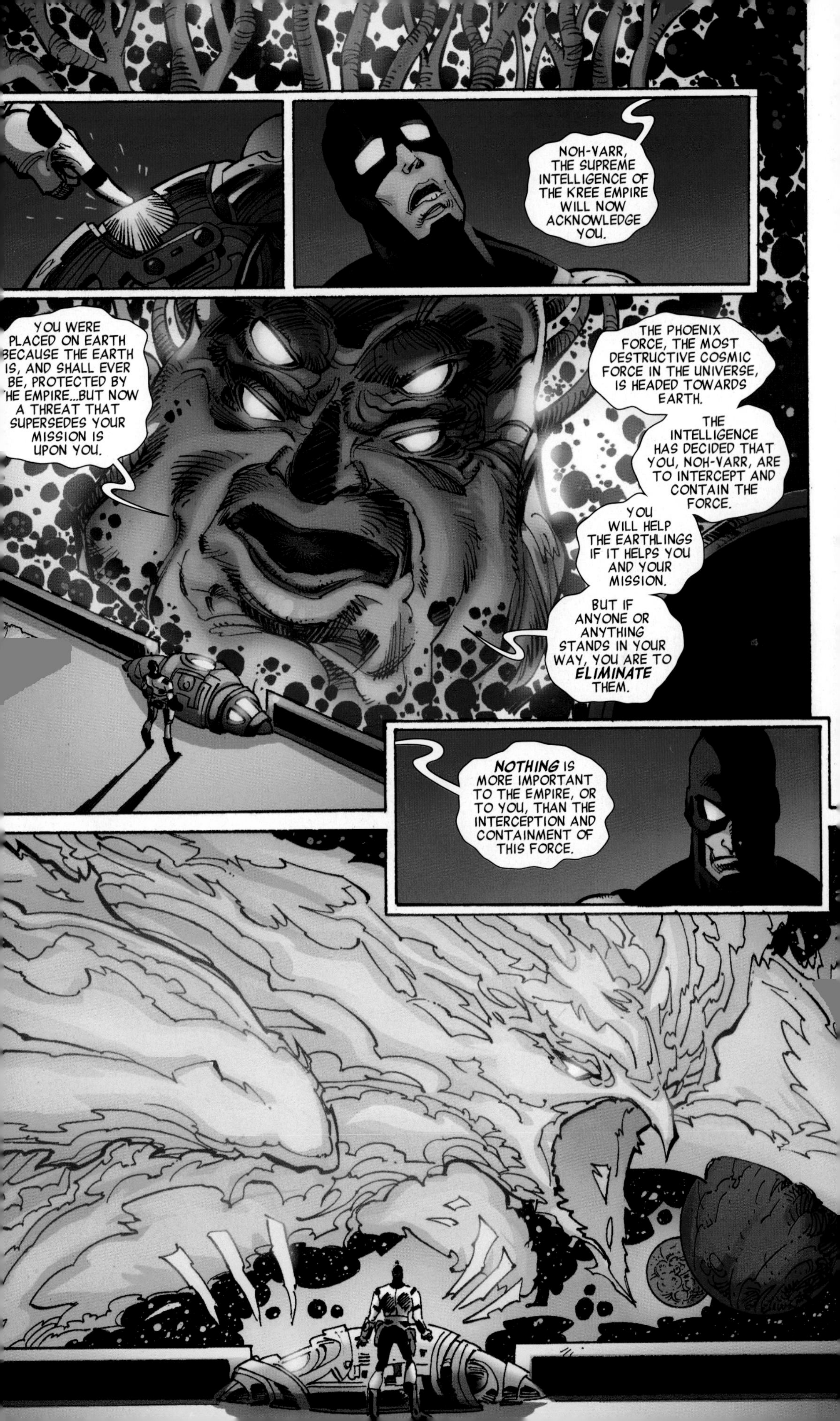
NOH-VARR, THE SUPREME INTELLIGENCE OF THE KREE EMPIRE WILL NOW ACKNOWLEDGE YOU.
YOU WERE PLACED ON EARTH BECAUSE THE EARTH IS, AND SHALL EVER BE, PROTECTED BY THE EMPIRE...BUT NOW A THREAT THAT SUPERSEDES YOUR MISSION IS UPON YOU.
THE PHOENIX FORCE, THE MOST DESTRUCTIVE COSMIC FORCE IN THE UNIVERSE, IS HEADED TOWARDS EARTH.
THE INTELLIGENCE HAS DECIDED THAT YOU, NOH-VARR, ARE TO INTERCEPT AND CONTAIN THE FORCE.
YOU WILL HELP THE EARTHLINGS IF IT HELPS YOU AND YOUR MISSION.
BUT IF ANYONE OR ANYTHING STANDS IN YOUR WAY, YOU ARE TO ***ELIMINATE*** THEM.
NOTHING IS MORE IMPORTANT TO THE EMPIRE, OR TO YOU, THAN THE INTERCEPTION AND CONTAINMENT OF THIS FORCE.

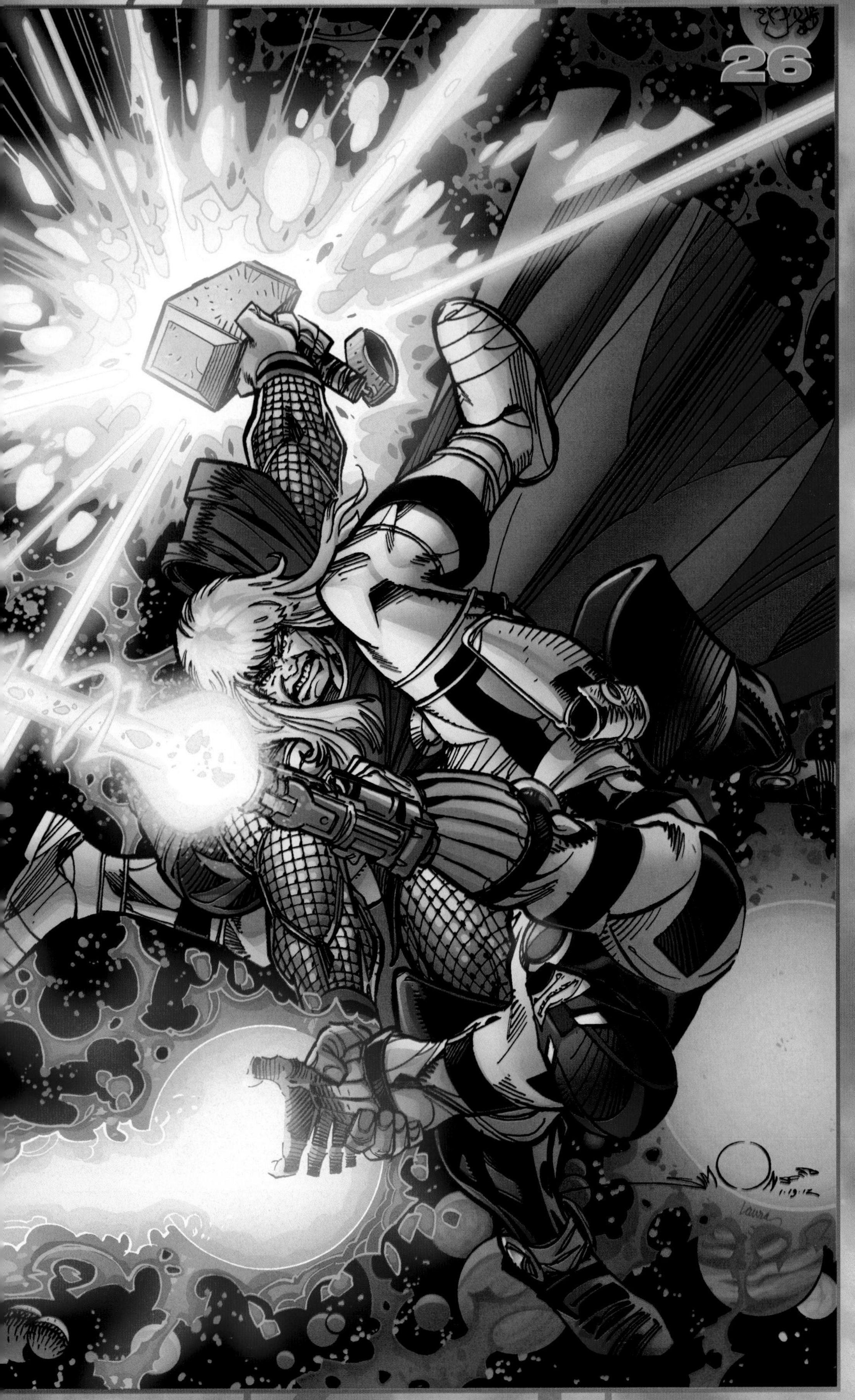
26

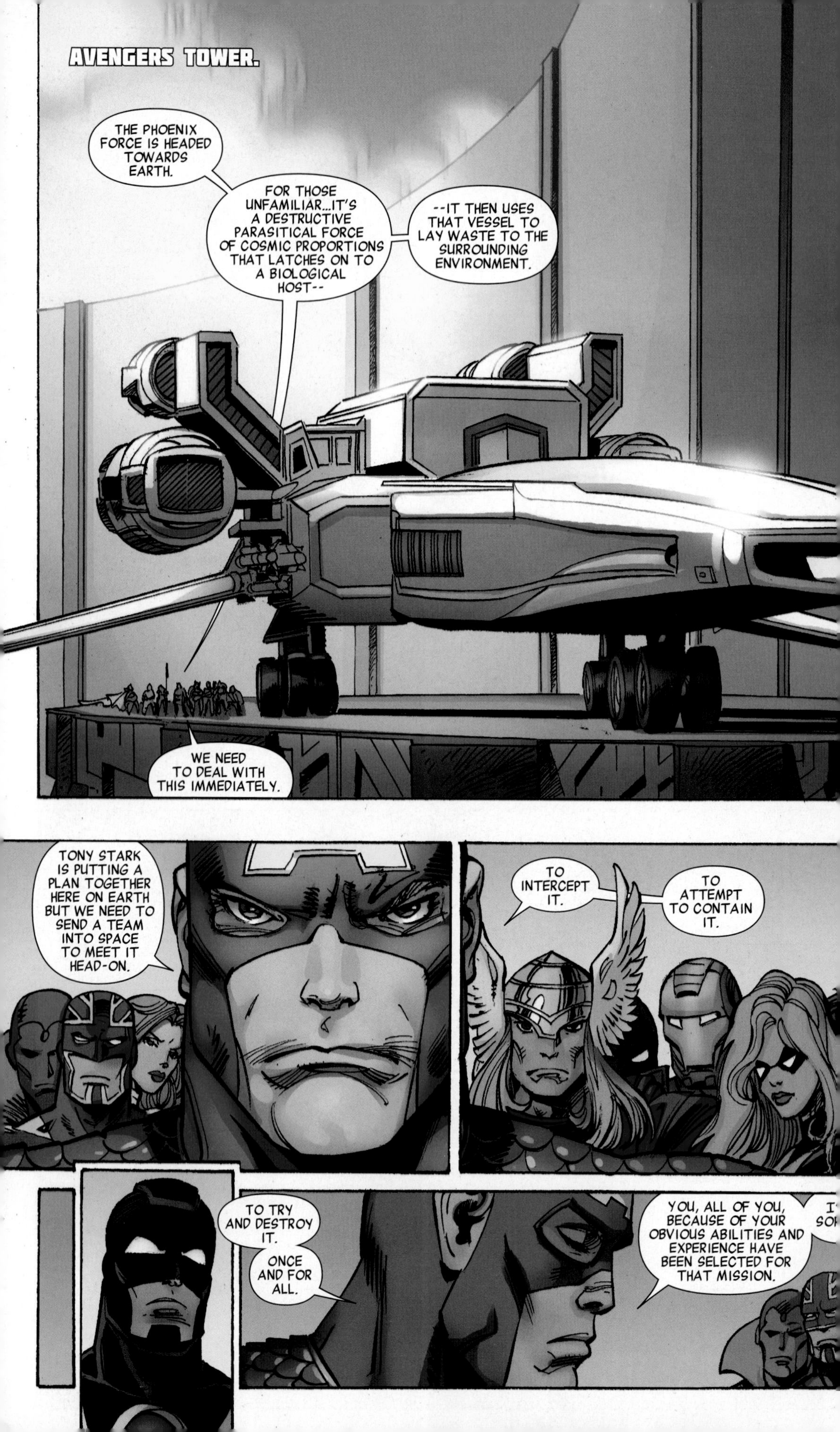
AVENGERS TOWER.
THE PHOENIX FORCE IS HEADED TOWARDS EARTH.
FOR THOSE UNFAMILIAR...IT'S A DESTRUCTIVE PARASITICAL FORCE OF COSMIC PROPORTIONS THAT LATCHES ON TO A BIOLOGICAL HOST--
--IT THEN USES THAT VESSEL TO LAY WASTE TO THE SURROUNDING ENVIRONMENT.
WE NEED TO DEAL WITH THIS IMMEDIATELY.
TONY STARK IS PUTTING A PLAN TOGETHER HERE ON EARTH BUT WE NEED TO SEND A TEAM INTO SPACE TO MEET IT HEAD-ON.
TO INTERCEPT IT.
TO ATTEMPT TO CONTAIN IT.
TO TRY AND DESTROY IT.
ONCE AND FOR ALL.
YOU, ALL OF YOU, BECAUSE OF YOUR OBVIOUS ABILITIES AND EXPERIENCE HAVE BEEN SELECTED FOR THAT MISSION.

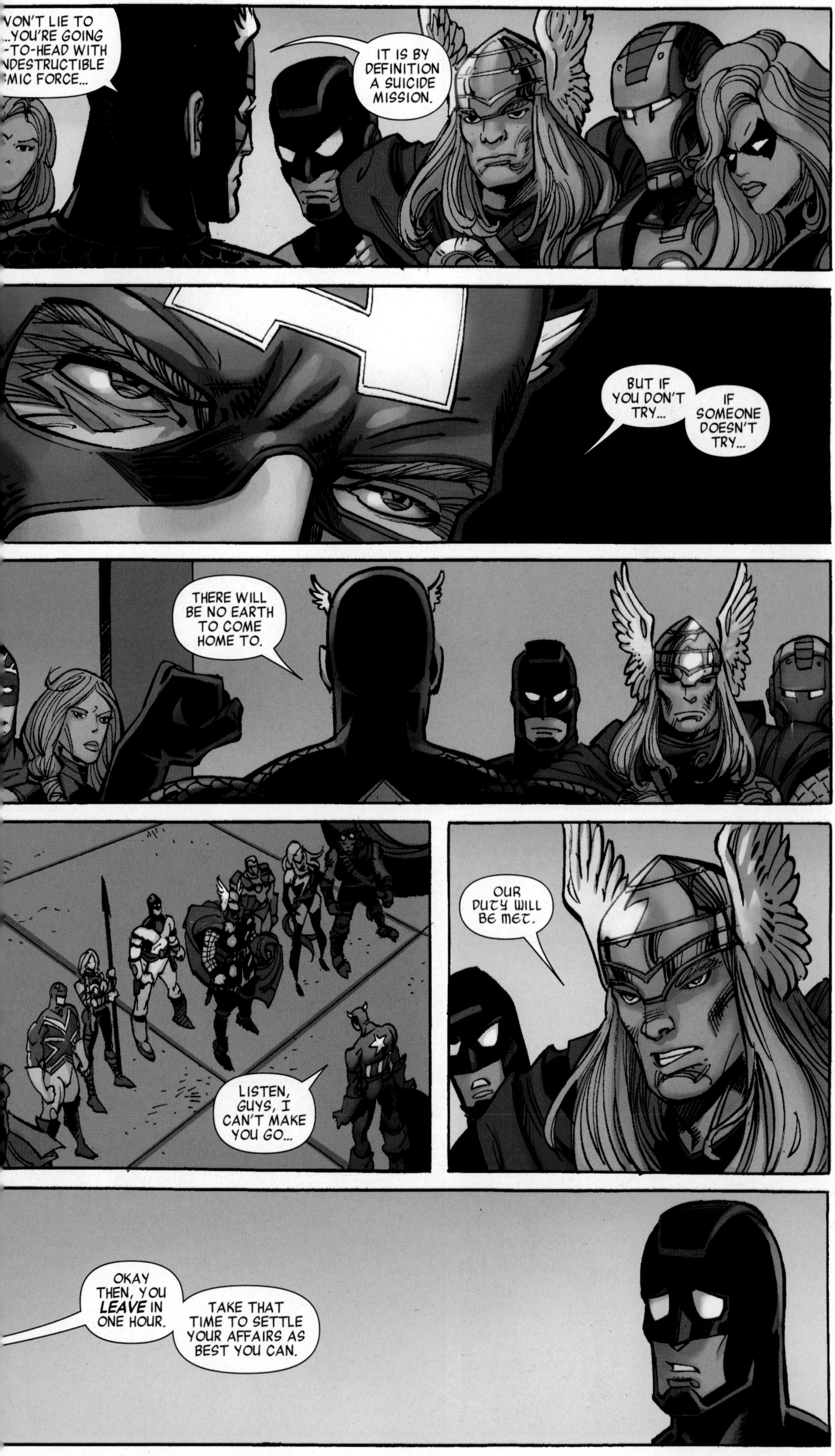

VON'T LIE TO ...YOU'RE GOING -TO-HEAD WITH NDESTRUCTIBLE MIC FORCE...
IT IS BY DEFINITION A SUICIDE MISSION.
BUT IF YOU DON'T TRY...
IF SOMEONE DOESN'T TRY...
THERE WILL BE NO EARTH TO COME HOME TO.
LISTEN, GUYS, I CAN'T MAKE YOU GO...
OUR DUTY WILL BE MET.
OKAY THEN, YOU LEAVE IN ONE HOUR.
TAKE THAT TIME TO SETTLE YOUR AFFAIRS AS BEST YOU CAN.

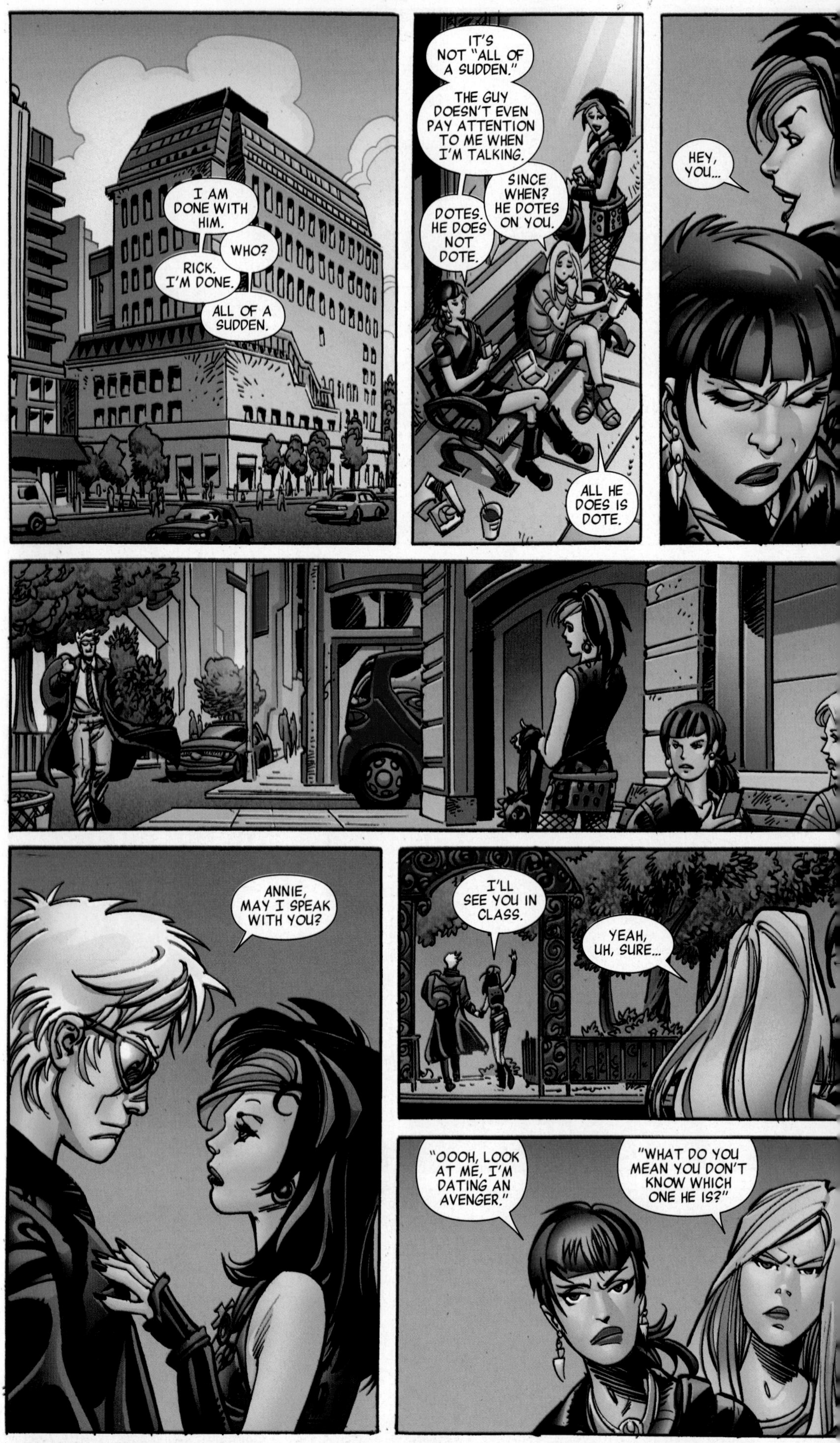
I AM DONE WITH HIM.
WHO?
RICK. I'M DONE.
ALL OF A SUDDEN.
IT'S NOT "ALL OF A SUDDEN."
THE GUY DOESN'T EVEN PAY ATTENTION TO ME WHEN I'M TALKING.
SINCE WHEN? HE DOTES ON YOU.
DOTES. HE DOES NOT DOTE.
ALL HE DOES IS DOTE.
HEY, YOU...
ANNIE, MAY I SPEAK WITH YOU?
I'LL SEE YOU IN CLASS.
YEAH, UH, SURE...
"OOOH, LOOK AT ME, I'M DATING AN AVENGER."
"WHAT DO YOU MEAN YOU DON'T KNOW WHICH ONE HE IS?"

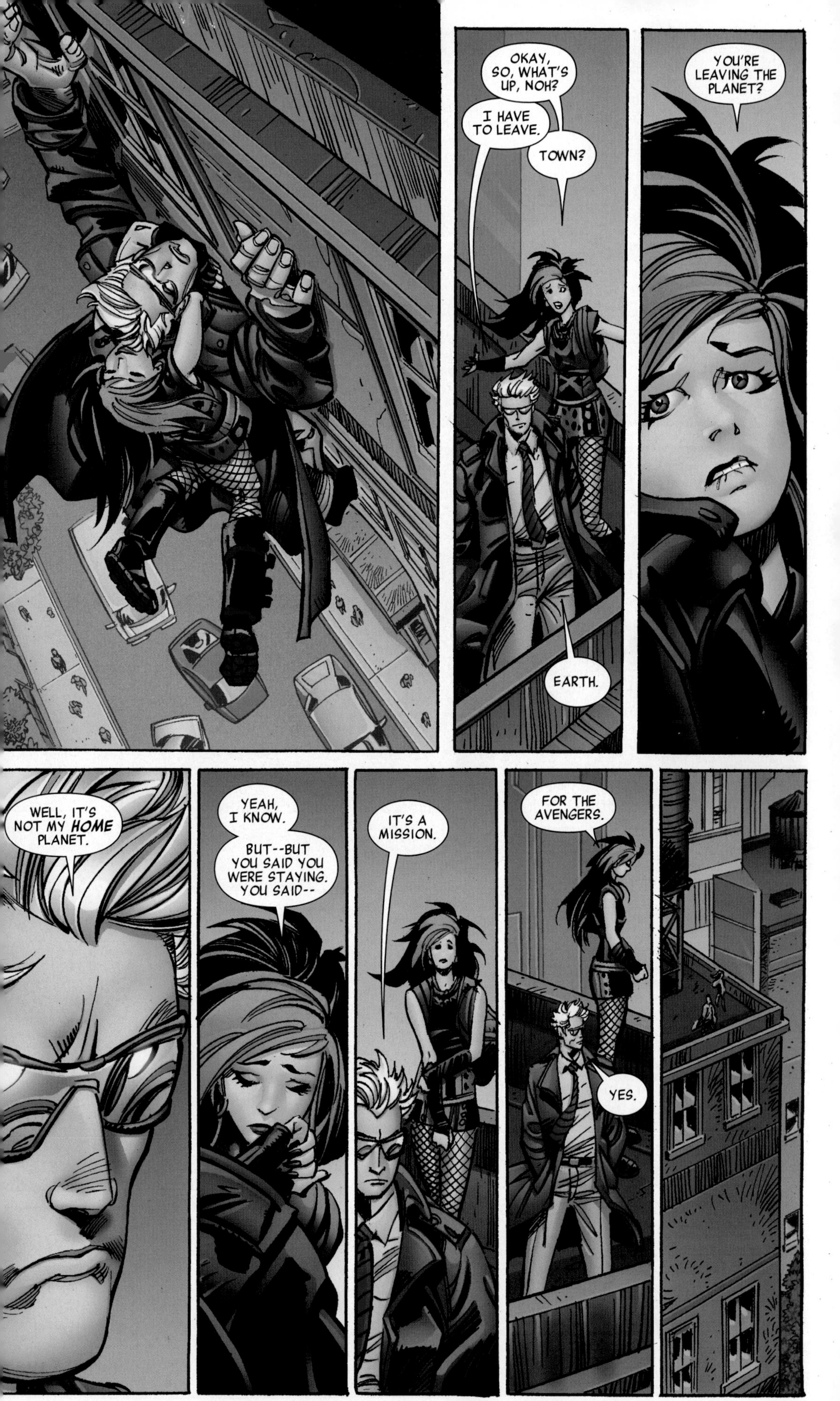
OKAY, SO, WHAT'S UP, NOH?
I HAVE TO LEAVE.
TOWN?
EARTH.
YOU'RE LEAVING THE PLANET?
WELL, IT'S NOT MY *HOME* PLANET.
YEAH, I KNOW.
BUT--BUT YOU SAID YOU WERE STAYING. YOU SAID--
IT'S A MISSION.
FOR THE AVENGERS.
YES.

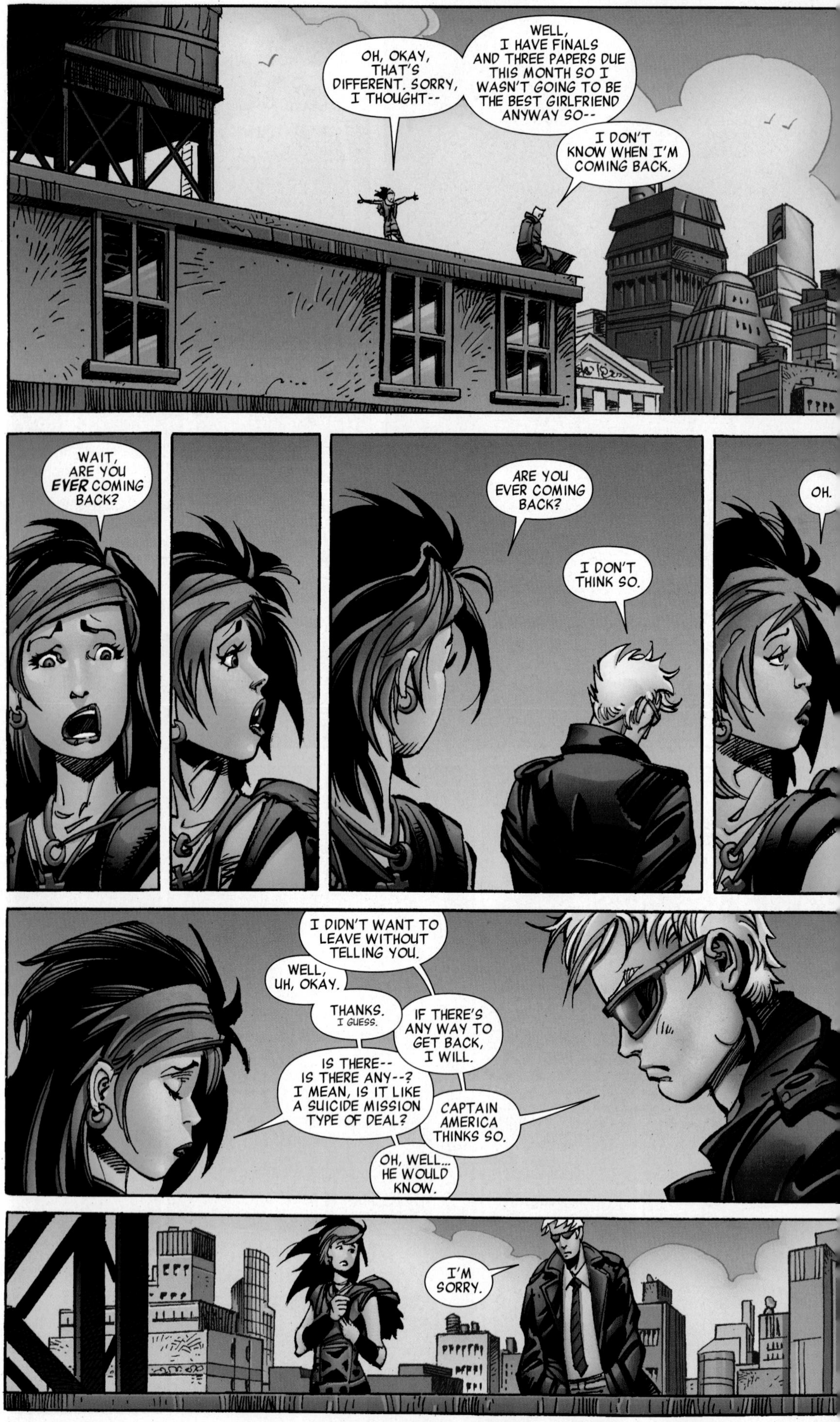
OH, OKAY, THAT'S DIFFERENT. SORRY, I THOUGHT--
WELL, I HAVE FINALS AND THREE PAPERS DUE THIS MONTH SO I WASN'T GOING TO BE THE BEST GIRLFRIEND ANYWAY SO--
I DON'T KNOW WHEN I'M COMING BACK.
WAIT, ARE YOU EVER COMING BACK?
ARE YOU EVER COMING BACK?
I DON'T THINK SO.
OH.
I DIDN'T WANT TO LEAVE WITHOUT TELLING YOU.
WELL, UH, OKAY.
THANKS. I GUESS.
IF THERE'S ANY WAY TO GET BACK, I WILL.
IS THERE-- IS THERE ANY--? I MEAN, IS IT LIKE A SUICIDE MISSION TYPE OF DEAL?
CAPTAIN AMERICA THINKS SO.
OH, WELL... HE WOULD KNOW.
I'M SORRY.

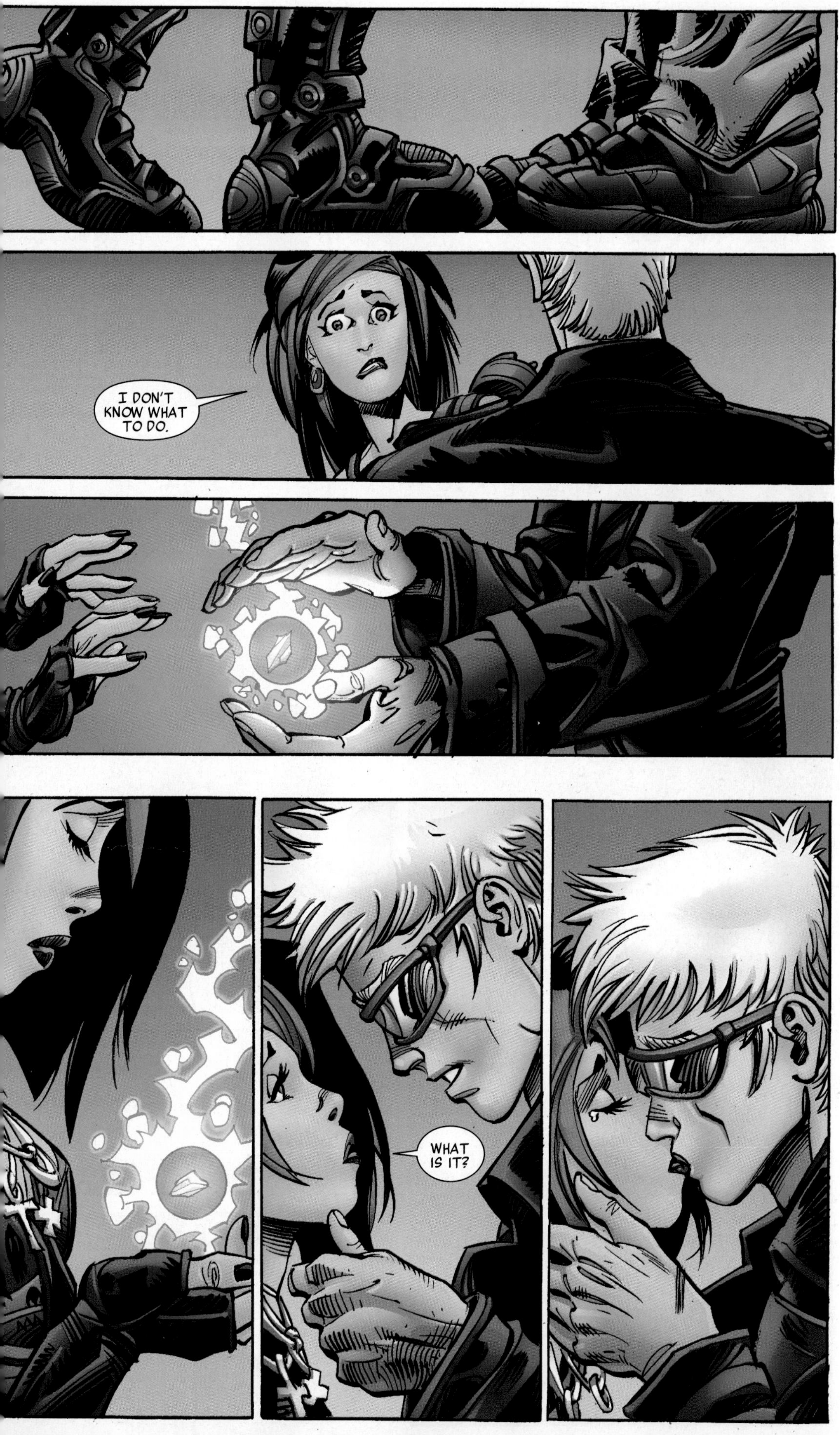

I DON'T KNOW WHAT TO DO.
WHAT IS IT?

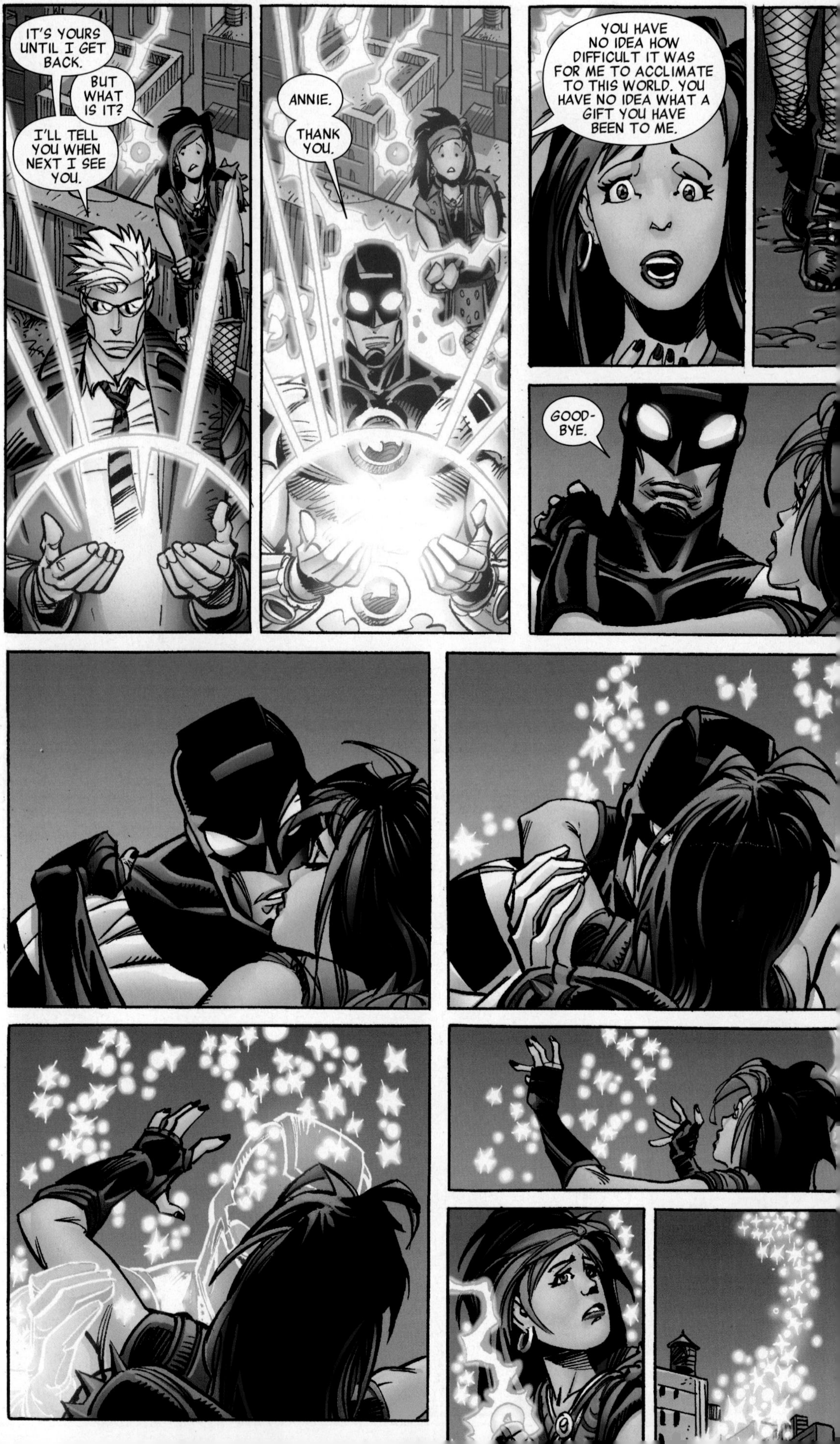
IT'S YOURS UNTIL I GET BACK.
BUT WHAT IS IT?
I'LL TELL YOU WHEN NEXT I SEE YOU.
ANNIE.
THANK YOU.
YOU HAVE NO IDEA HOW DIFFICULT IT WAS FOR ME TO ACCLIMATE TO THIS WORLD. YOU HAVE NO IDEA WHAT A GIFT YOU HAVE BEEN TO ME.
GOOD-BYE.

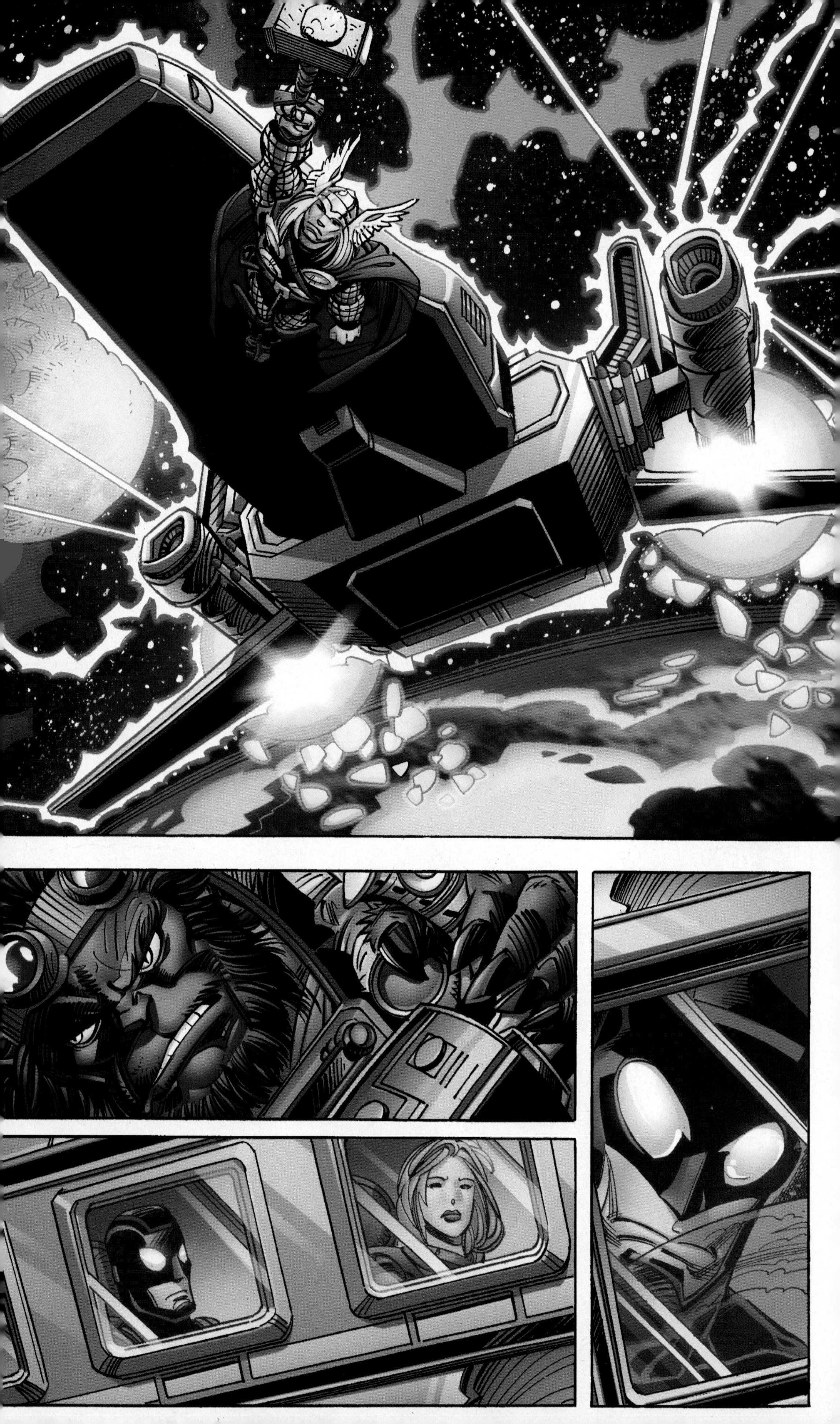

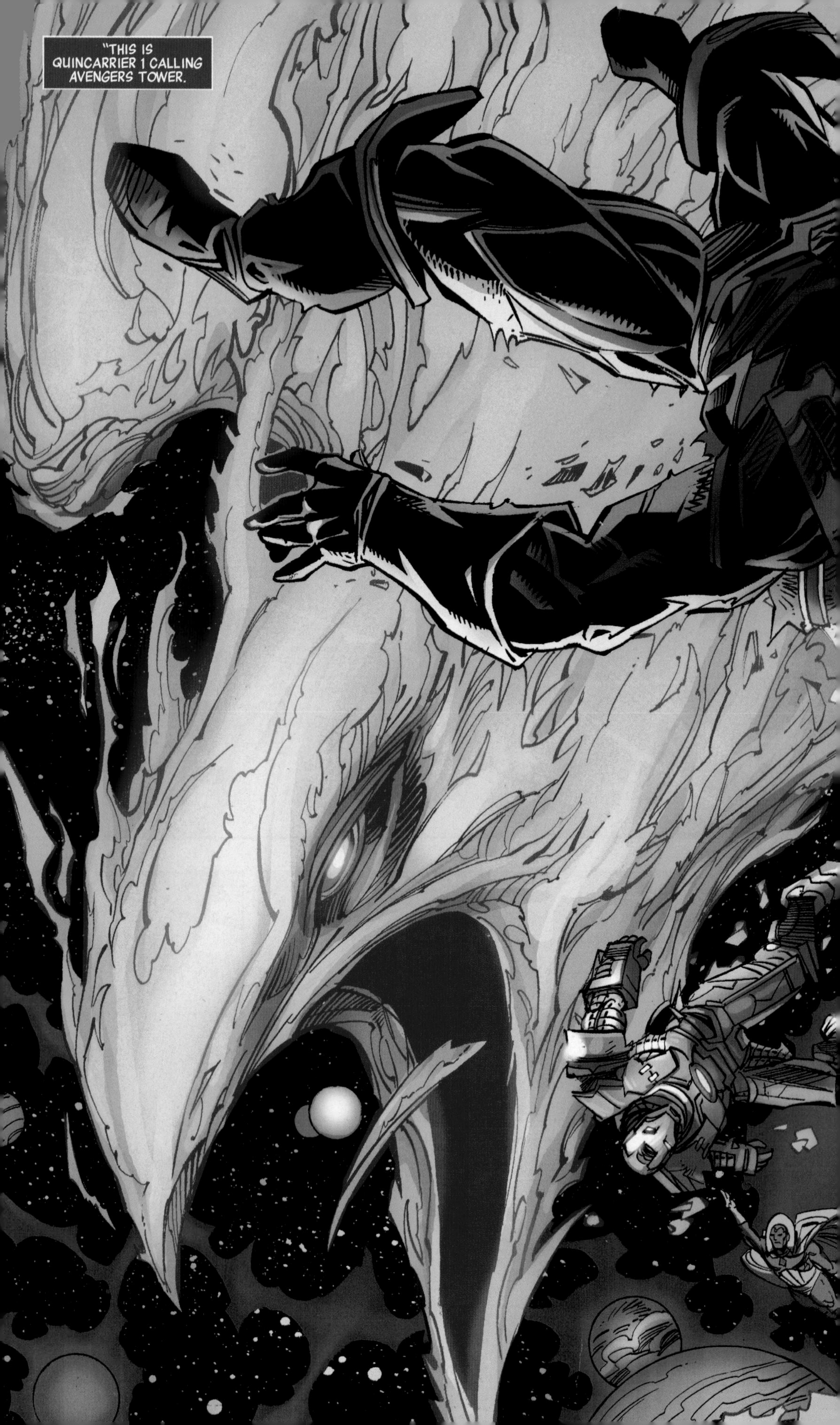
"THIS IS QUINCARRIER 1 CALLING AVENGERS TOWER.

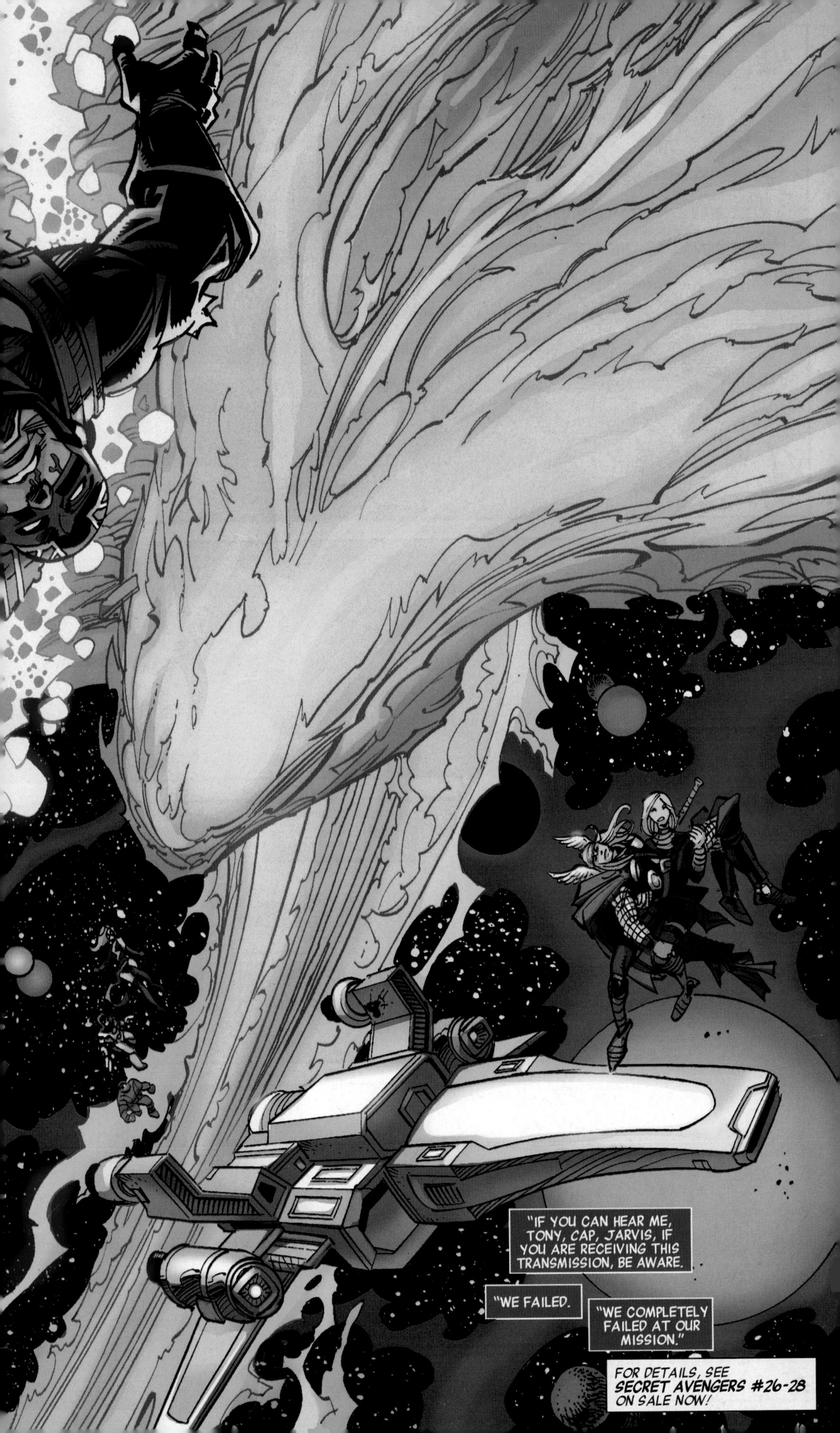
"IF YOU CAN HEAR ME, TONY, CAP, JARVIS, IF YOU ARE RECEIVING THIS TRANSMISSION, BE AWARE.
"WE FAILED.
"WE COMPLETELY FAILED AT OUR MISSION."
FOR DETAILS, SEE SECRET AVENGERS #26-28 ON SALE NOW!

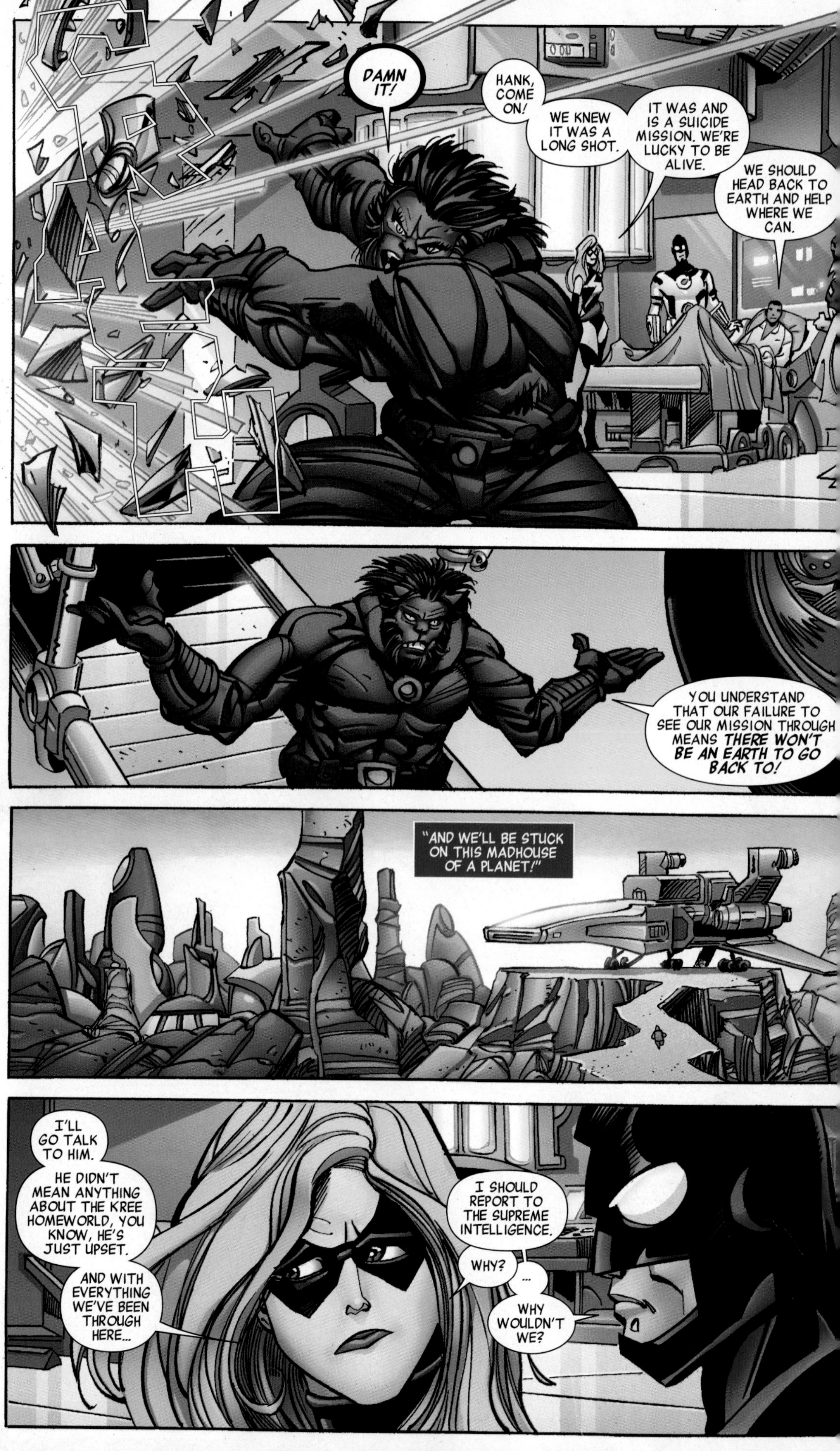
DAMN IT!
HANK, COME ON!
WE KNEW IT WAS A LONG SHOT.
IT WAS AND IS A SUICIDE MISSION. WE'RE LUCKY TO BE ALIVE.
WE SHOULD HEAD BACK TO EARTH AND HELP WHERE WE CAN.
YOU UNDERSTAND THAT OUR FAILURE TO SEE OUR MISSION THROUGH MEANS THERE WON'T BE AN EARTH TO GO BACK TO!
"AND WE'LL BE STUCK ON THIS MADHOUSE OF A PLANET!"
I'LL GO TALK TO HIM.
HE DIDN'T MEAN ANYTHING ABOUT THE KREE HOMEWORLD, YOU KNOW, HE'S JUST UPSET.
AND WITH EVERYTHING WE'VE BEEN THROUGH HERE...
I SHOULD REPORT TO THE SUPREME INTELLIGENCE.
WHY?
...
WHY WOULDN'T WE?

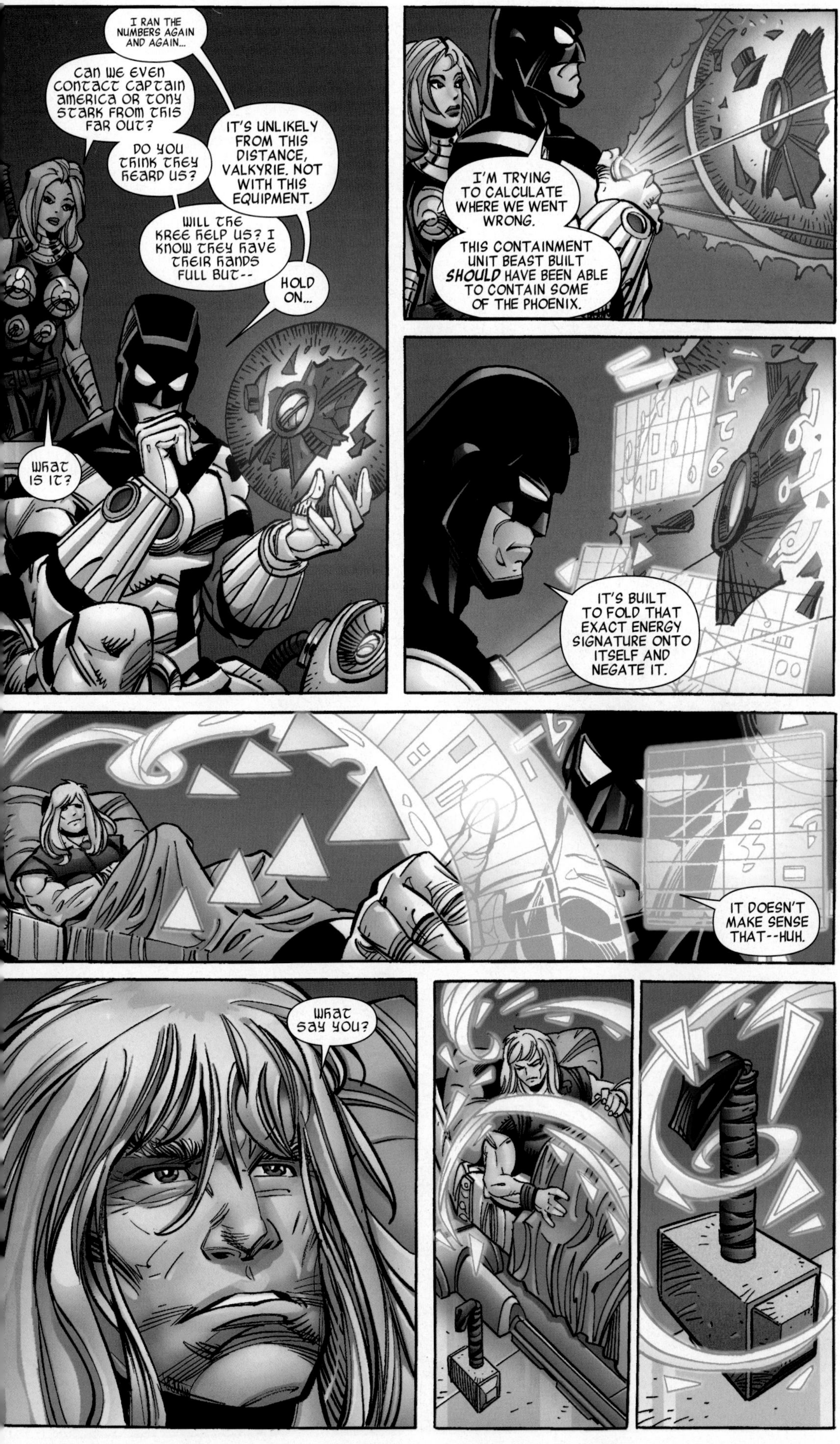
I RAN THE NUMBERS AGAIN AND AGAIN...
CAN WE EVEN CONTACT CAPTAIN AMERICA OR TONY STARK FROM THIS FAR OUT?
DO YOU THINK THEY HEARD US?
IT'S UNLIKELY FROM THIS DISTANCE, VALKYRIE. NOT WITH THIS EQUIPMENT.
WILL THE KREE HELP US? I KNOW THEY HAVE THEIR HANDS FULL BUT--
HOLD ON...
WHAT IS IT?
I'M TRYING TO CALCULATE WHERE WE WENT WRONG.
THIS CONTAINMENT UNIT BEAST BUILT SHOULD HAVE BEEN ABLE TO CONTAIN SOME OF THE PHOENIX.
IT'S BUILT TO FOLD THAT EXACT ENERGY SIGNATURE ONTO ITSELF AND NEGATE IT.
IT DOESN'T MAKE SENSE THAT--HUH.
WHAT SAY YOU?

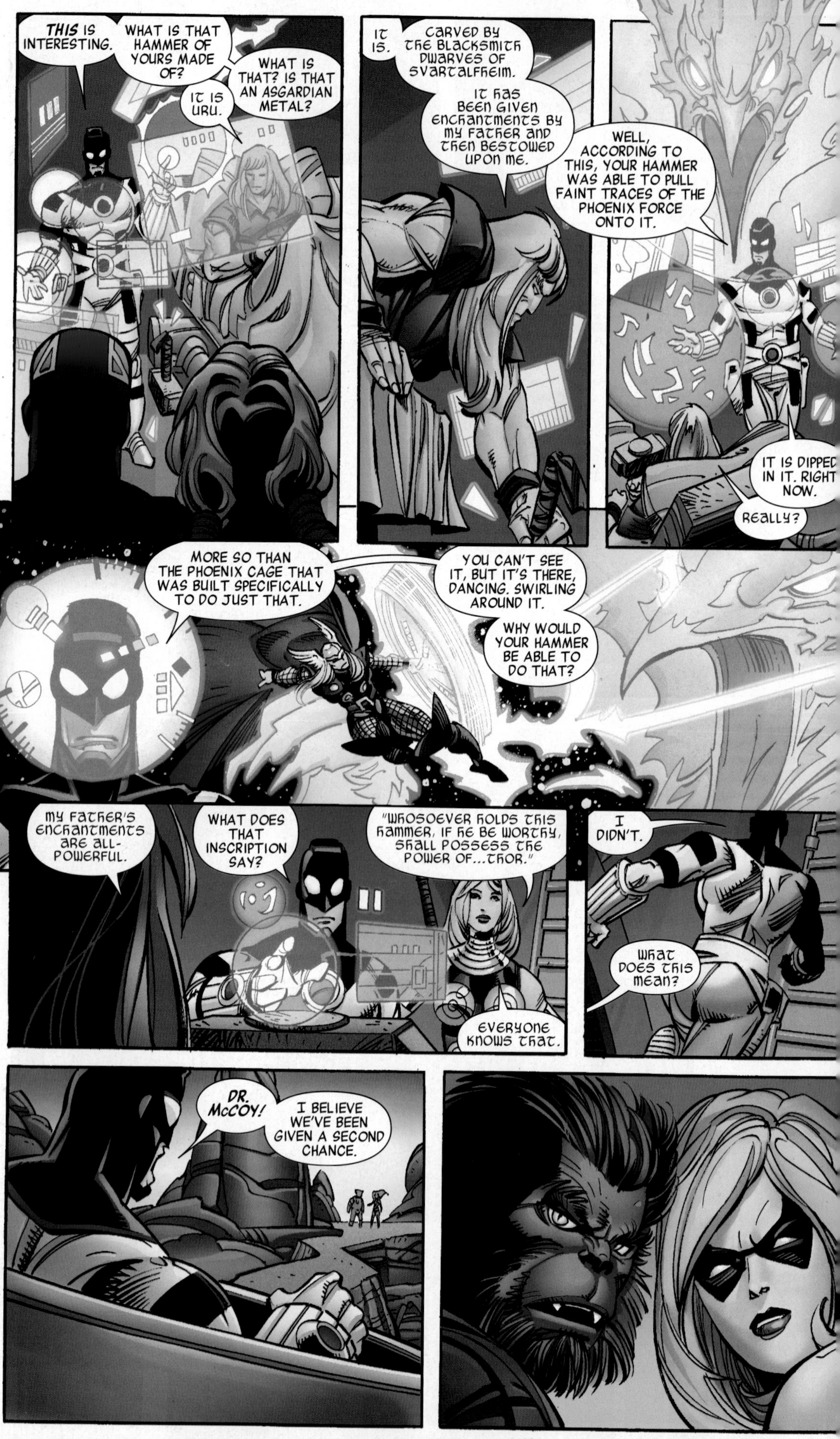
THIS is interesting.
What is that hammer of yours made of?
What is that? Is that an Asgardian metal?
It is Uru.
It is.
Carved by the blacksmith dwarves of Svartalfheim.
It has been given enchantments by my father and then bestowed upon me.
Well, according to this, your hammer was able to pull faint traces of the Phoenix Force onto it.
It is dipped in it. Right now.
Really?
More so than the Phoenix cage that was built specifically to do just that.
You can't see it, but it's there, dancing. Swirling around it.
Why would your hammer be able to do that?
My father's enchantments are all-powerful.
What does that inscription say?
"Whosoever holds this hammer, if he be worthy, shall possess the power of... Thor."
Everyone knows that.
I didn't.
What does this mean?
DR. McCOY!
I believe we've been given a second chance.

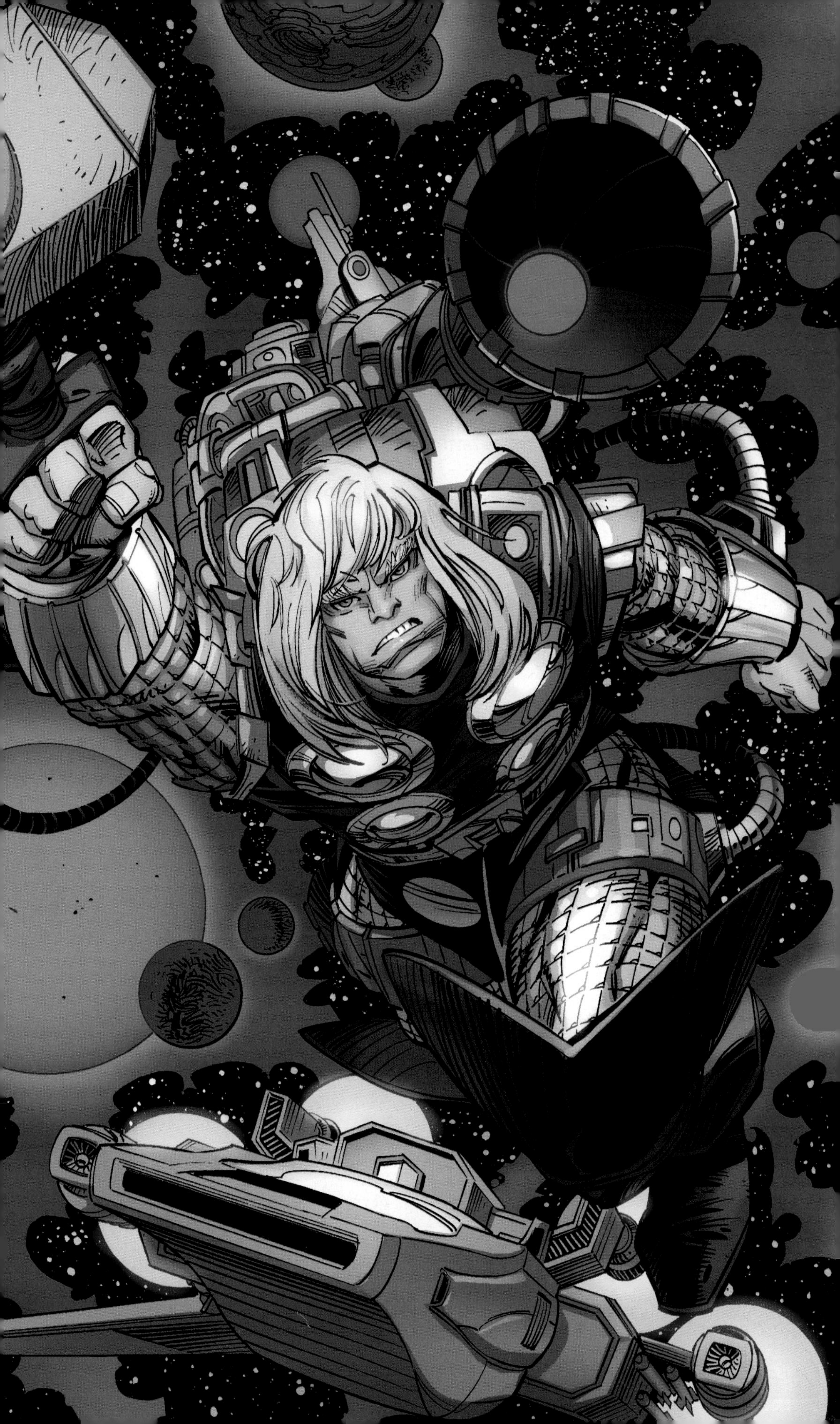

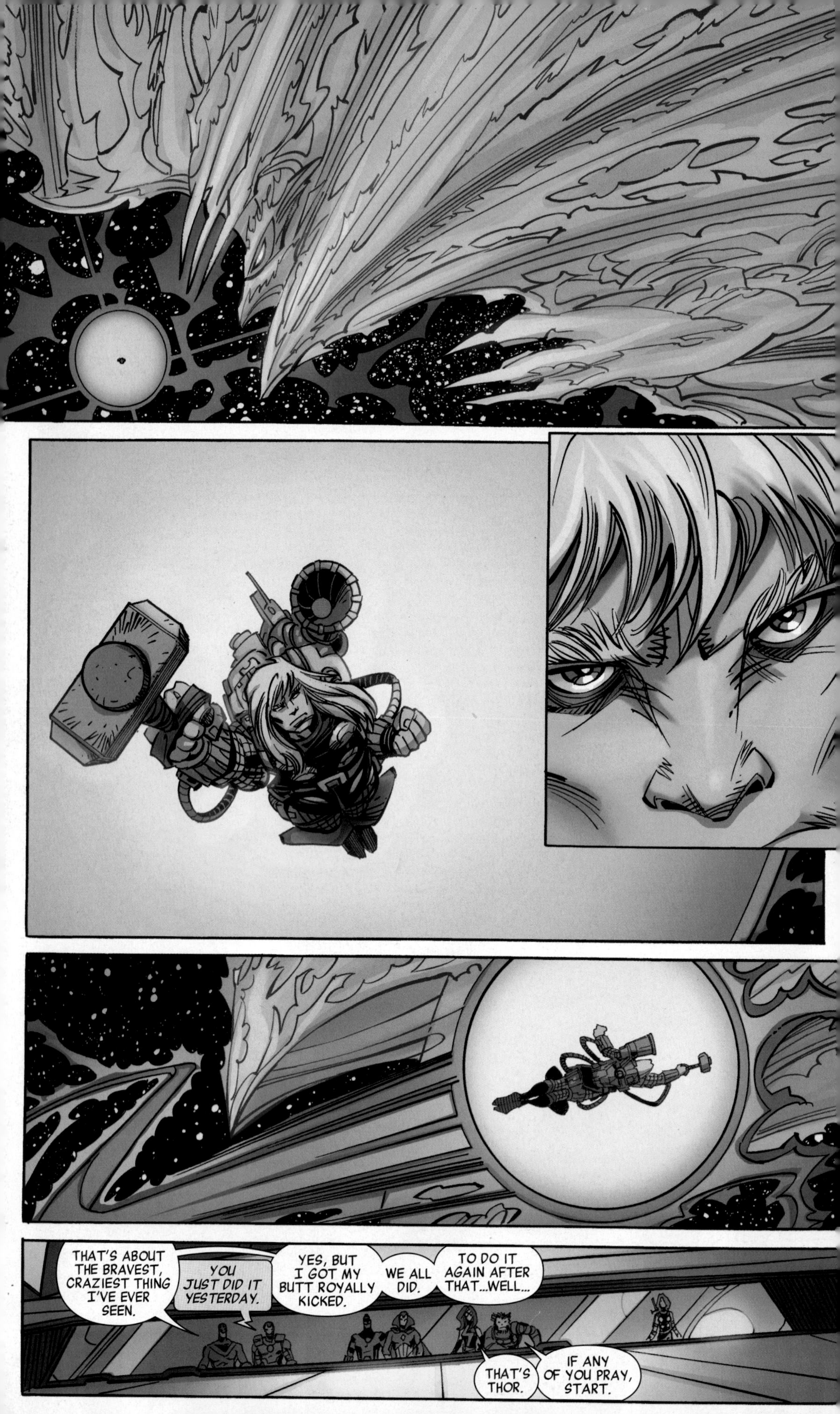
THAT'S ABOUT THE BRAVEST, CRAZIEST THING I'VE EVER SEEN.
YOU JUST DID IT YESTERDAY.
YES, BUT I GOT MY BUTT ROYALLY KICKED.
WE ALL DID.
TO DO IT AGAIN AFTER THAT...WELL...
THAT'S THOR.
IF ANY OF YOU PRAY, START.

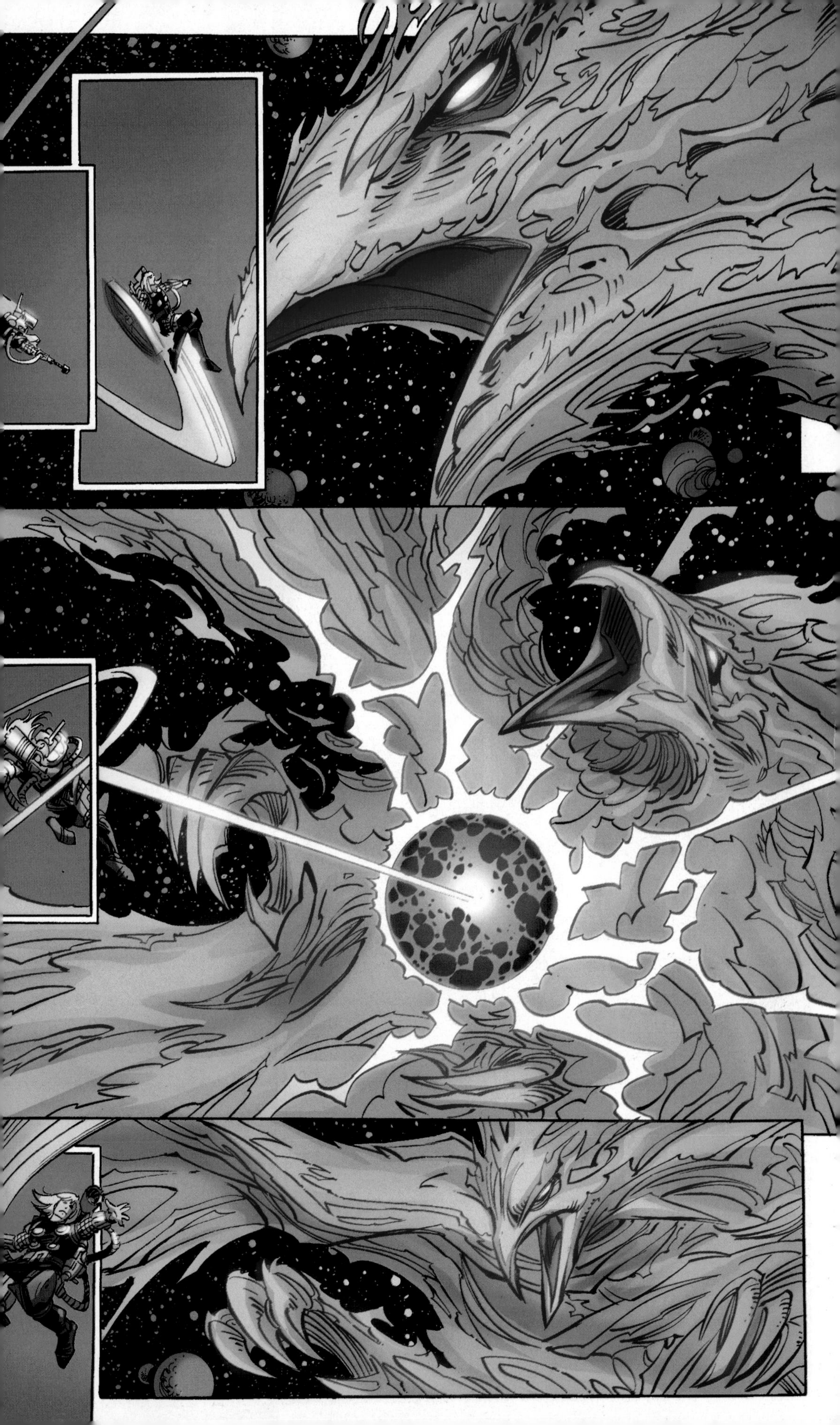

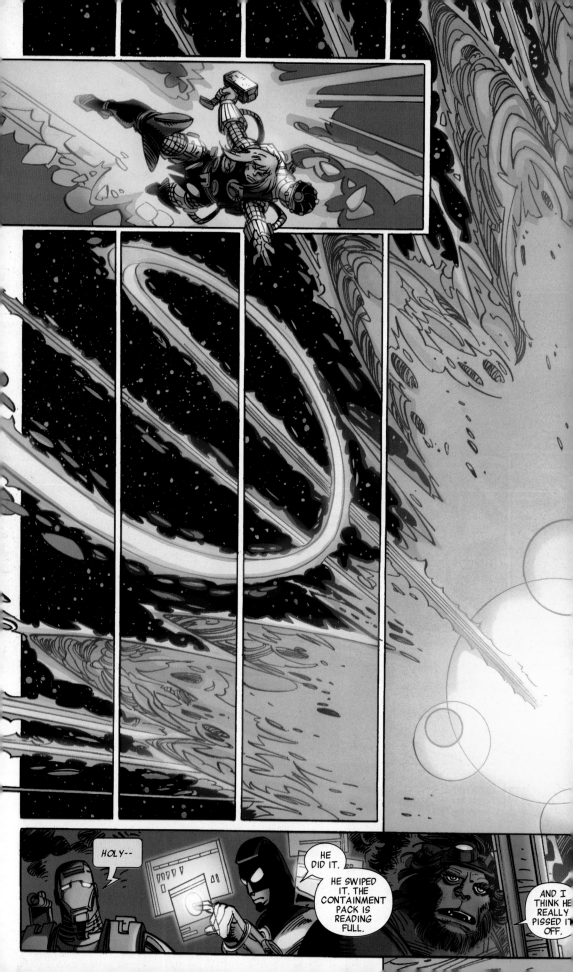

HOLY--

HE DID IT.

HE SWIPED IT. THE CONTAINMENT PACK IS READING FULL.

AND I THINK HE REALLY PISSED IT OFF.

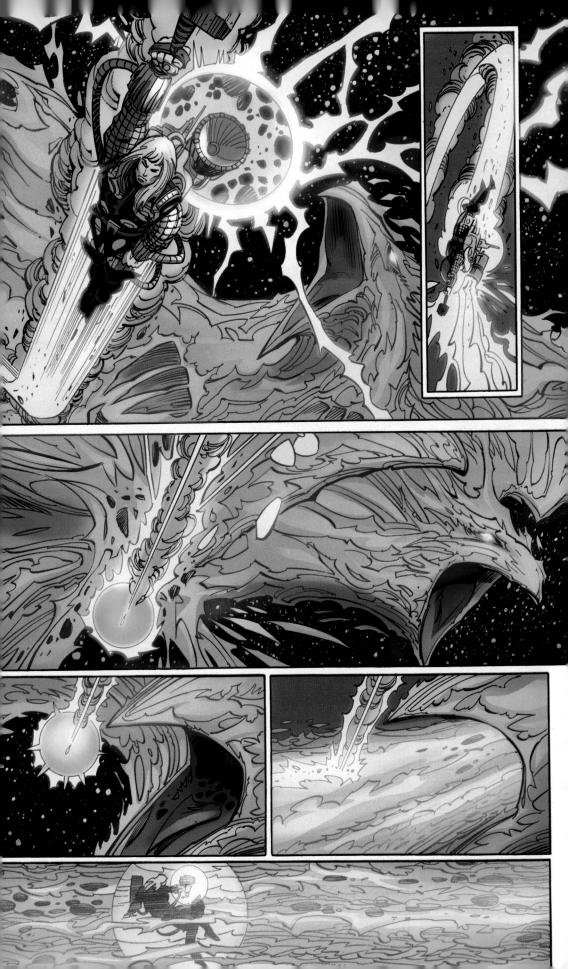

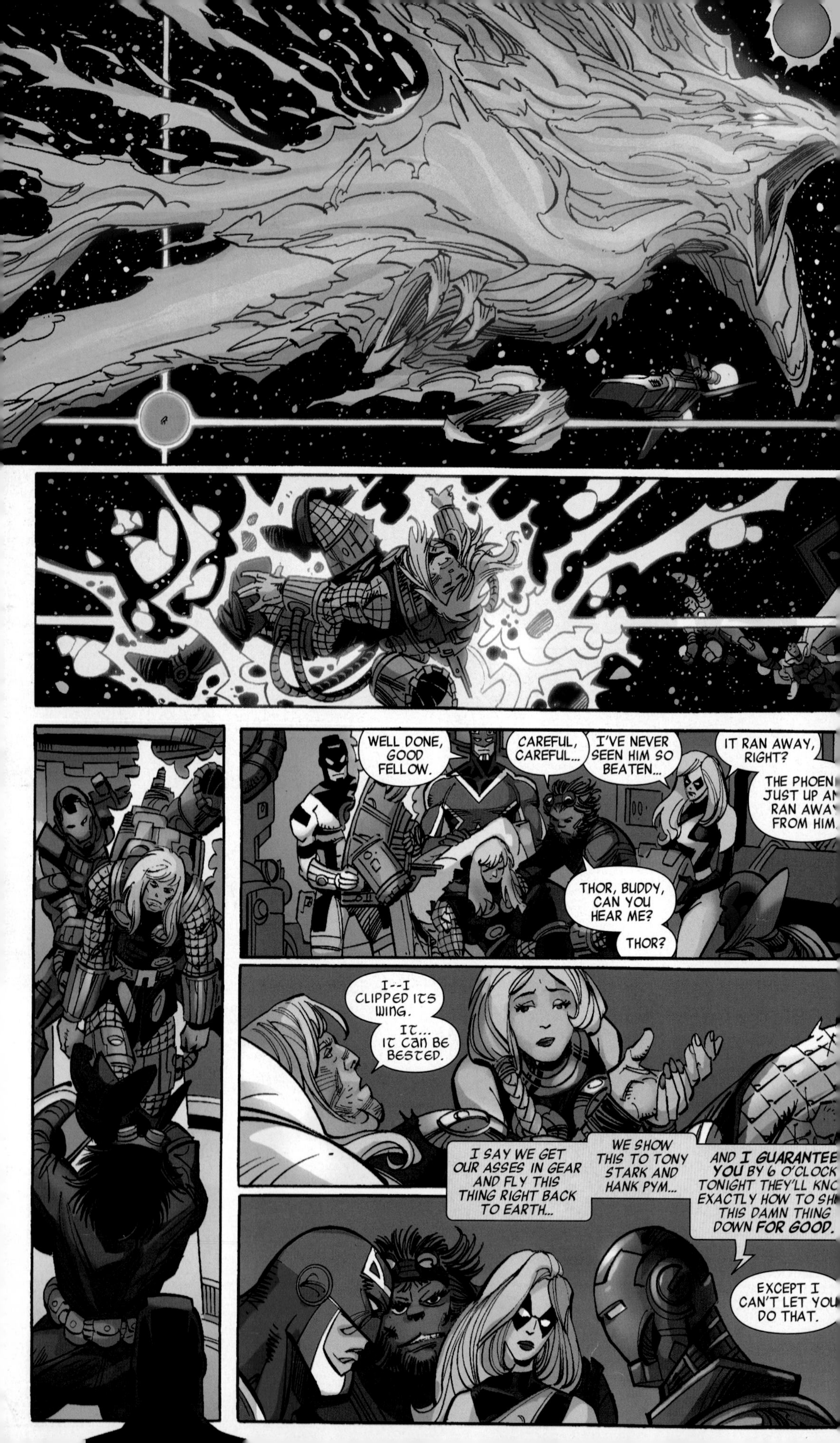
WELL DONE, GOOD FELLOW.
CAREFUL, CAREFUL...
I'VE NEVER SEEN HIM SO BEATEN...
IT RAN AWAY, RIGHT?
THE PHOEN JUST UP AN RAN AWA FROM HIM.
THOR, BUDDY, CAN YOU HEAR ME?
THOR?
I--I CLIPPED ITS WING.
IT... IT CAN BE BESTED.
I SAY WE GET OUR ASSES IN GEAR AND FLY THIS THING RIGHT BACK TO EARTH...
WE SHOW THIS TO TONY STARK AND HANK PYM...
AND I GUARANTEE YOU BY 6 O'CLOCK TONIGHT THEY'LL KNO EXACTLY HOW TO SH THIS DAMN THING DOWN FOR GOOD.
EXCEPT I CAN'T LET YOU DO THAT.

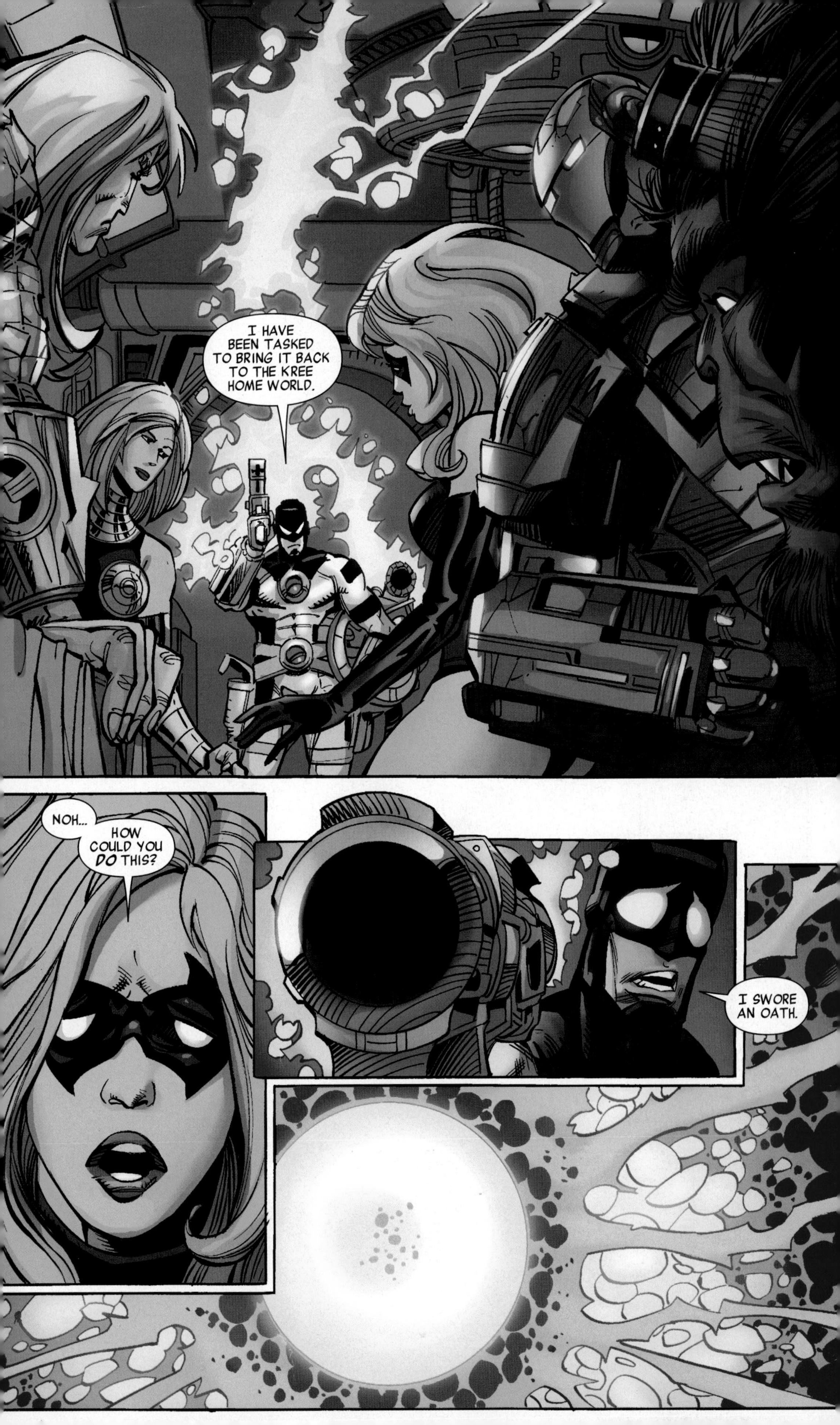
I HAVE BEEN TASKED TO BRING IT BACK TO THE KREE HOME WORLD.
NOH...
HOW COULD YOU DO THIS?
I SWORE AN OATH.

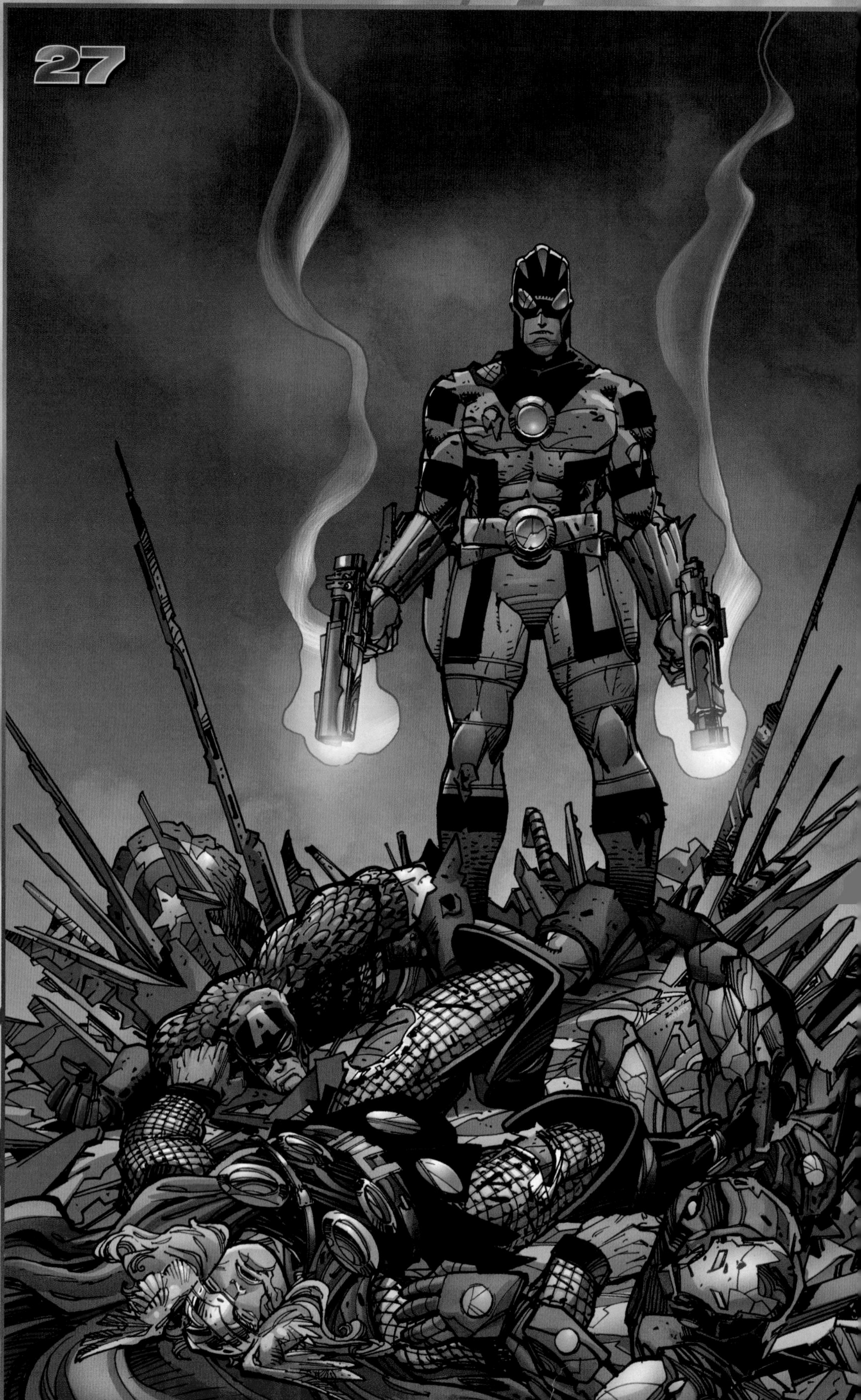
27

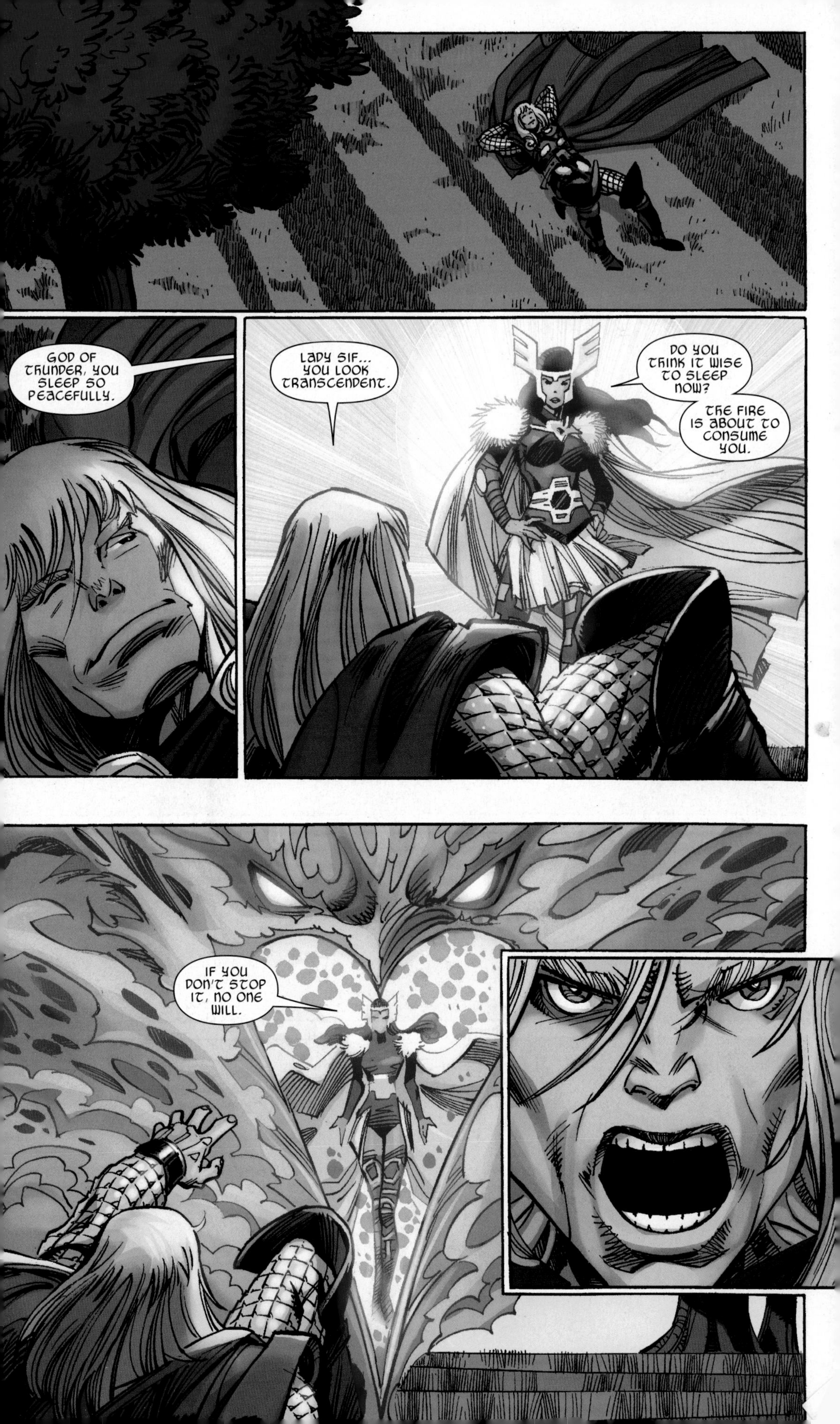
GOD OF THUNDER, YOU SLEEP SO PEACEFULLY.
LADY SIF... YOU LOOK TRANSCENDENT.
DO YOU THINK IT WISE TO SLEEP NOW?
THE FIRE IS ABOUT TO CONSUME YOU.
IF YOU DON'T STOP IT, NO ONE WILL.

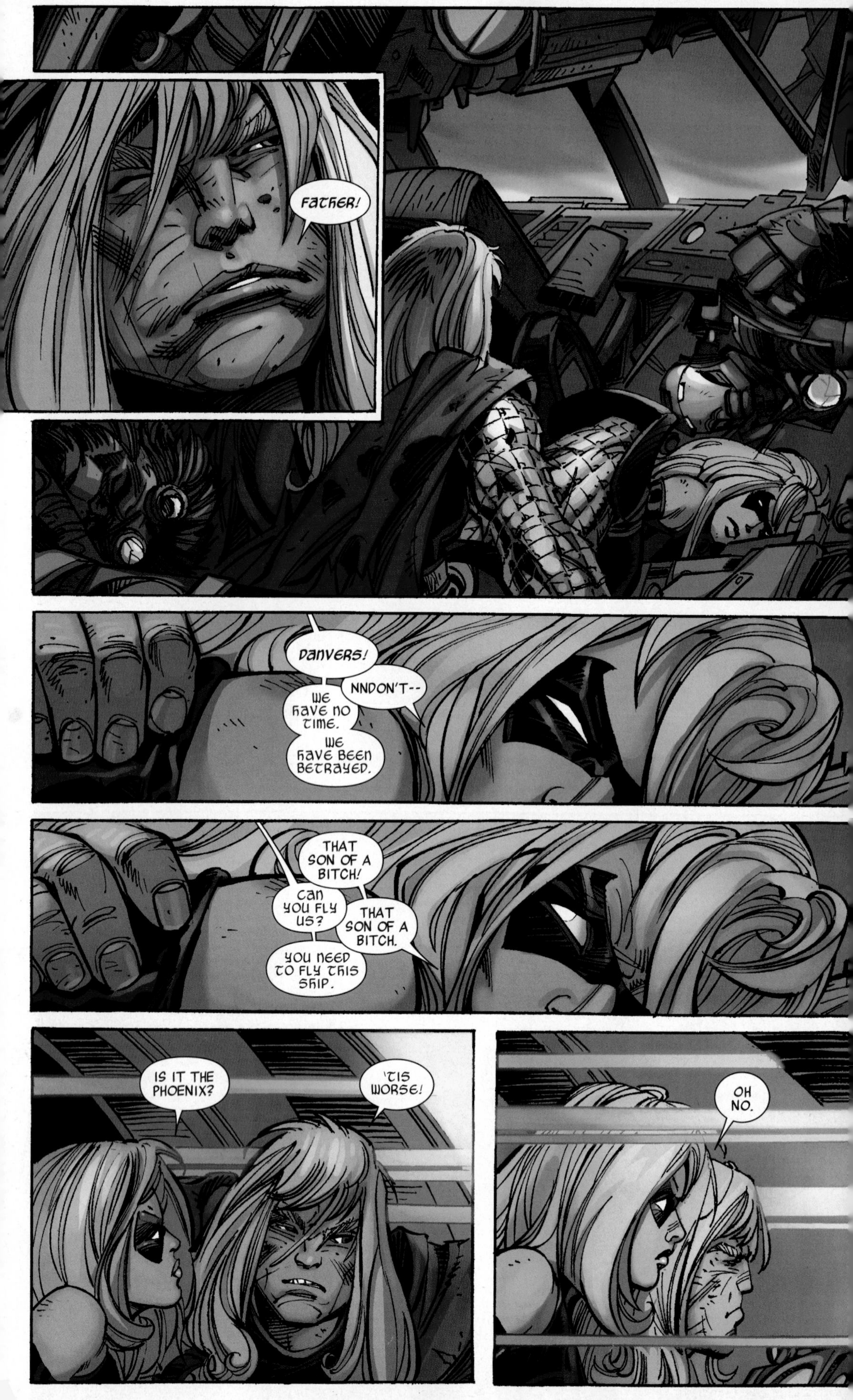
FATHER!
DANVERS!
NNDON'T--
WE HAVE NO TIME.
WE HAVE BEEN BETRAYED.
THAT SON OF A BITCH!
CAN YOU FLY US?
THAT SON OF A BITCH.
YOU NEED TO FLY THIS SHIP.
IS IT THE PHOENIX?
'TIS WORSE!
OH NO.

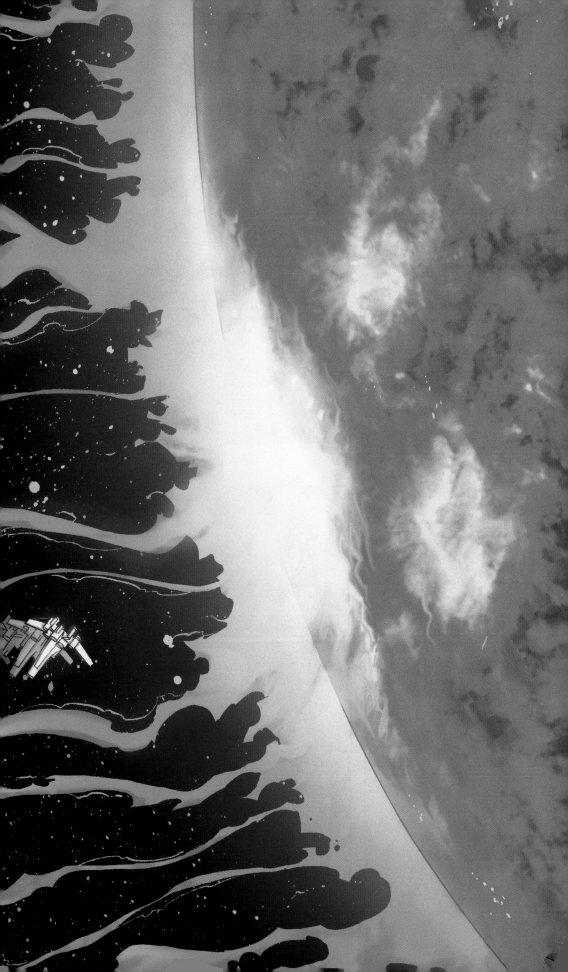

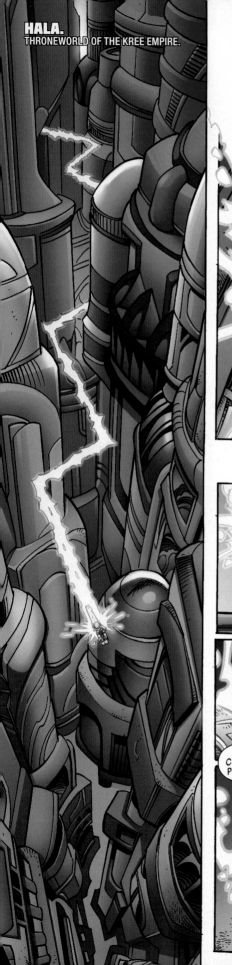

I AM NOH-VARR OF THE KREE.

I AM HERE TO SEE THE SUPREME INTELLIGENCE AT HIS REQUEST.

WE KNOW EXACTLY WHO YOU ARE AND WHAT YOU BRING US, NOH-VARR.

HOW COULD YOU POSSIBLY?

THE SUPREME INTELLIGENCE HAS BEEN OBSERVING YOUR QUEST.

I AM SINTA THE ACCUSER. PLEASE FOLLOW ME.

YOU HAVE BROUGHT US A MOST GLORIOUS DAY OF HOPE.

NOH-VA I PRESEN YOU.

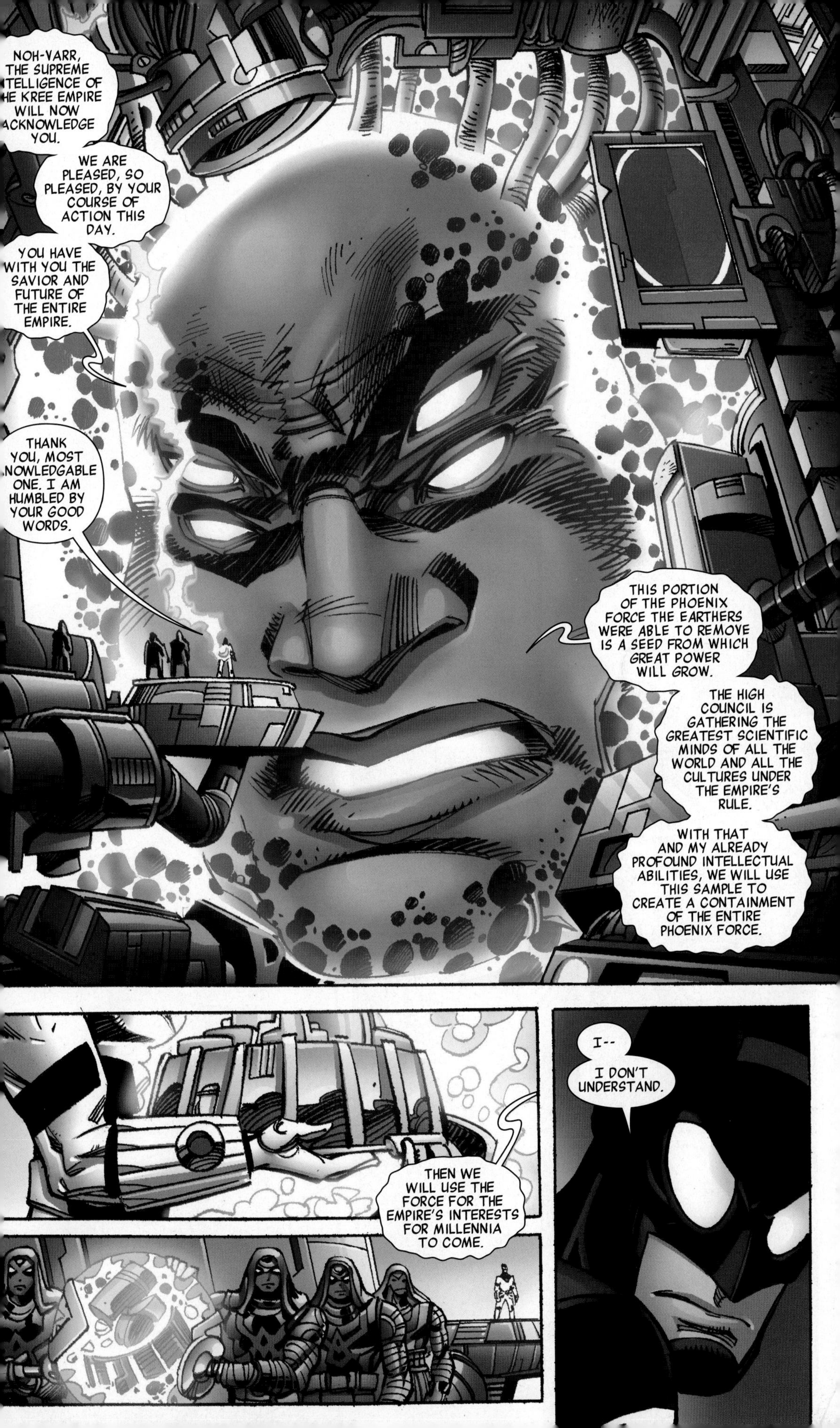
NOH-VARR, THE SUPREME INTELLIGENCE OF THE KREE EMPIRE WILL NOW ACKNOWLEDGE YOU.
WE ARE PLEASED, SO PLEASED, BY YOUR COURSE OF ACTION THIS DAY.
YOU HAVE WITH YOU THE SAVIOR AND FUTURE OF THE ENTIRE EMPIRE.
THANK YOU, MOST NOWLEDGABLE ONE. I AM HUMBLED BY YOUR GOOD WORDS.
THIS PORTION OF THE PHOENIX FORCE THE EARTHERS WERE ABLE TO REMOVE IS A SEED FROM WHICH GREAT POWER WILL GROW.
THE HIGH COUNCIL IS GATHERING THE GREATEST SCIENTIFIC MINDS OF ALL THE WORLD AND ALL THE CULTURES UNDER THE EMPIRE'S RULE.
WITH THAT AND MY ALREADY PROFOUND INTELLECTUAL ABILITIES, WE WILL USE THIS SAMPLE TO CREATE A CONTAINMENT OF THE ENTIRE PHOENIX FORCE.
THEN WE WILL USE THE FORCE FOR THE EMPIRE'S INTERESTS FOR MILLENNIA TO COME.
I--
I DON'T UNDERSTAND.

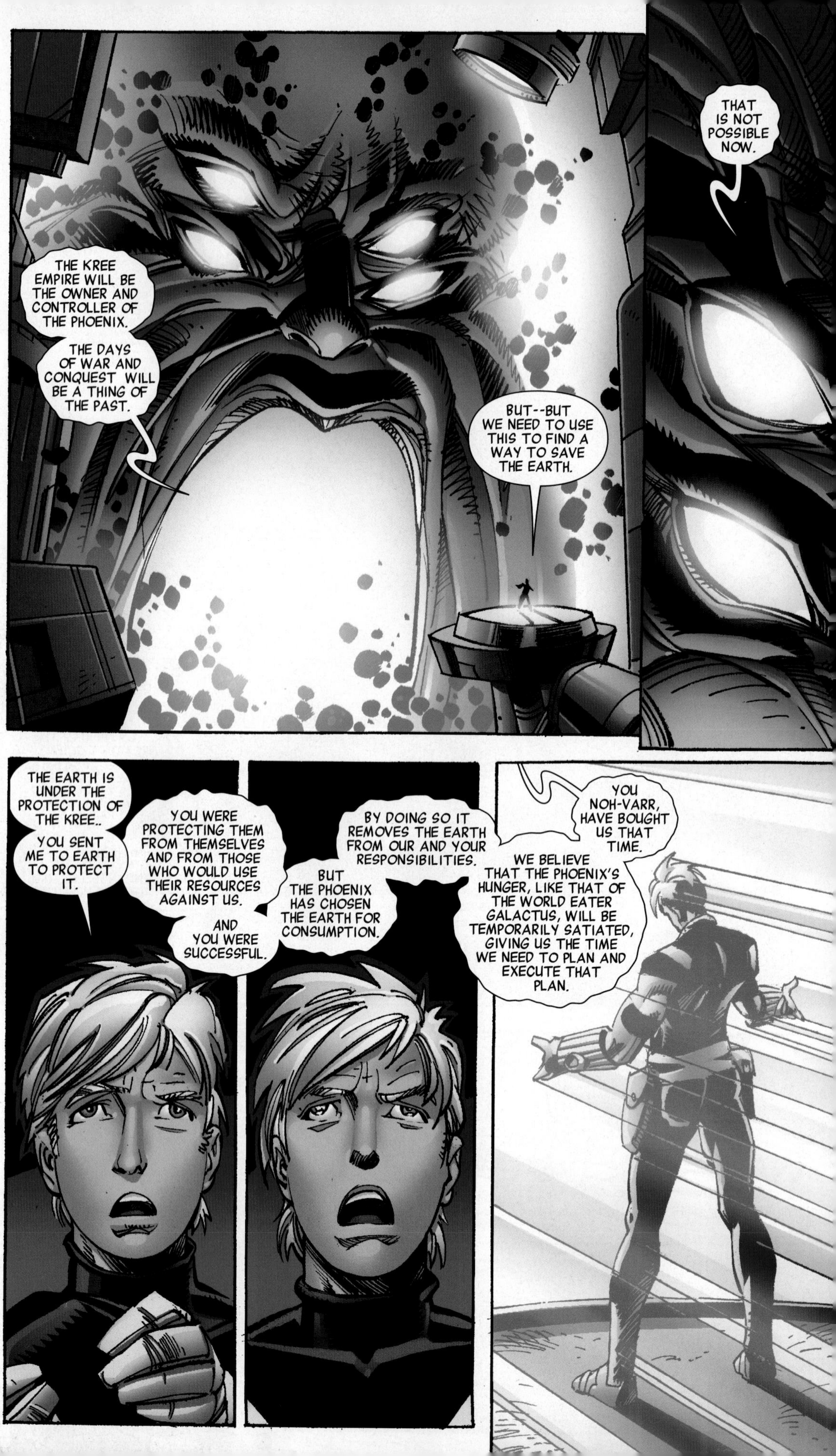

THE KREE EMPIRE WILL BE THE OWNER AND CONTROLLER OF THE PHOENIX.
THE DAYS OF WAR AND CONQUEST WILL BE A THING OF THE PAST.
BUT--BUT WE NEED TO USE THIS TO FIND A WAY TO SAVE THE EARTH.
THAT IS NOT POSSIBLE NOW.
THE EARTH IS UNDER THE PROTECTION OF THE KREE..
YOU SENT ME TO EARTH TO PROTECT IT.
YOU WERE PROTECTING THEM FROM THEMSELVES AND FROM THOSE WHO WOULD USE THEIR RESOURCES AGAINST US.
AND YOU WERE SUCCESSFUL.
BUT THE PHOENIX HAS CHOSEN THE EARTH FOR CONSUMPTION.
BY DOING SO IT REMOVES THE EARTH FROM OUR AND YOUR RESPONSIBILITIES.
YOU NOH-VARR, HAVE BOUGHT US THAT TIME.
WE BELIEVE THAT THE PHOENIX'S HUNGER, LIKE THAT OF THE WORLD EATER GALACTUS, WILL BE TEMPORARILY SATIATED, GIVING US THE TIME WE NEED TO PLAN AND EXECUTE THAT PLAN.

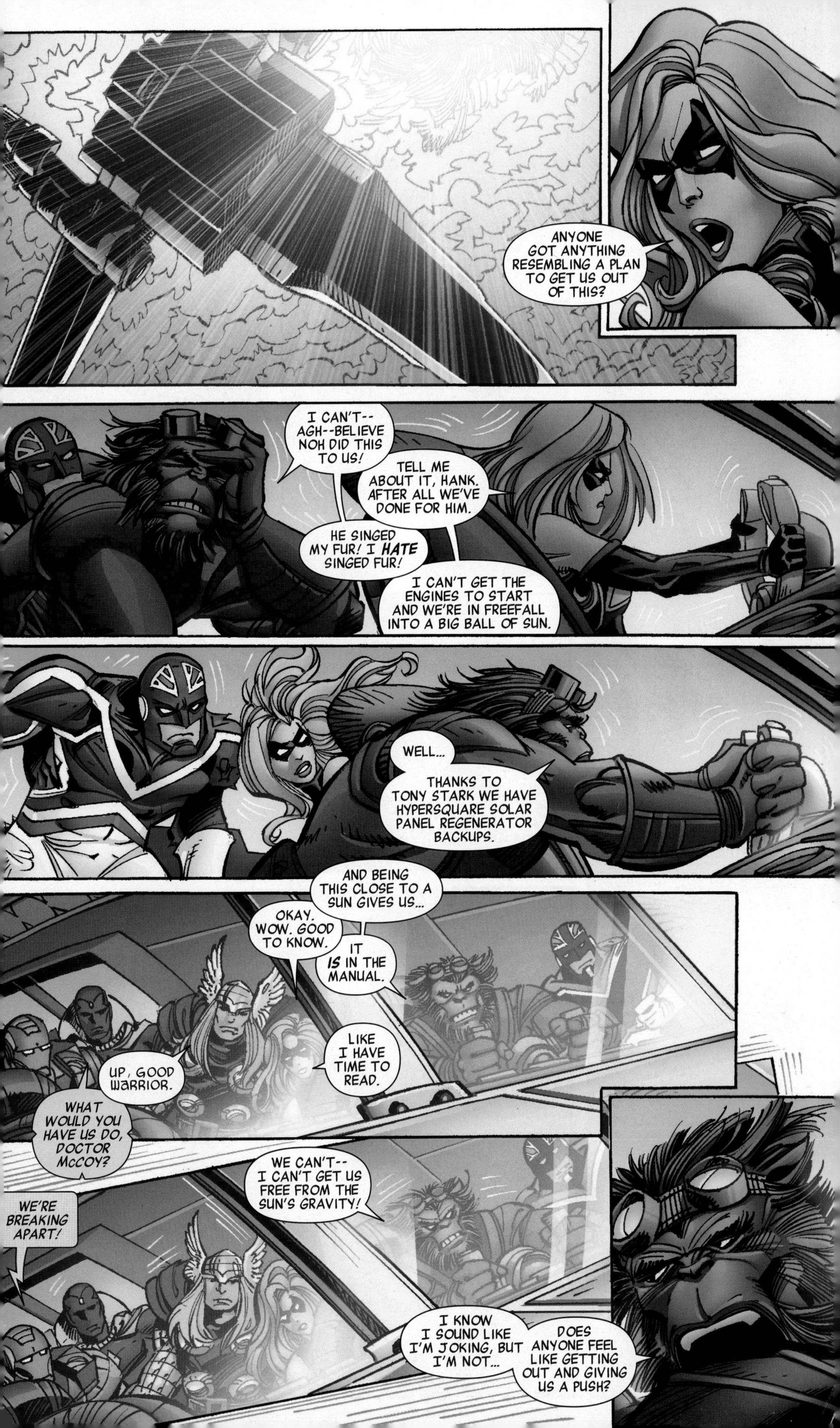
ANYONE GOT ANYTHING RESEMBLING A PLAN TO GET US OUT OF THIS?
I CAN'T--AGH--BELIEVE NOH DID THIS TO US!
TELL ME ABOUT IT, HANK. AFTER ALL WE'VE DONE FOR HIM.
HE SINGED MY FUR! I HATE SINGED FUR!
I CAN'T GET THE ENGINES TO START AND WE'RE IN FREEFALL INTO A BIG BALL OF SUN.
WELL...
THANKS TO TONY STARK WE HAVE HYPERSQUARE SOLAR PANEL REGENERATOR BACKUPS.
AND BEING THIS CLOSE TO A SUN GIVES US...
OKAY. WOW. GOOD TO KNOW.
IT IS IN THE MANUAL.
LIKE I HAVE TIME TO READ.
UP, GOOD WARRIOR.
WHAT WOULD YOU HAVE US DO, DOCTOR McCOY?
WE'RE BREAKING APART!
WE CAN'T-- I CAN'T GET US FREE FROM THE SUN'S GRAVITY!
I KNOW I SOUND LIKE I'M JOKING, BUT I'M NOT...
DOES ANYONE FEEL LIKE GETTING OUT AND GIVING US A PUSH?

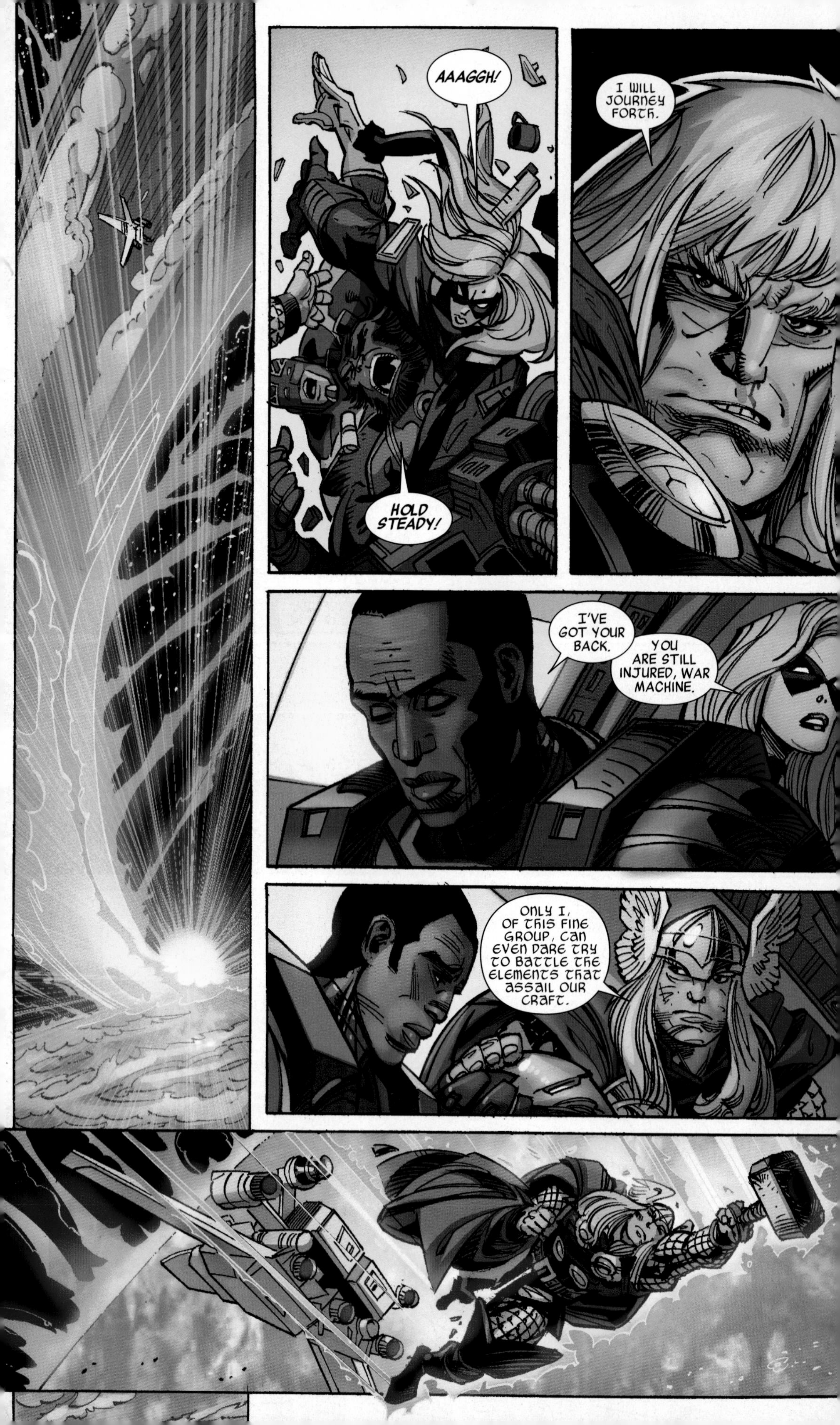
AAAGGH!
HOLD STEADY!
I WILL JOURNEY FORTH.
I'VE GOT YOUR BACK.
YOU ARE STILL INJURED, WAR MACHINE.
ONLY I, OF THIS FINE GROUP, CAN EVEN DARE TRY TO BATTLE THE ELEMENTS THAT ASSAIL OUR CRAFT.

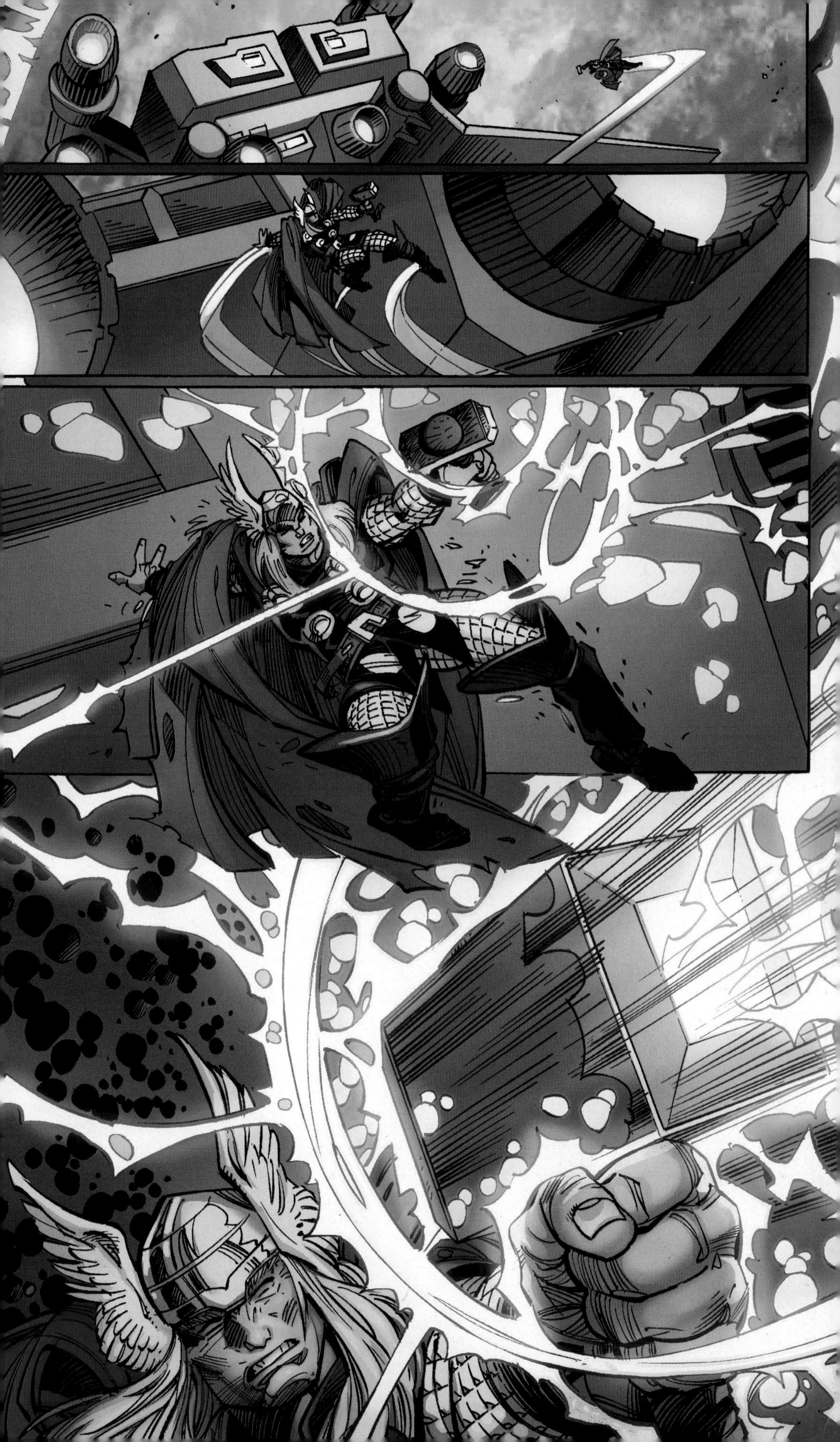

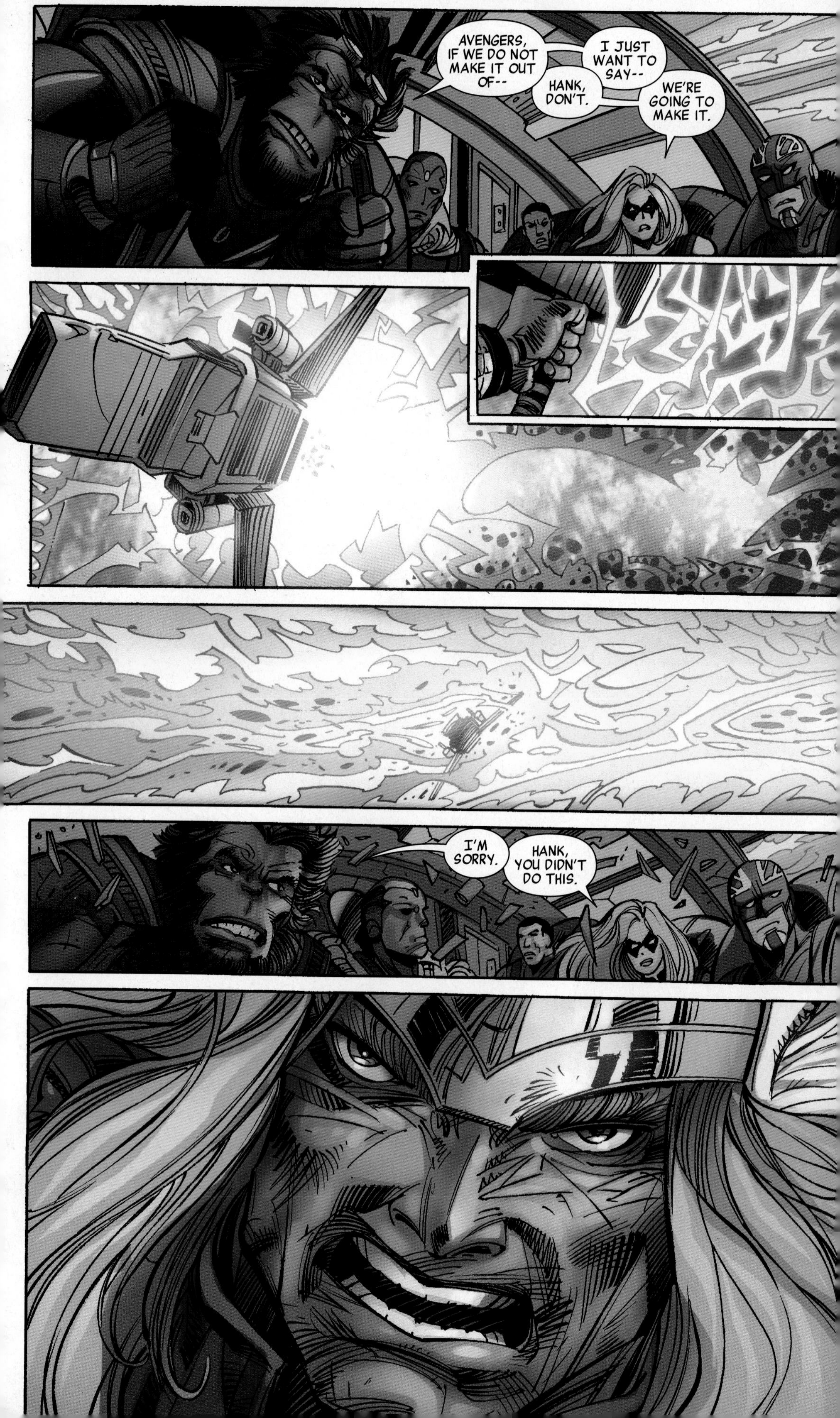
AVENGERS, IF WE DO NOT MAKE IT OUT OF--
I JUST WANT TO SAY--
HANK, DON'T.
WE'RE GOING TO MAKE IT.
I'M SORRY.
HANK, YOU DIDN'T DO THIS.

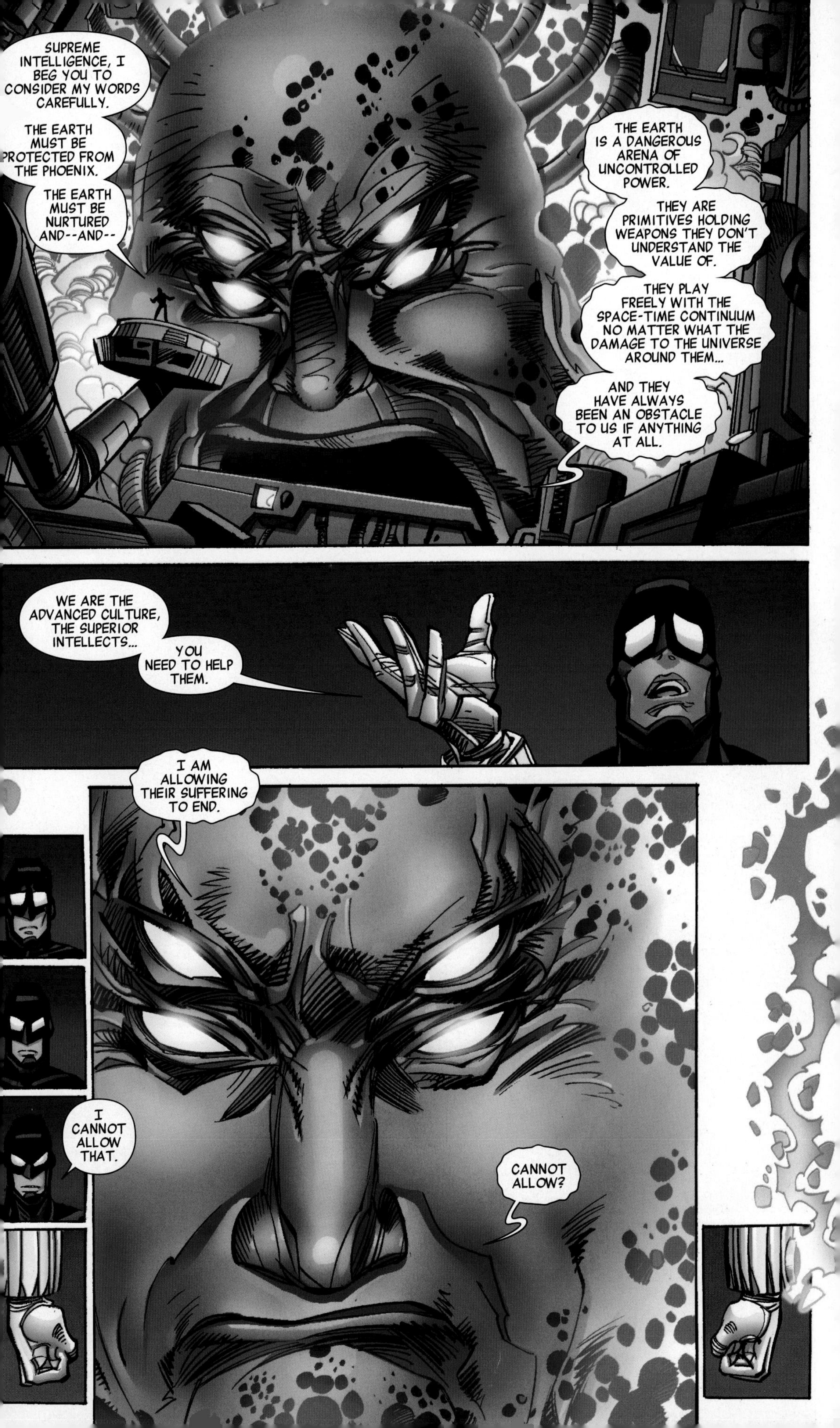
SUPREME INTELLIGENCE, I BEG YOU TO CONSIDER MY WORDS CAREFULLY.
THE EARTH MUST BE PROTECTED FROM THE PHOENIX.
THE EARTH MUST BE NURTURED AND--AND--
THE EARTH IS A DANGEROUS ARENA OF UNCONTROLLED POWER.
THEY ARE PRIMITIVES HOLDING WEAPONS THEY DON'T UNDERSTAND THE VALUE OF.
THEY PLAY FREELY WITH THE SPACE-TIME CONTINUUM NO MATTER WHAT THE DAMAGE TO THE UNIVERSE AROUND THEM...
AND THEY HAVE ALWAYS BEEN AN OBSTACLE TO US IF ANYTHING AT ALL.
WE ARE THE ADVANCED CULTURE, THE SUPERIOR INTELLECTS...
YOU NEED TO HELP THEM.
I AM ALLOWING THEIR SUFFERING TO END.
I CANNOT ALLOW THAT.
CANNOT ALLOW?

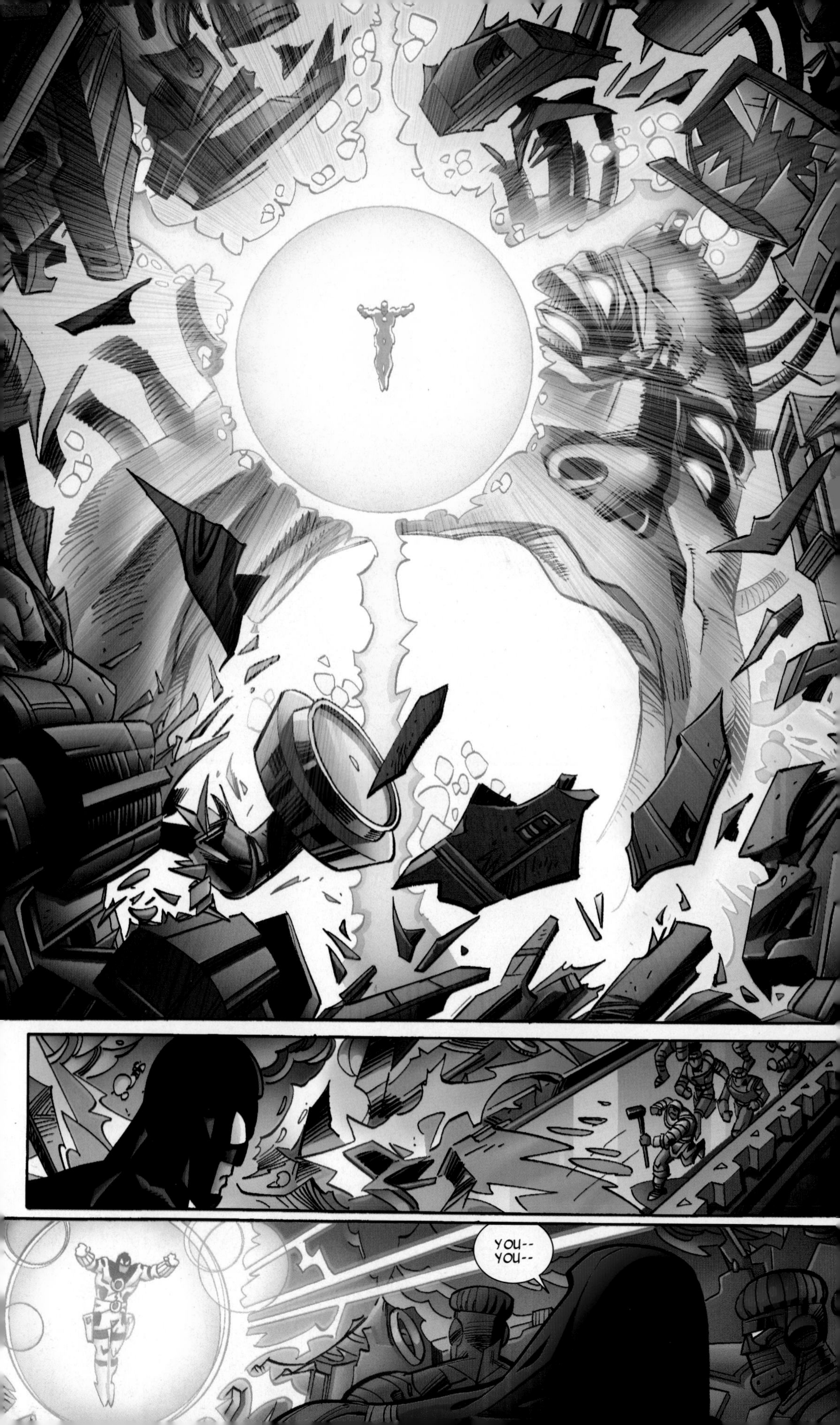
YOU--
YOU--

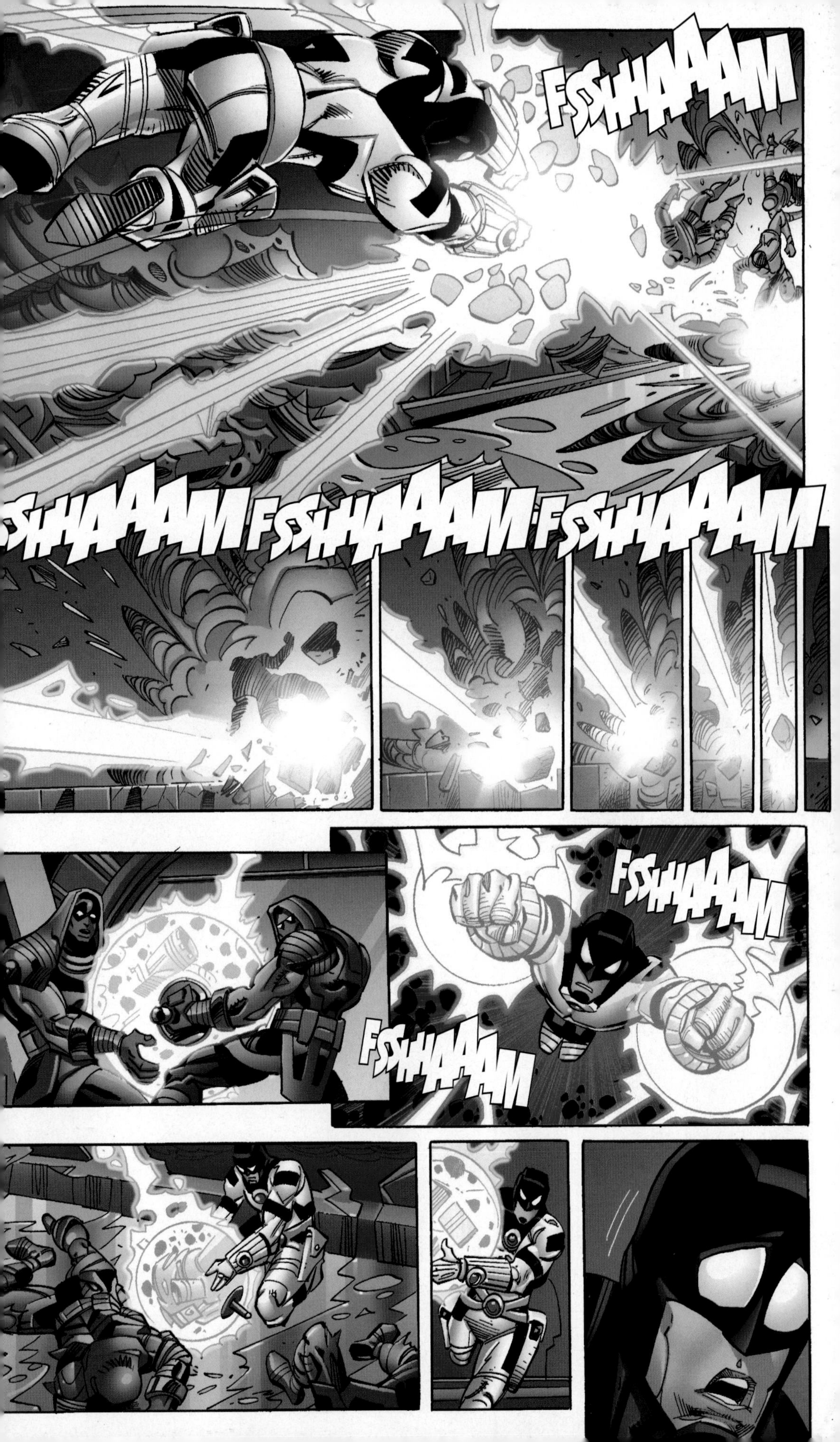
FSSHAAAAM
FSSHAAAAM
FSSHAAAAM
FSSHAAAAM
FSSHAAAAM
FSSHAAAAM

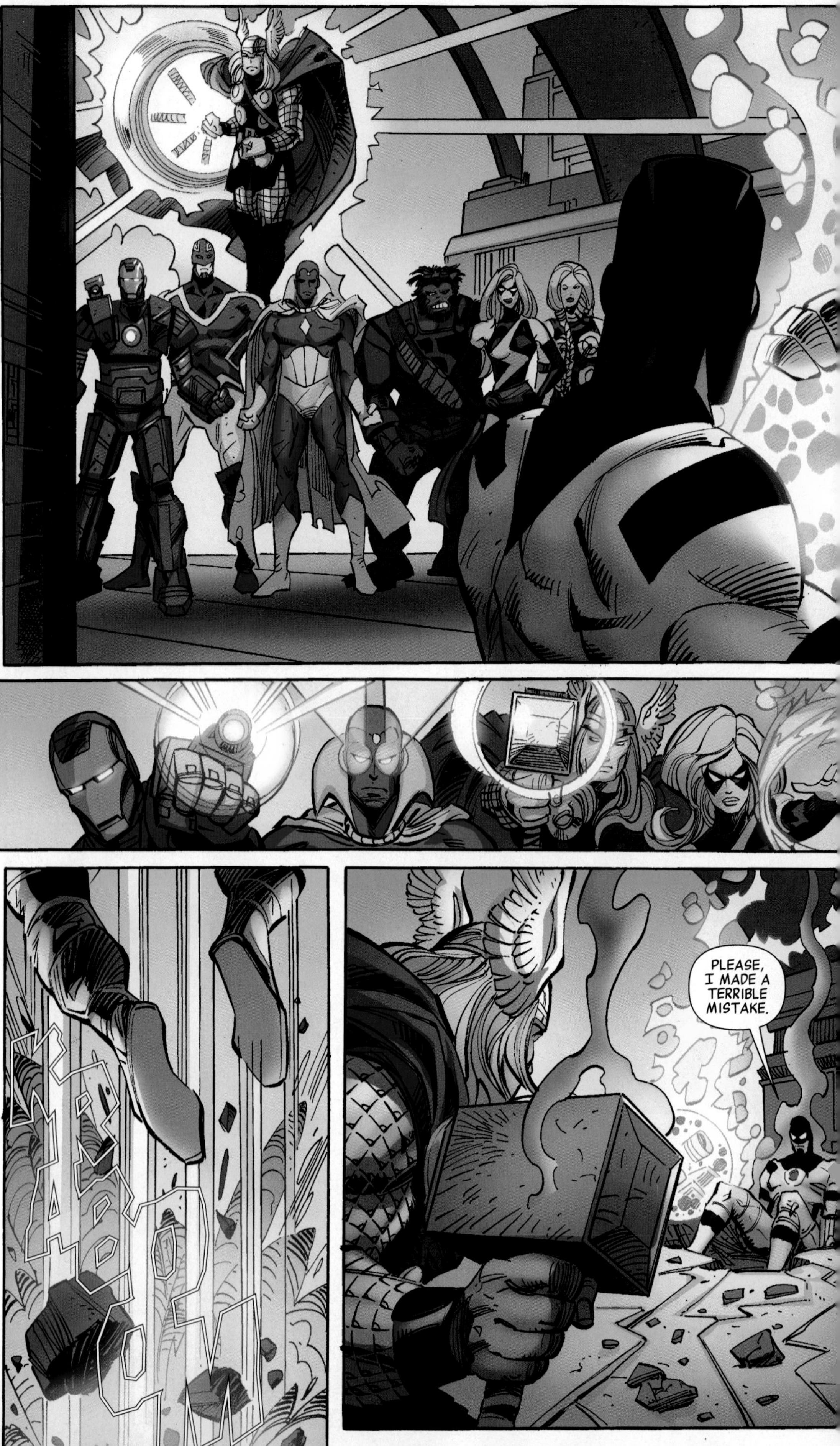
PLEASE, I MADE A TERRIBLE MISTAKE.

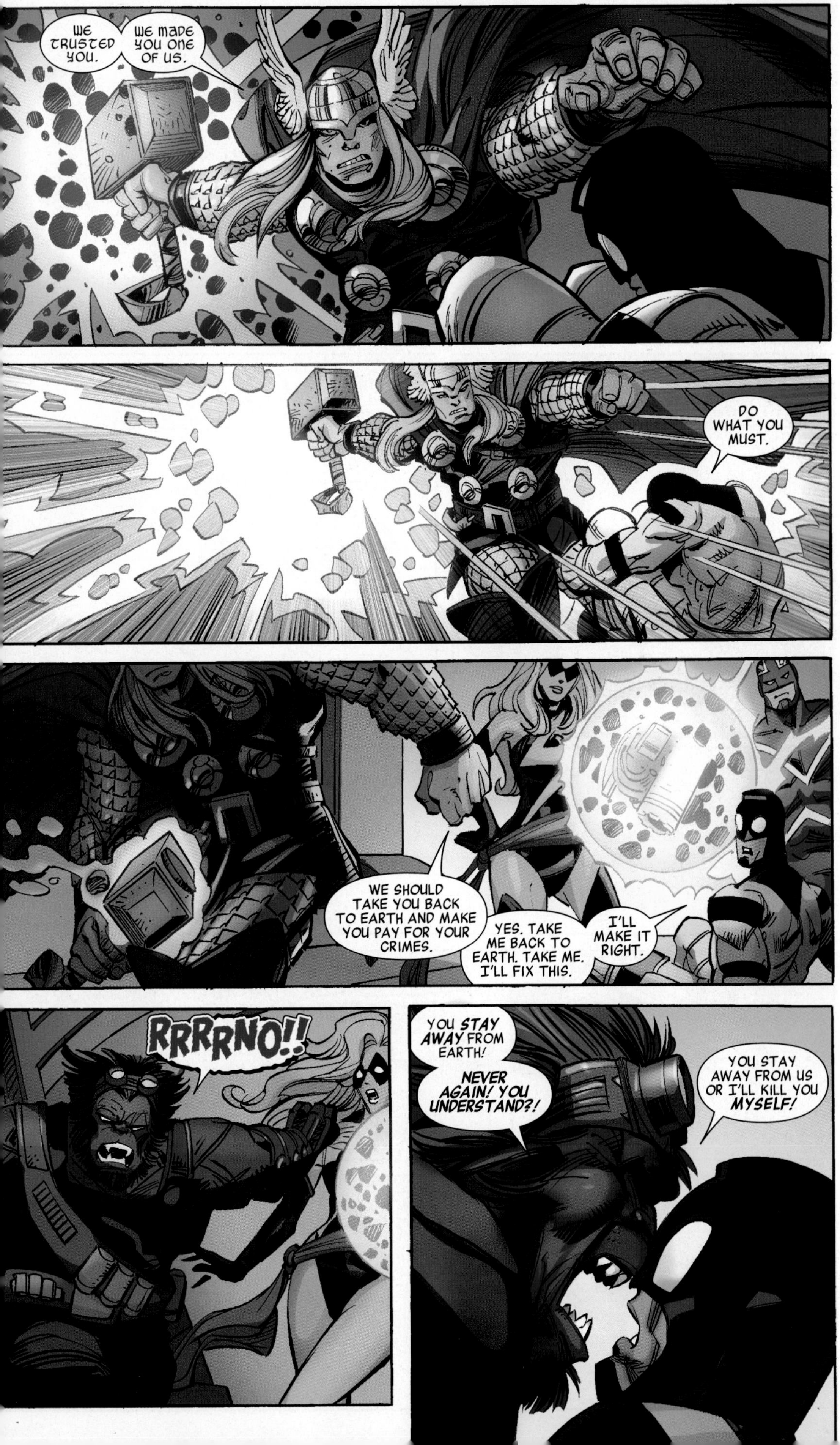
WE TRUSTED YOU.
WE MADE YOU ONE OF US.
DO WHAT YOU MUST.
WE SHOULD TAKE YOU BACK TO EARTH AND MAKE YOU PAY FOR YOUR CRIMES.
YES. TAKE ME BACK TO EARTH. TAKE ME. I'LL FIX THIS.
I'LL MAKE IT RIGHT.
RRRRNO!!
YOU STAY AWAY FROM EARTH!
NEVER AGAIN! YOU UNDERSTAND?!
YOU STAY AWAY FROM US OR I'LL KILL YOU MYSELF!

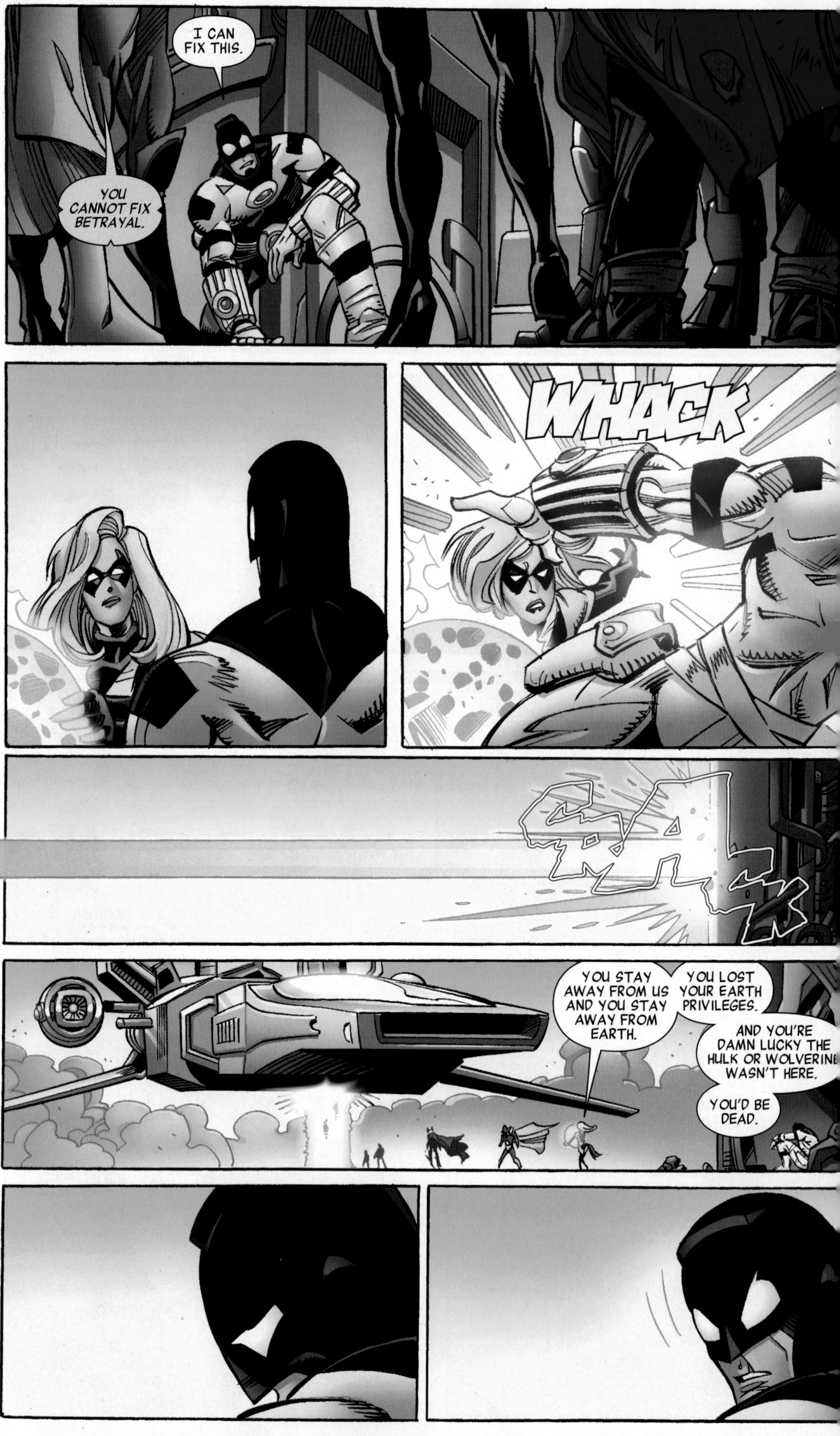
I CAN FIX THIS.
YOU CANNOT FIX BETRAYAL.
WHACK
YOU STAY AWAY FROM US AND YOU STAY AWAY FROM EARTH.
YOU LOST YOUR EARTH PRIVILEGES.
AND YOU'RE DAMN LUCKY THE HULK OR WOLVERINE WASN'T HERE.
YOU'D BE DEAD.

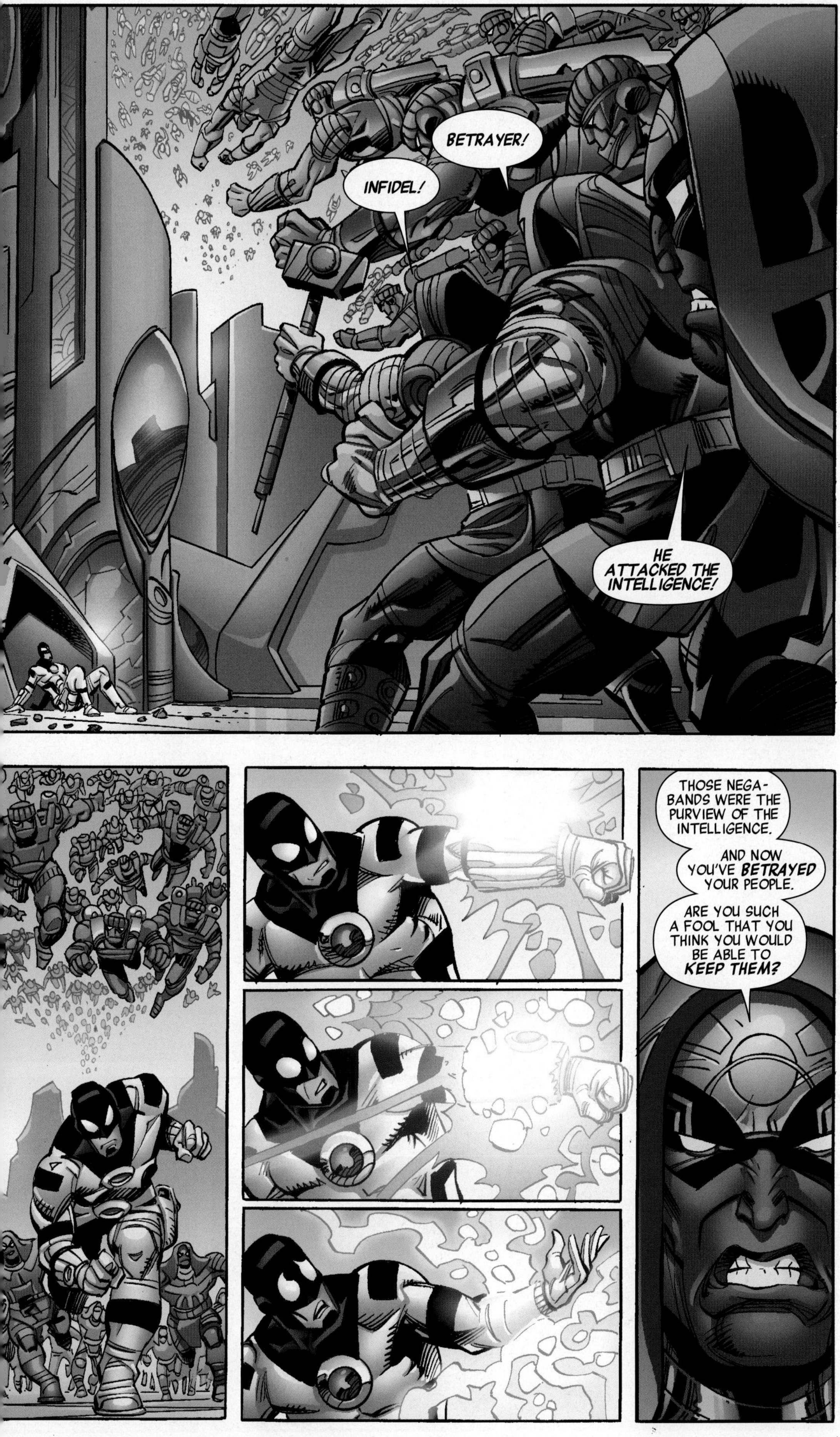
BETRAYER!
INFIDEL!
HE ATTACKED THE INTELLIGENCE!
THOSE NEGA-BANDS WERE THE PURVIEW OF THE INTELLIGENCE.
AND NOW YOU'VE BETRAYED YOUR PEOPLE.
ARE YOU SUCH A FOOL THAT YOU THINK YOU WOULD BE ABLE TO KEEP THEM?

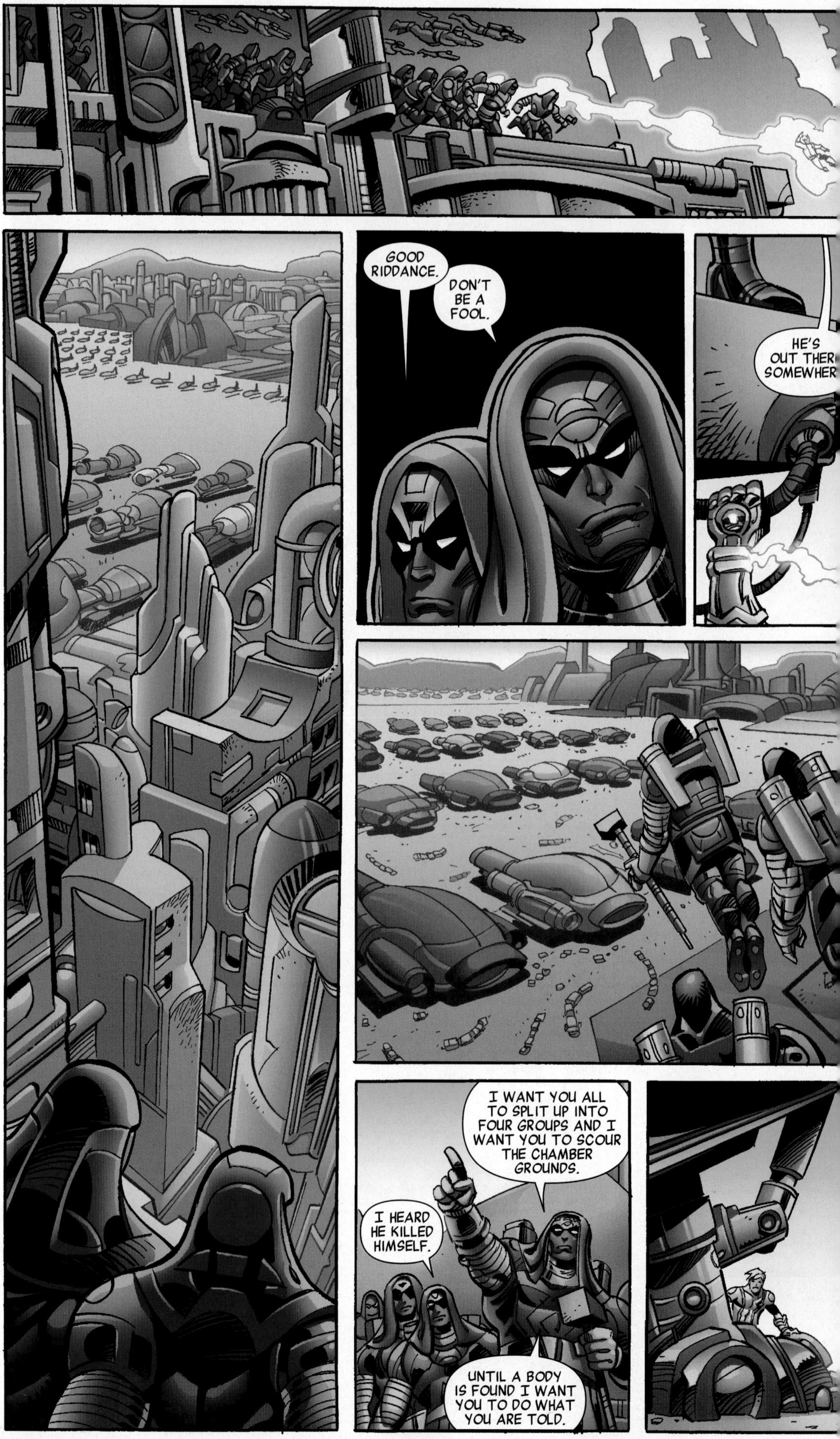
GOOD RIDDANCE.
DON'T BE A FOOL.
HE'S OUT THER SOMEWHER
I WANT YOU ALL TO SPLIT UP INTO FOUR GROUPS AND I WANT YOU TO SCOUR THE CHAMBER GROUNDS.
I HEARD HE KILLED HIMSELF.
UNTIL A BODY IS FOUND I WANT YOU TO DO WHAT YOU ARE TOLD.

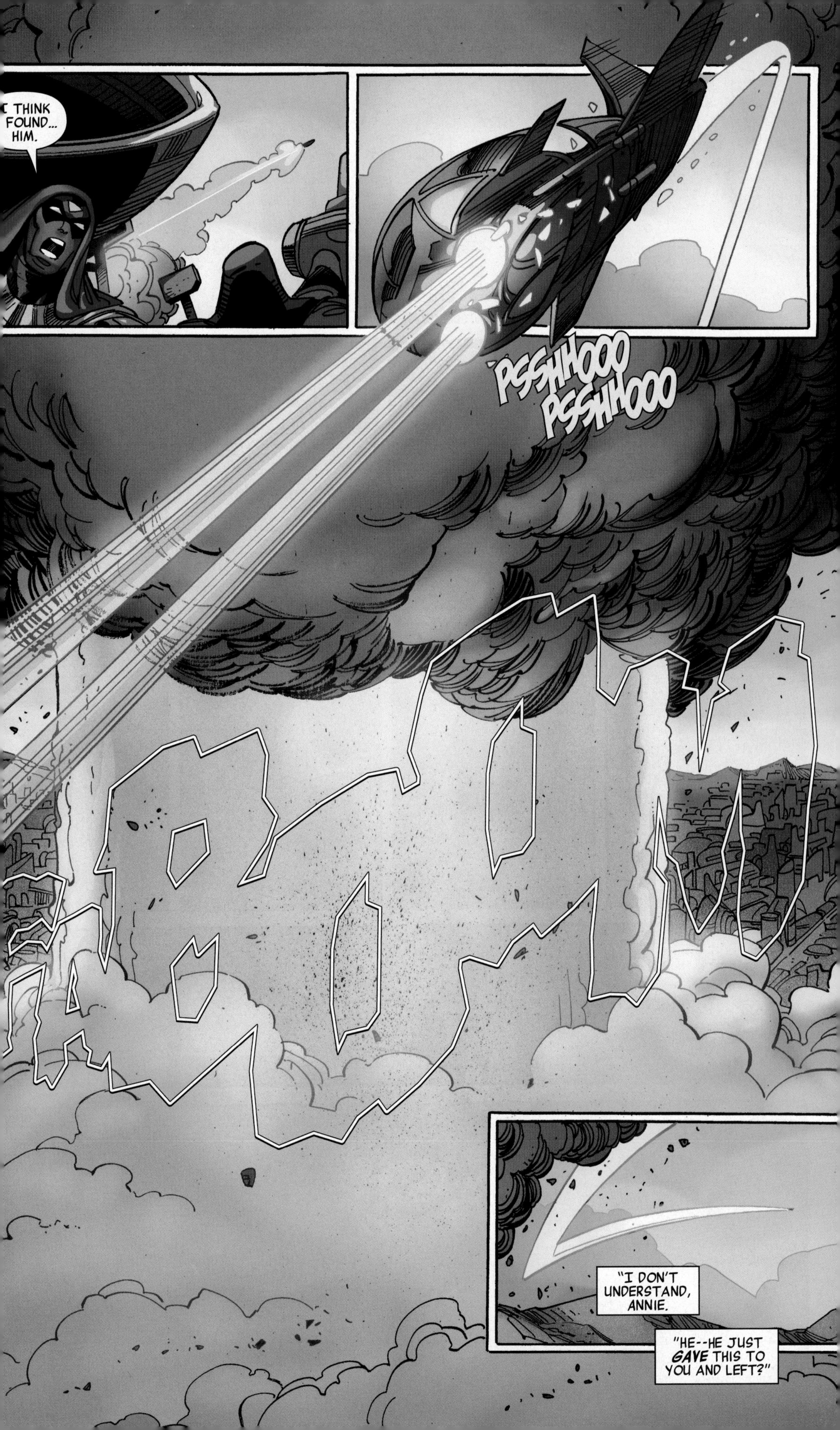

I THINK I FOUND... HIM.
PSSHHOOO
PSSHHOOO
"I DON'T UNDERSTAND, ANNIE.
"HE--HE JUST *GAVE* THIS TO YOU AND LEFT?"

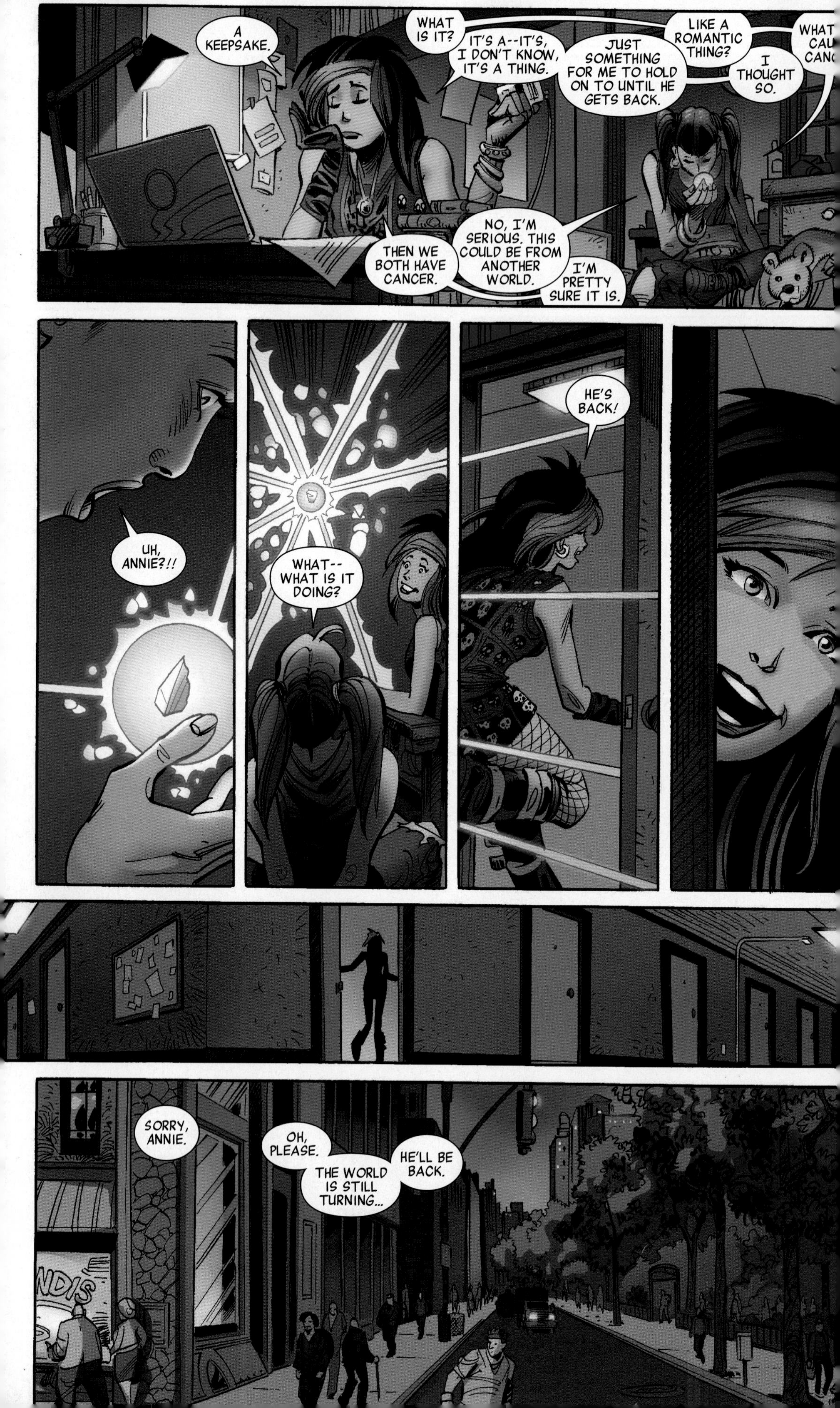
A KEEPSAKE.
WHAT IS IT?
IT'S A--IT'S, I DON'T KNOW, IT'S A THING.
JUST SOMETHING FOR ME TO HOLD ON TO UNTIL HE GETS BACK.
LIKE A ROMANTIC THING?
I THOUGHT SO.
THEN WE BOTH HAVE CANCER.
NO, I'M SERIOUS. THIS COULD BE FROM ANOTHER WORLD.
I'M PRETTY SURE IT IS.
UH, ANNIE?!!
WHAT--WHAT IS IT DOING?
HE'S BACK!
SORRY, ANNIE.
OH, PLEASE.
THE WORLD IS STILL TURNING...
HE'LL BE BACK.

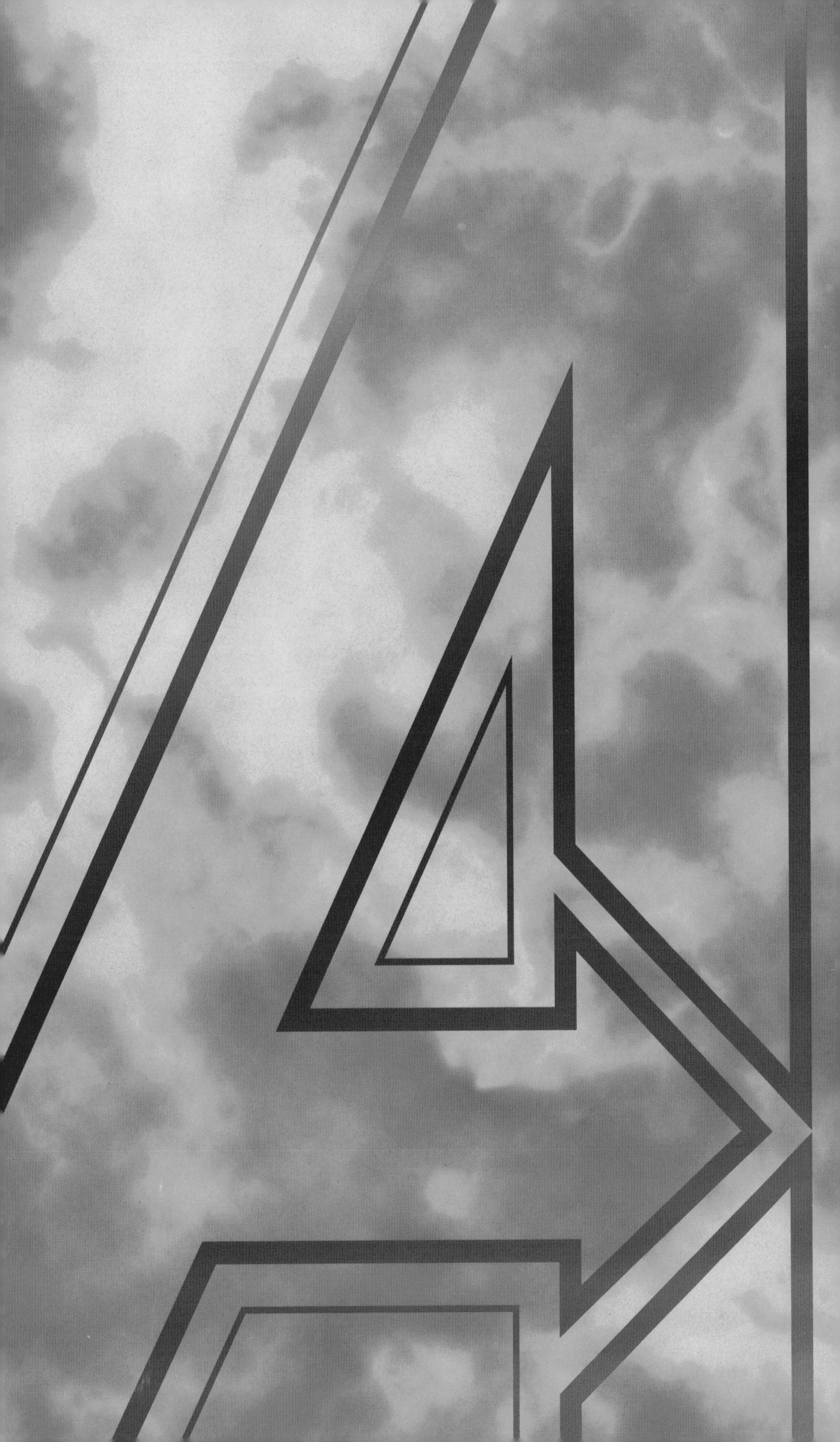

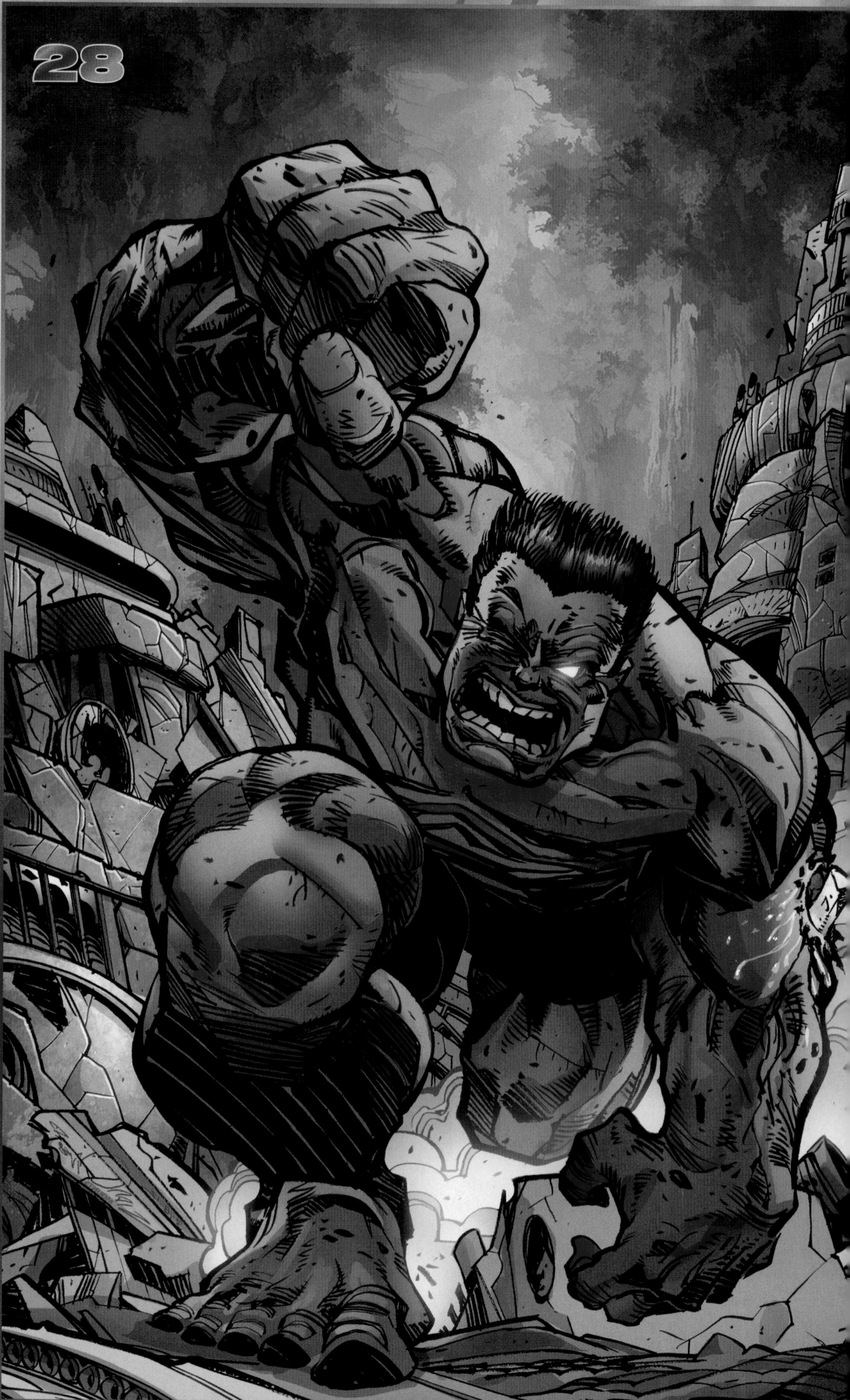
28

EARTH'S MIGHTIEST
HEROES, UNITED
AINST A COMMON
HREAT! ON THAT
Y THE AVENGERS
RE BORN, TO FIGHT
ES THAT NO SINGLE
HERO COULD
WITHSTAND!

THE AVENGERS

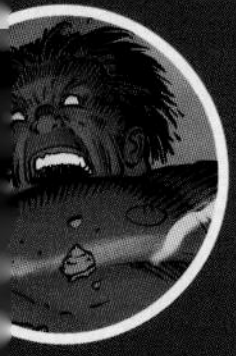
RED
ULK

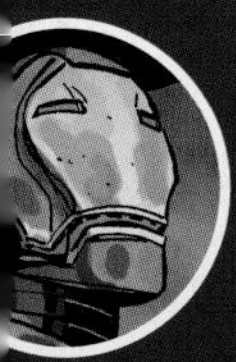
RON
MAN

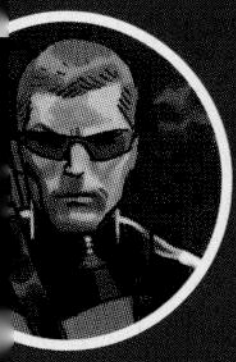
WKEYE

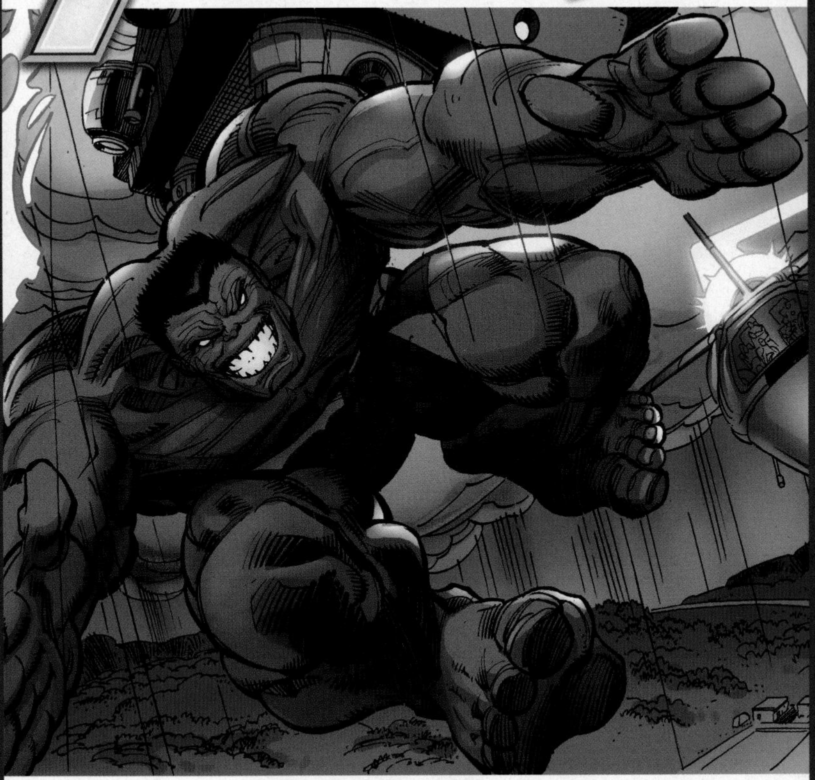

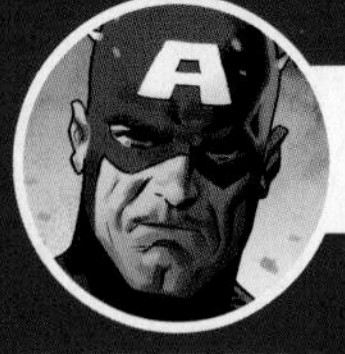
CAPTAIN
AMERICA

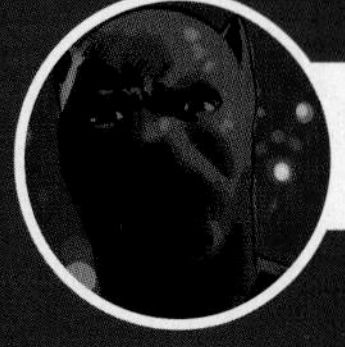
BLACK
PANTHER

PREVIOUSLY:

THE PHOENIX FORCE HAS ARRIVED, IMBUING FIVE OF THE MOST ICONIC MUTANTS -- CYCLOPS, EMMA FROST, NAMOR, COLOSSUS AND MAGIK -- WITH WORLD-ALTERING POWERS.

THE AVENGERS WISH TO NEUTRALIZE THE COSMIC FORCE, BUT ARE PUT IN A PRECARIOUS SITUATION AS THE MUTANTS HAVE THUS FAR BEEN USING THEIR POWERS FOR HUMANITARIAN EFFORTS ACROSS THE GLOBE. AS EARTH'S MIGHTIEST HEROES SEEM OVERPOWERED AND OUTMANEUVERED IN EVERY HEAD-TO-HEAD CONFRONTATION, SOME SEE A SHIFT IN TACTICS AS THE ONLY POSSIBLE SOLUTION.

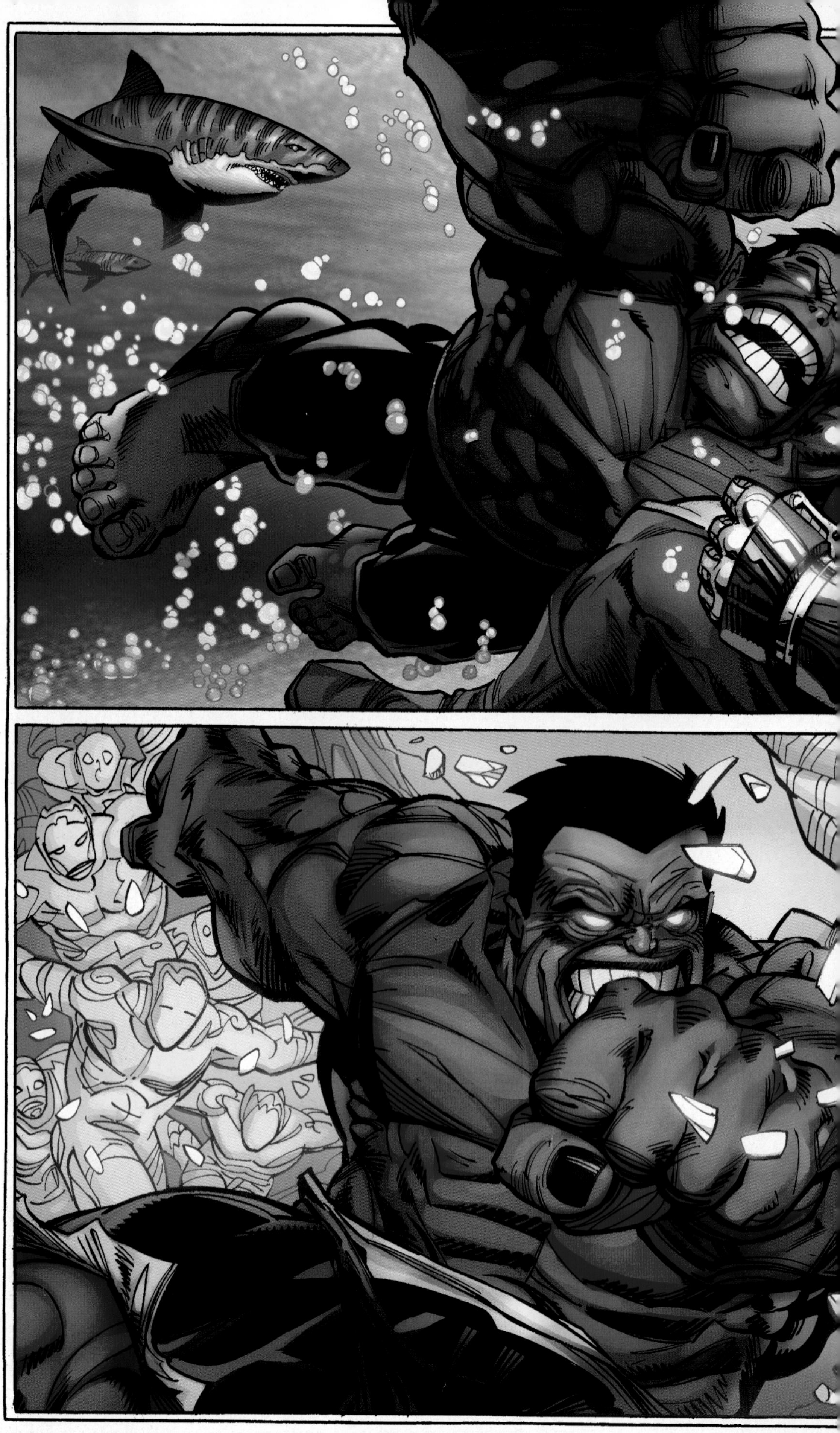

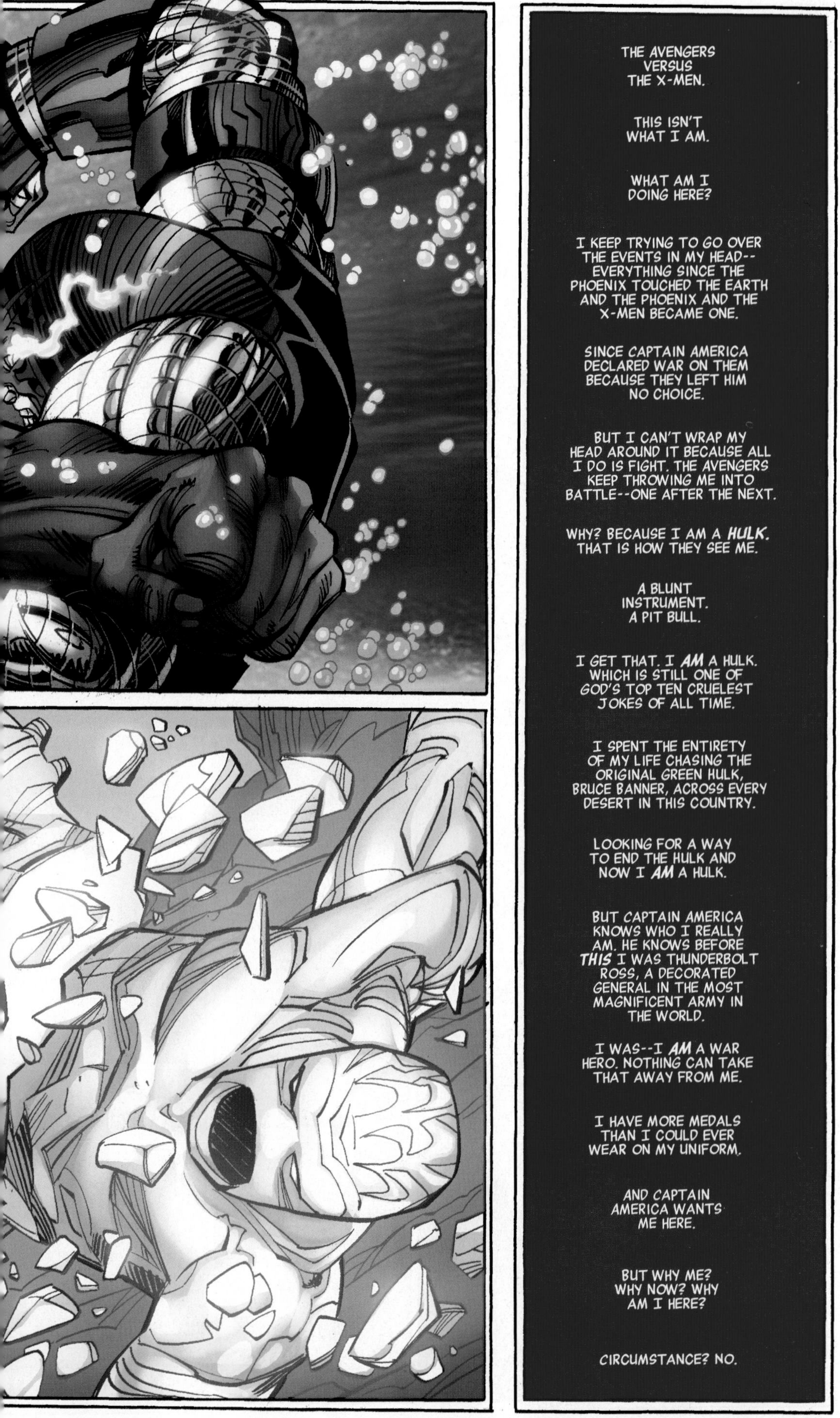
THE AVENGERS VERSUS THE X-MEN.
THIS ISN'T WHAT I AM.
WHAT AM I DOING HERE?
I KEEP TRYING TO GO OVER THE EVENTS IN MY HEAD--EVERYTHING SINCE THE PHOENIX TOUCHED THE EARTH AND THE PHOENIX AND THE X-MEN BECAME ONE.
SINCE CAPTAIN AMERICA DECLARED WAR ON THEM BECAUSE THEY LEFT HIM NO CHOICE.
BUT I CAN'T WRAP MY HEAD AROUND IT BECAUSE ALL I DO IS FIGHT. THE AVENGERS KEEP THROWING ME INTO BATTLE--ONE AFTER THE NEXT.
WHY? BECAUSE I AM A *HULK.* THAT IS HOW THEY SEE ME.
A BLUNT INSTRUMENT. A PIT BULL.
I GET THAT. I *AM* A HULK. WHICH IS STILL ONE OF GOD'S TOP TEN CRUELEST JOKES OF ALL TIME.
I SPENT THE ENTIRETY OF MY LIFE CHASING THE ORIGINAL GREEN HULK, BRUCE BANNER, ACROSS EVERY DESERT IN THIS COUNTRY.
LOOKING FOR A WAY TO END THE HULK AND NOW I *AM* A HULK.
BUT CAPTAIN AMERICA KNOWS WHO I REALLY AM. HE KNOWS BEFORE *THIS* I WAS THUNDERBOLT ROSS, A DECORATED GENERAL IN THE MOST MAGNIFICENT ARMY IN THE WORLD.
I WAS--I *AM* A WAR HERO. NOTHING CAN TAKE THAT AWAY FROM ME.
I HAVE MORE MEDALS THAN I COULD EVER WEAR ON MY UNIFORM.
AND CAPTAIN AMERICA WANTS ME HERE.
BUT WHY ME? WHY NOW? WHY AM I HERE?
CIRCUMSTANCE? NO.

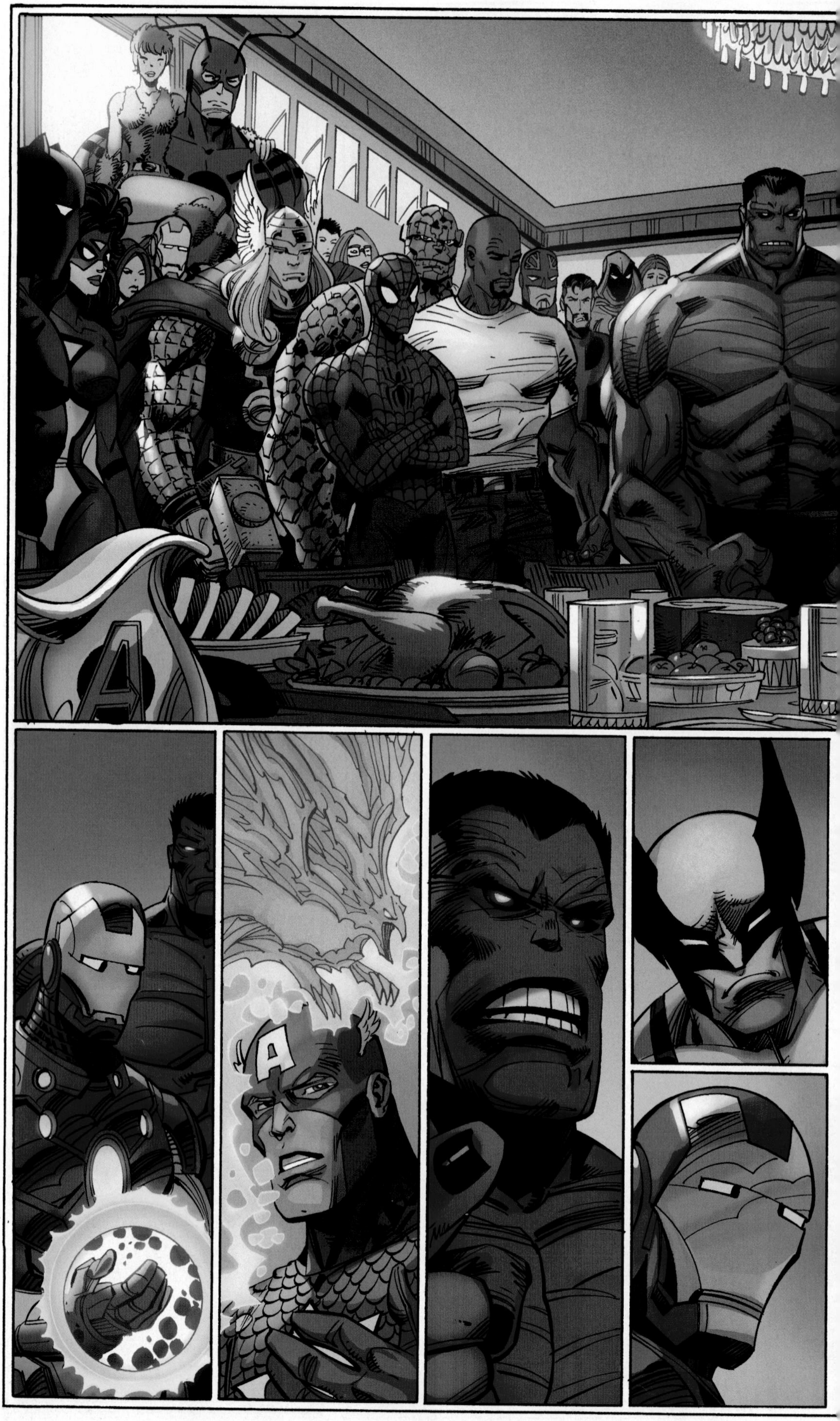

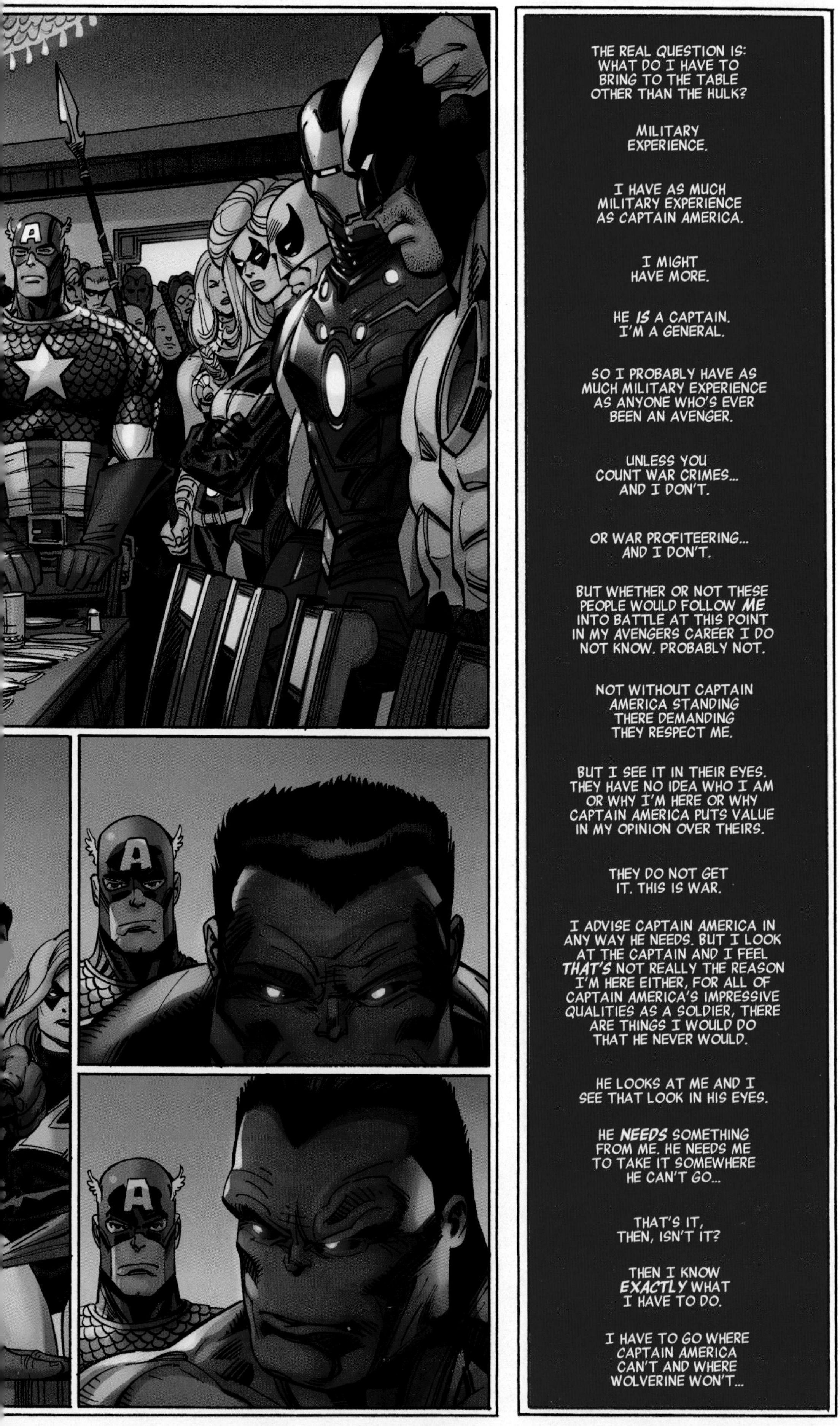
THE REAL QUESTION IS: WHAT DO I HAVE TO BRING TO THE TABLE OTHER THAN THE HULK?
MILITARY EXPERIENCE.
I HAVE AS MUCH MILITARY EXPERIENCE AS CAPTAIN AMERICA.
I MIGHT HAVE MORE.
HE *IS* A CAPTAIN. I'M A GENERAL.
SO I PROBABLY HAVE AS MUCH MILITARY EXPERIENCE AS ANYONE WHO'S EVER BEEN AN AVENGER.
UNLESS YOU COUNT WAR CRIMES... AND I DON'T.
OR WAR PROFITEERING... AND I DON'T.
BUT WHETHER OR NOT THESE PEOPLE WOULD FOLLOW *ME* INTO BATTLE AT THIS POINT IN MY AVENGERS CAREER I DO NOT KNOW. PROBABLY NOT.
NOT WITHOUT CAPTAIN AMERICA STANDING THERE DEMANDING THEY RESPECT ME.
BUT I SEE IT IN THEIR EYES. THEY HAVE NO IDEA WHO I AM OR WHY I'M HERE OR WHY CAPTAIN AMERICA PUTS VALUE IN MY OPINION OVER THEIRS.
THEY DO NOT GET IT. THIS IS WAR.
I ADVISE CAPTAIN AMERICA IN ANY WAY HE NEEDS. BUT I LOOK AT THE CAPTAIN AND I FEEL *THAT'S* NOT REALLY THE REASON I'M HERE EITHER, FOR ALL OF CAPTAIN AMERICA'S IMPRESSIVE QUALITIES AS A SOLDIER, THERE ARE THINGS I WOULD DO THAT HE NEVER WOULD.
HE LOOKS AT ME AND I SEE THAT LOOK IN HIS EYES.
HE *NEEDS* SOMETHING FROM ME. HE NEEDS ME TO TAKE IT SOMEWHERE HE CAN'T GO...
THAT'S IT, THEN, ISN'T IT?
THEN I KNOW *EXACTLY* WHAT I HAVE TO DO.
I HAVE TO GO WHERE CAPTAIN AMERICA CAN'T AND WHERE WOLVERINE WON'T...

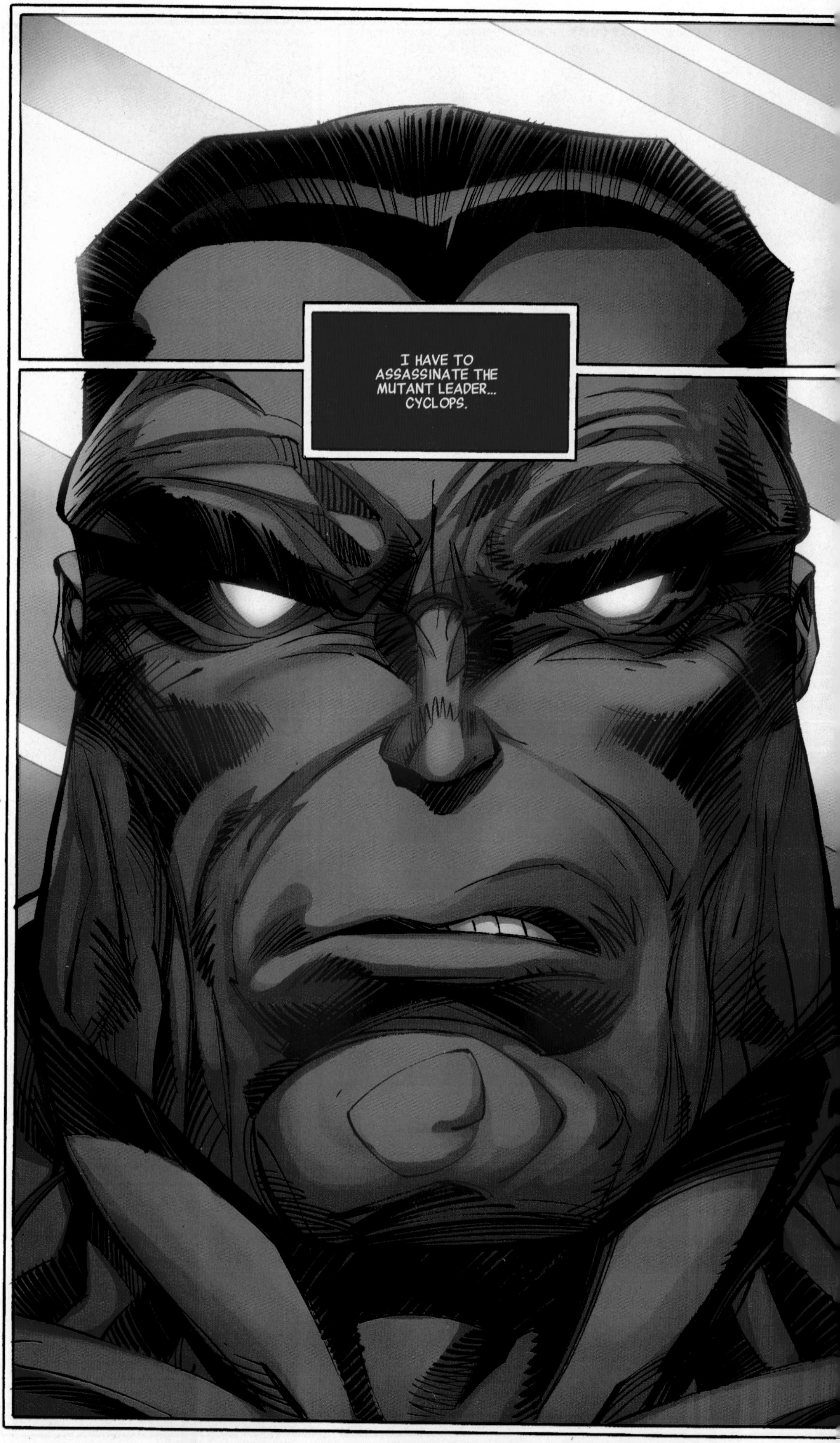
I HAVE TO ASSASSINATE THE MUTANT LEADER... CYCLOPS.

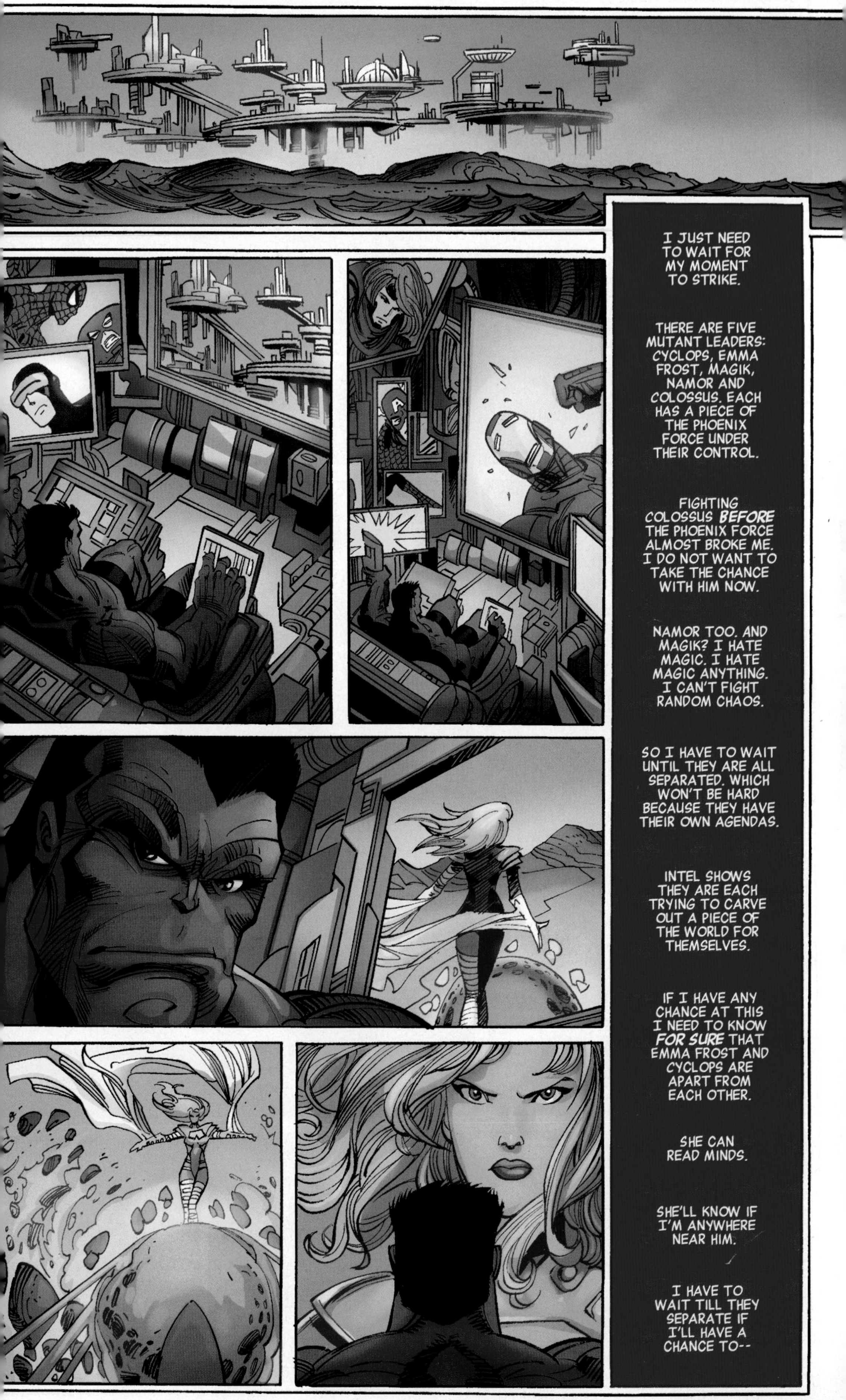

I JUST NEED TO WAIT FOR MY MOMENT TO STRIKE.
THERE ARE FIVE MUTANT LEADERS: CYCLOPS, EMMA FROST, MAGIK, NAMOR AND COLOSSUS. EACH HAS A PIECE OF THE PHOENIX FORCE UNDER THEIR CONTROL.
FIGHTING COLOSSUS **BEFORE** THE PHOENIX FORCE ALMOST BROKE ME. I DO NOT WANT TO TAKE THE CHANCE WITH HIM NOW.
NAMOR TOO. AND MAGIK? I HATE MAGIC. I HATE MAGIC ANYTHING. I CAN'T FIGHT RANDOM CHAOS.
SO I HAVE TO WAIT UNTIL THEY ARE ALL SEPARATED. WHICH WON'T BE HARD BECAUSE THEY HAVE THEIR OWN AGENDAS.
INTEL SHOWS THEY ARE EACH TRYING TO CARVE OUT A PIECE OF THE WORLD FOR THEMSELVES.
IF I HAVE ANY CHANCE AT THIS I NEED TO KNOW **FOR SURE** THAT EMMA FROST AND CYCLOPS ARE APART FROM EACH OTHER.
SHE CAN READ MINDS.
SHE'LL KNOW IF I'M ANYWHERE NEAR HIM.
I HAVE TO WAIT TILL THEY SEPARATE IF I'LL HAVE A CHANCE TO--

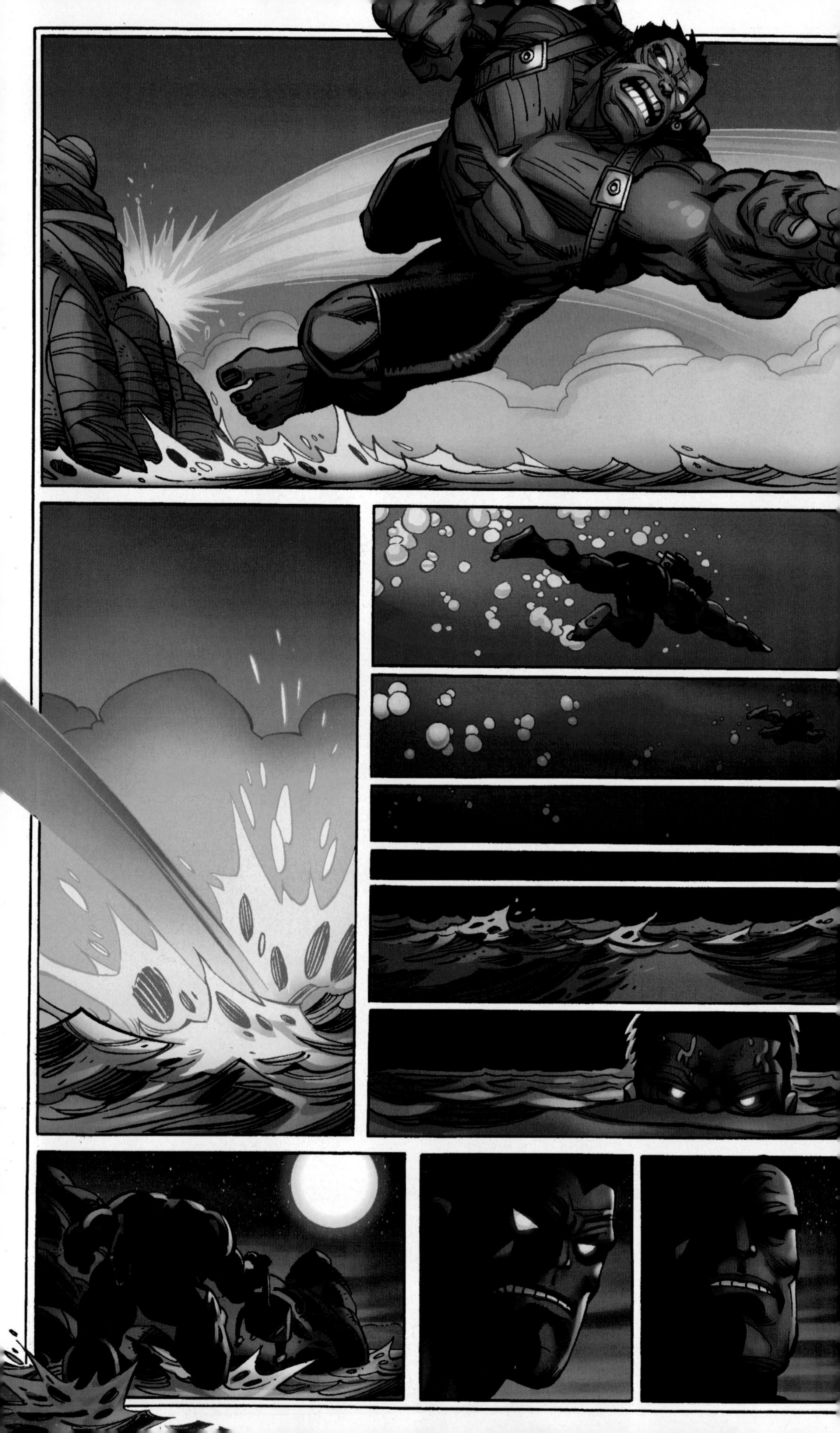

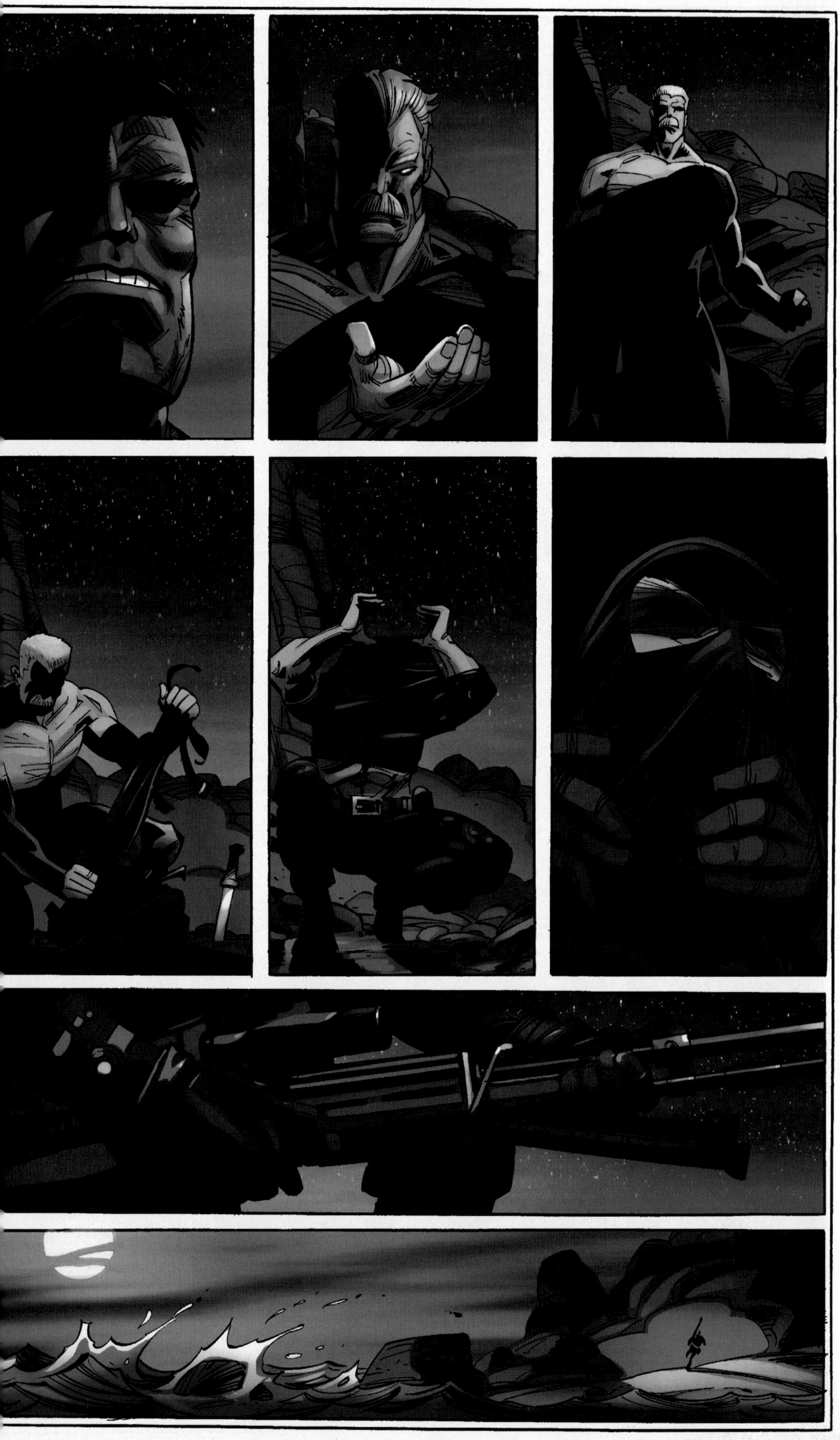

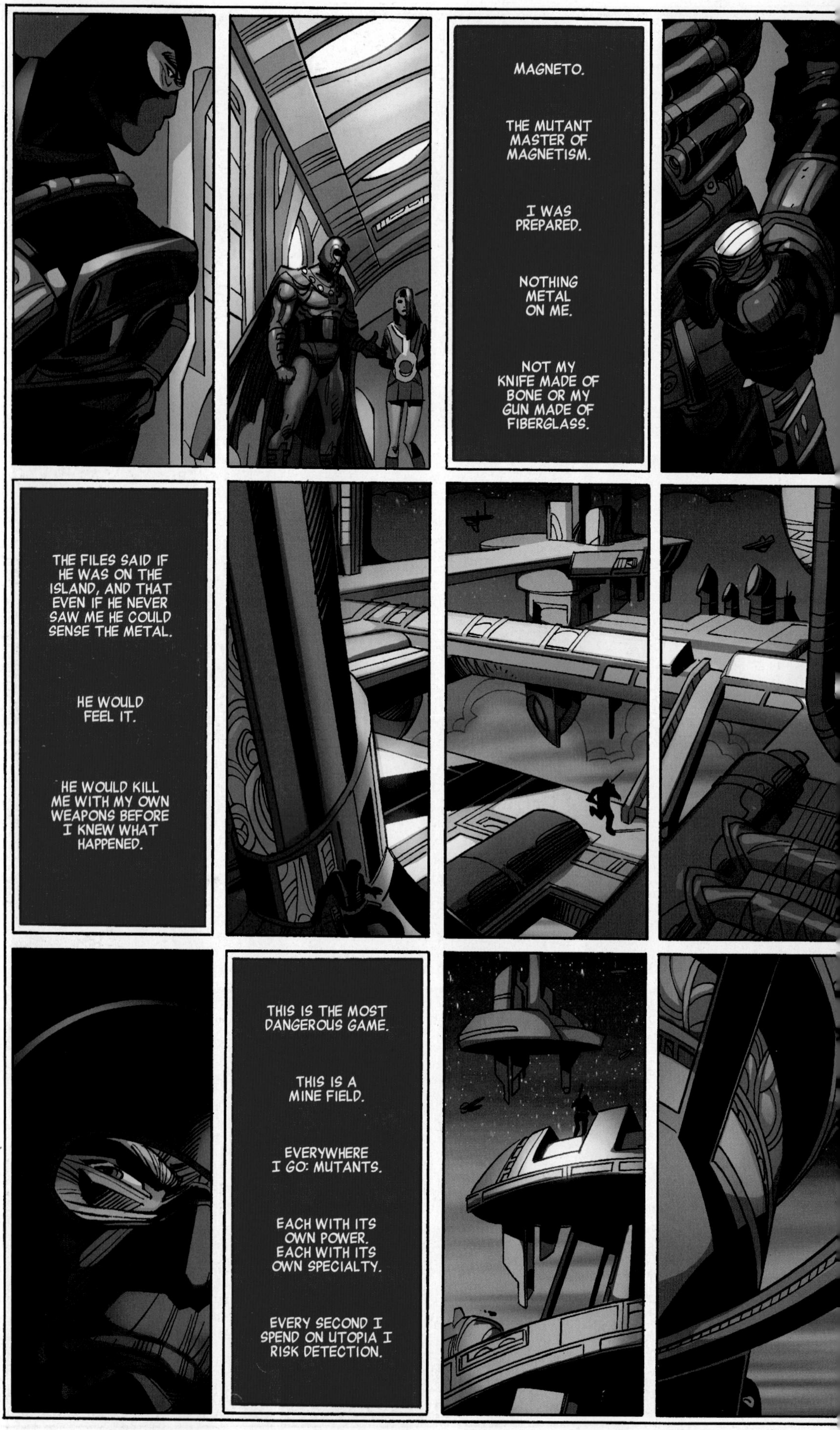
MAGNETO.
THE MUTANT MASTER OF MAGNETISM.
I WAS PREPARED.
NOTHING METAL ON ME.
NOT MY KNIFE MADE OF BONE OR MY GUN MADE OF FIBERGLASS.
THE FILES SAID IF HE WAS ON THE ISLAND, AND THAT EVEN IF HE NEVER SAW ME HE COULD SENSE THE METAL.
HE WOULD FEEL IT.
HE WOULD KILL ME WITH MY OWN WEAPONS BEFORE I KNEW WHAT HAPPENED.
THIS IS THE MOST DANGEROUS GAME.
THIS IS A MINE FIELD.
EVERYWHERE I GO: MUTANTS.
EACH WITH ITS OWN POWER. EACH WITH ITS OWN SPECIALTY.
EVERY SECOND I SPEND ON UTOPIA I RISK DETECTION.

THERE HE IS: CYCLOPS, LEADER OF THE X-MEN, IN MY SIGHTS. I TAKE THIS DECISION VERY SERIOUSLY.

THIS IS A MAN'S LIFE. I HAVE TO WEIGH THE GREATER GOOD. I KNOW THIS MOMENT WILL HAUNT ME FOR THE REST OF MY LIFE. LIKE ALL THE OTHERS. I HAVE TO IMAGINE THE LIVES SAVED BY THIS ONE SACRIFICE. I KNOW THIS MAN WAS A HERO. I KNOW HE HAS SACRIFICED HIS LIFE FOR THE ENTIRE PLANET, OVER AND OVER. I KNOW HE HAS LOVED. I KNOW HE HAS LOST. I KNOW HE IS A COMPLICATED MAN IN A COMPLICATED TIME. BUT IT DOESN'T MATTER WHAT HE *DID*. IT MATTERS WHAT HE IS DOING *NOW*. HE IS PUTTING THE ENTIRE WORLD IN GRAVE DANGER. HE WON'T STOP SO I HAVE TO STOP HIM. I HAVE TO PUT HIM DOWN SO THE REST OF US CAN SEE TOMORROW.

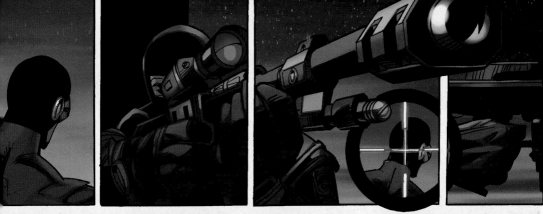

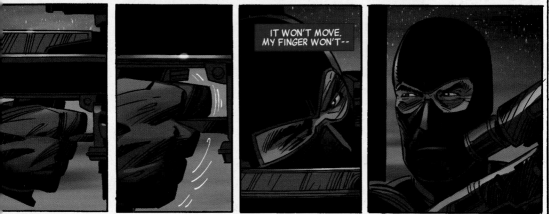

IT WON'T MOVE. MY FINGER WON'T--

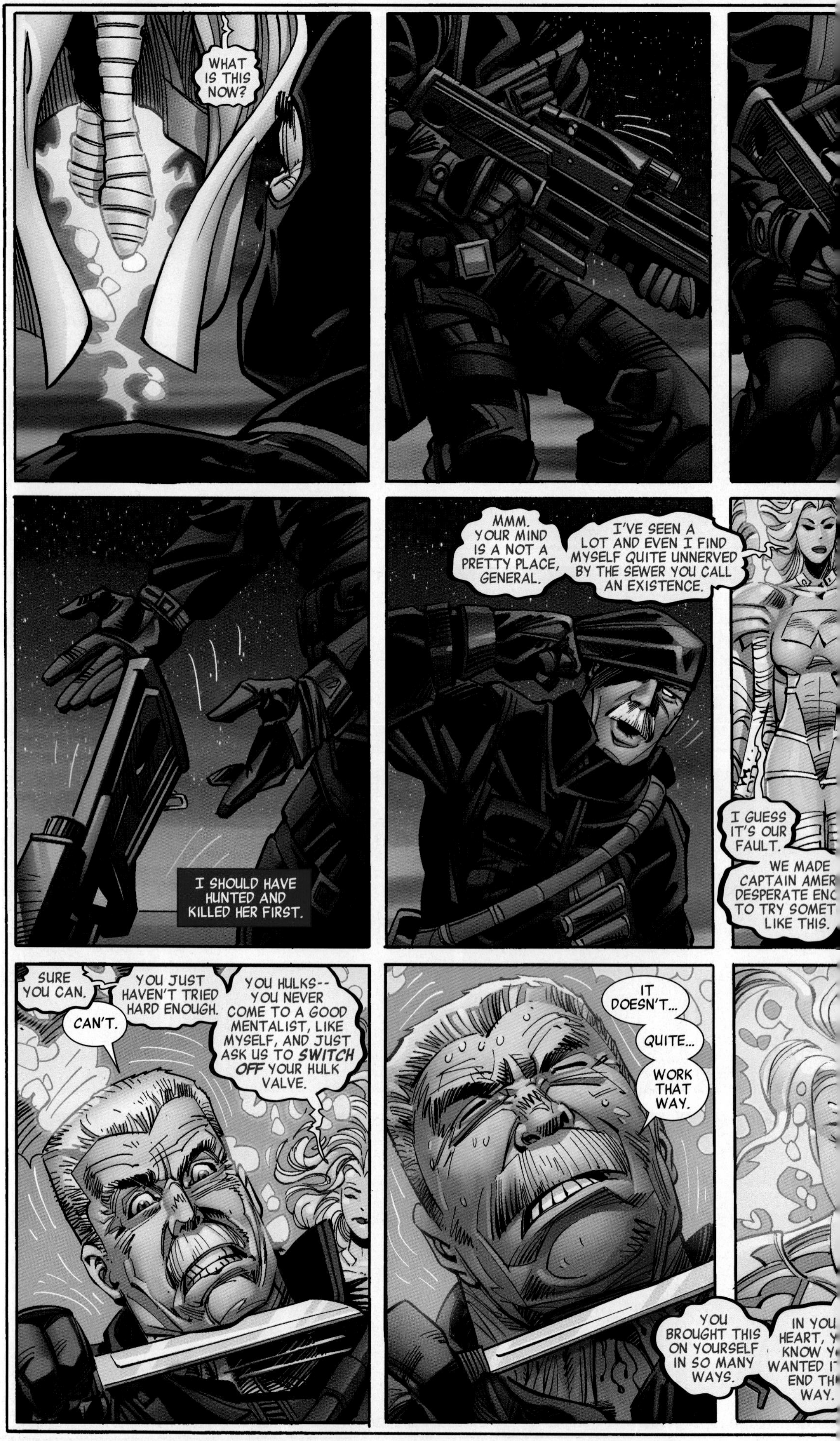
WHAT IS THIS NOW?
I SHOULD HAVE HUNTED AND KILLED HER FIRST.
MMM. YOUR MIND IS A NOT A PRETTY PLACE, GENERAL.
I'VE SEEN A LOT AND EVEN I FIND MYSELF QUITE UNNERVED BY THE SEWER YOU CALL AN EXISTENCE.
I GUESS IT'S OUR FAULT.
SURE YOU CAN.
CAN'T.
YOU JUST HAVEN'T TRIED HARD ENOUGH.
YOU HULKS-- YOU NEVER COME TO A GOOD MENTALIST, LIKE MYSELF, AND JUST ASK US TO SWITCH OFF YOUR HULK VALVE.
IT DOESN'T...
QUITE...
WORK THAT WAY.
YOU BROUGHT THIS ON YOURSELF IN SO MANY WAYS.

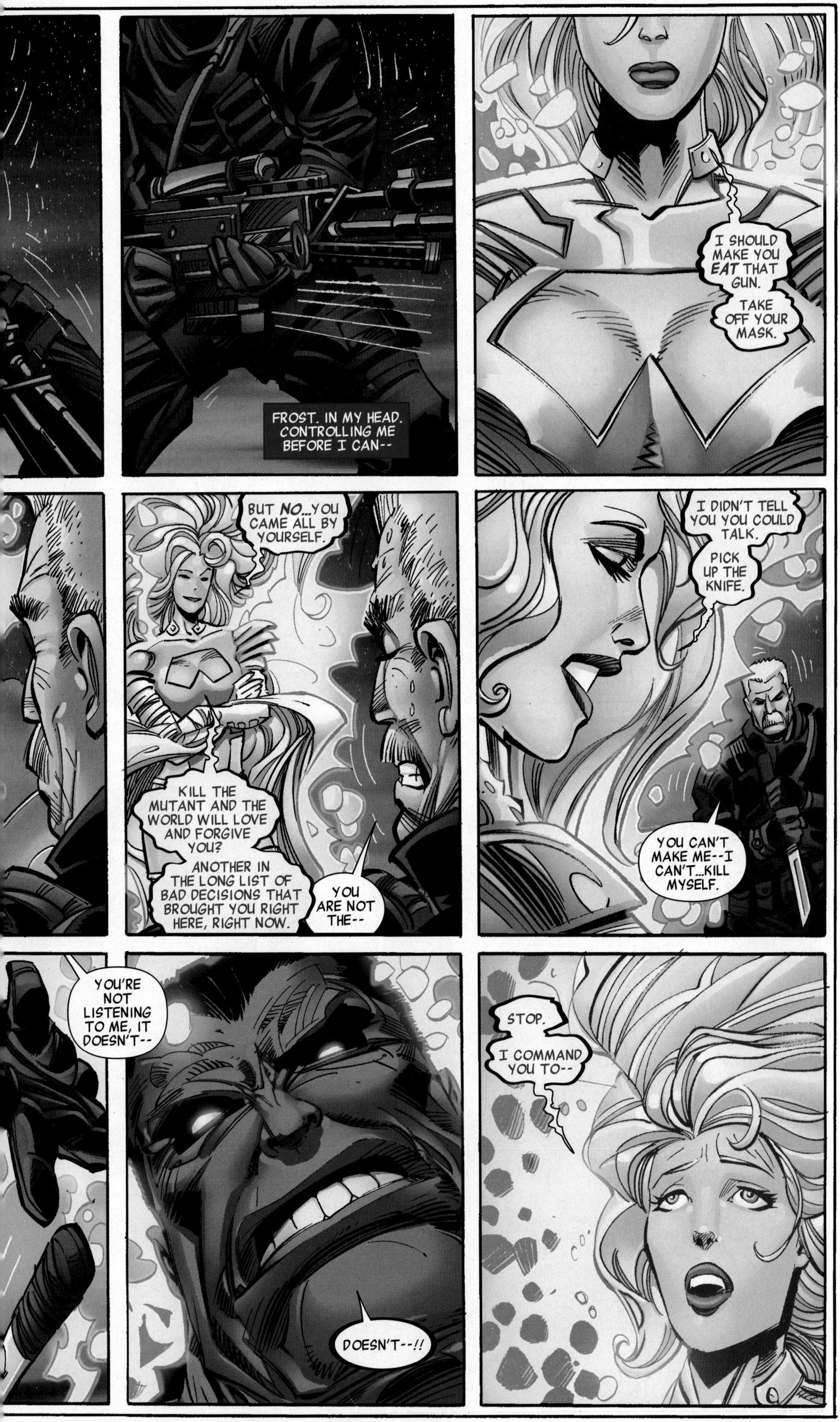
FROST. IN MY HEAD. CONTROLLING ME BEFORE I CAN--
I SHOULD MAKE YOU EAT THAT GUN.
TAKE OFF YOUR MASK.
BUT NO...YOU CAME ALL BY YOURSELF.
KILL THE MUTANT AND THE WORLD WILL LOVE AND FORGIVE YOU?
ANOTHER IN THE LONG LIST OF BAD DECISIONS THAT BROUGHT YOU RIGHT HERE, RIGHT NOW.
YOU ARE NOT THE--
I DIDN'T TELL YOU YOU COULD TALK.
PICK UP THE KNIFE.
YOU CAN'T MAKE ME--I CAN'T...KILL MYSELF.
YOU'RE NOT LISTENING TO ME, IT DOESN'T--
DOESN'T--!!
STOP.
I COMMAND YOU TO--

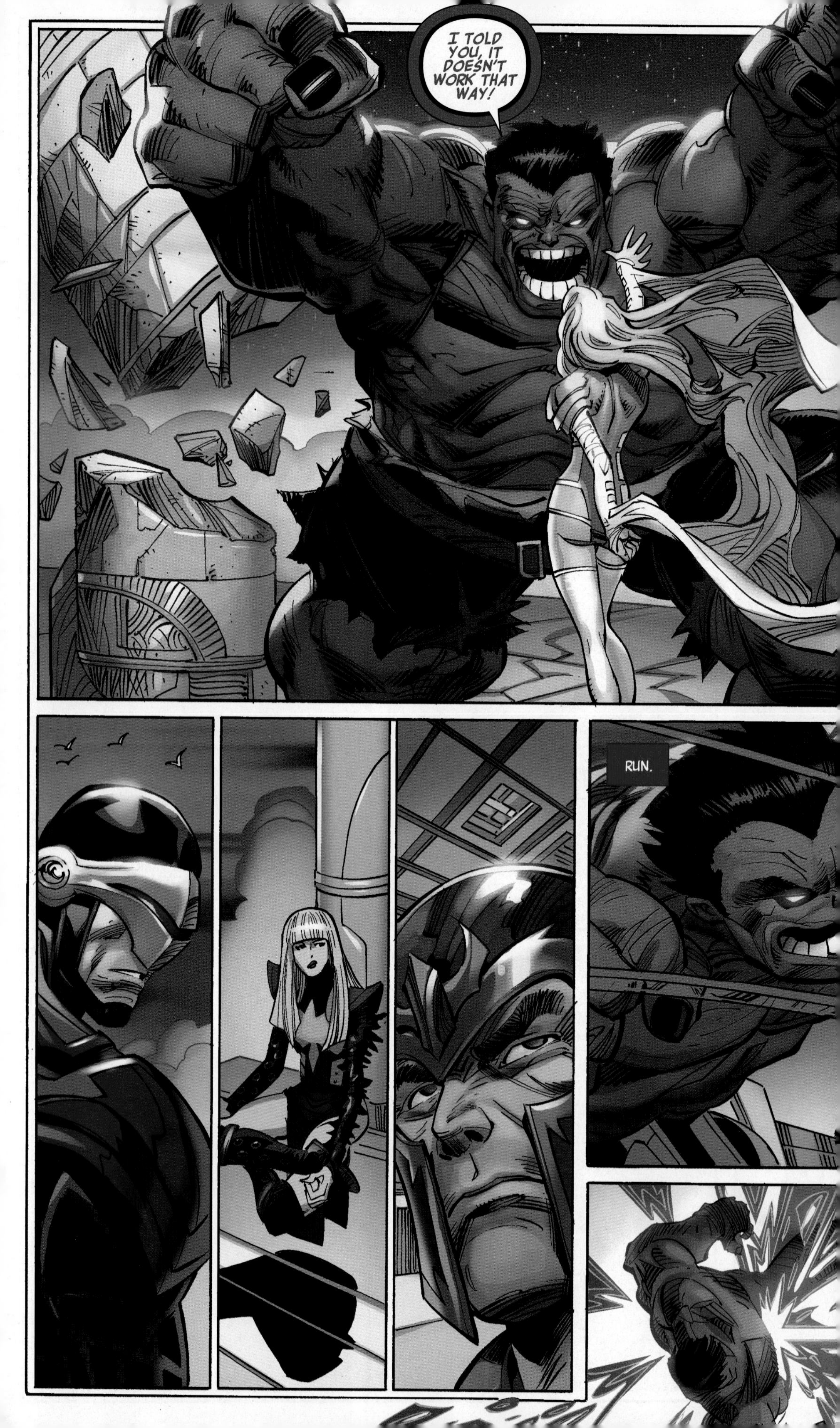
I TOLD YOU, IT DOESN'T WORK THAT WAY!
RUN.

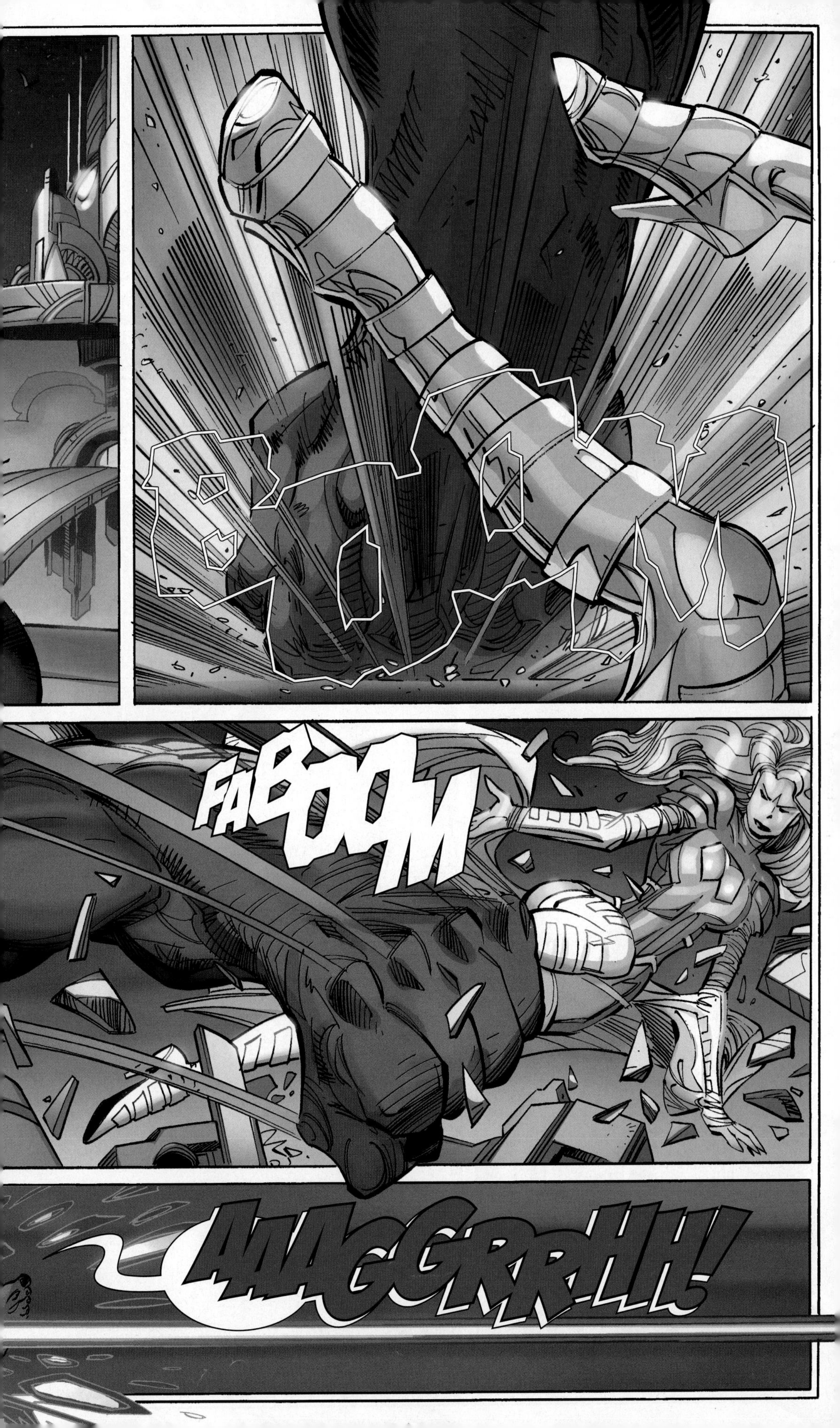
FABOOM
AAAGGRRHH!

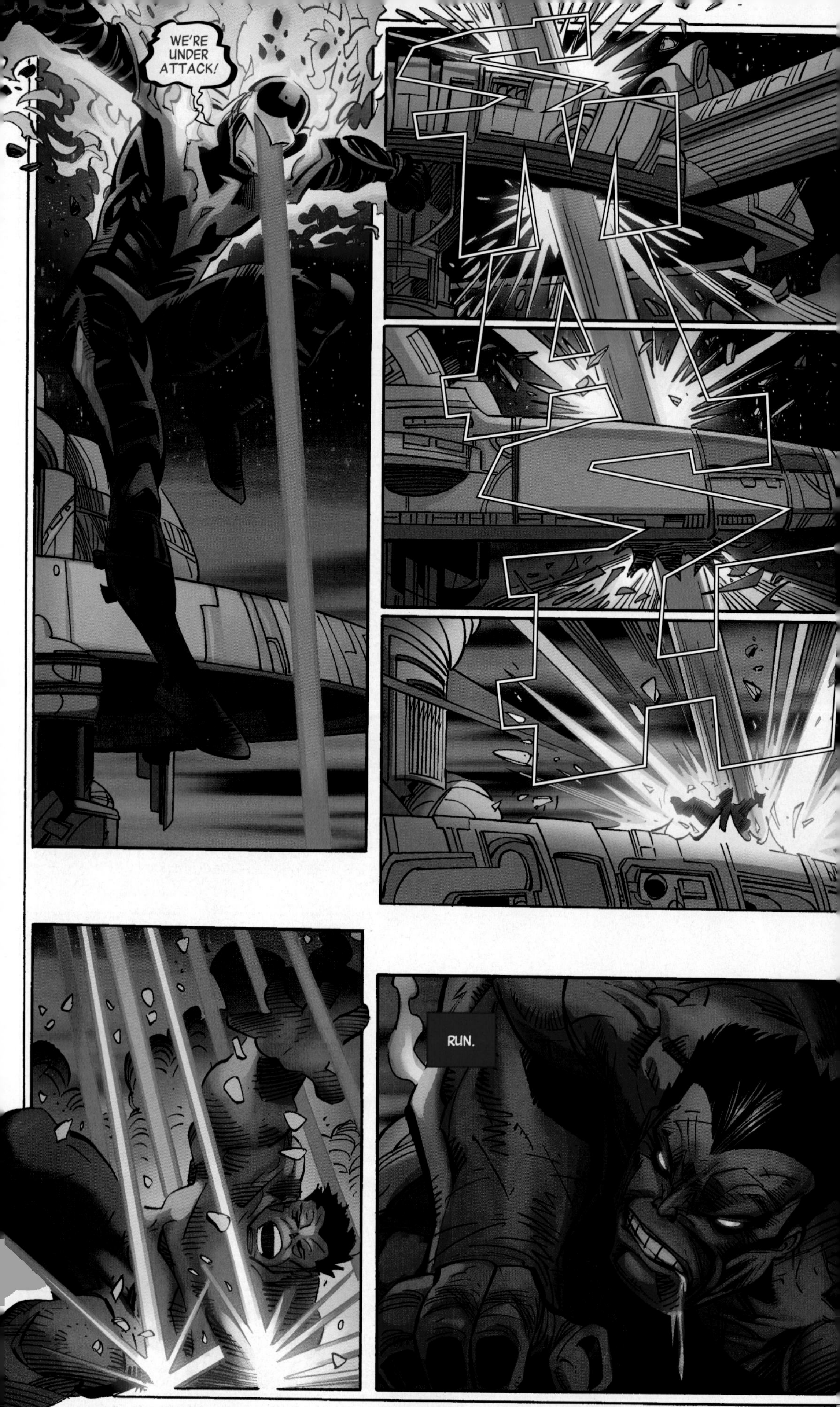
WE'RE UNDER ATTACK!
RUN.

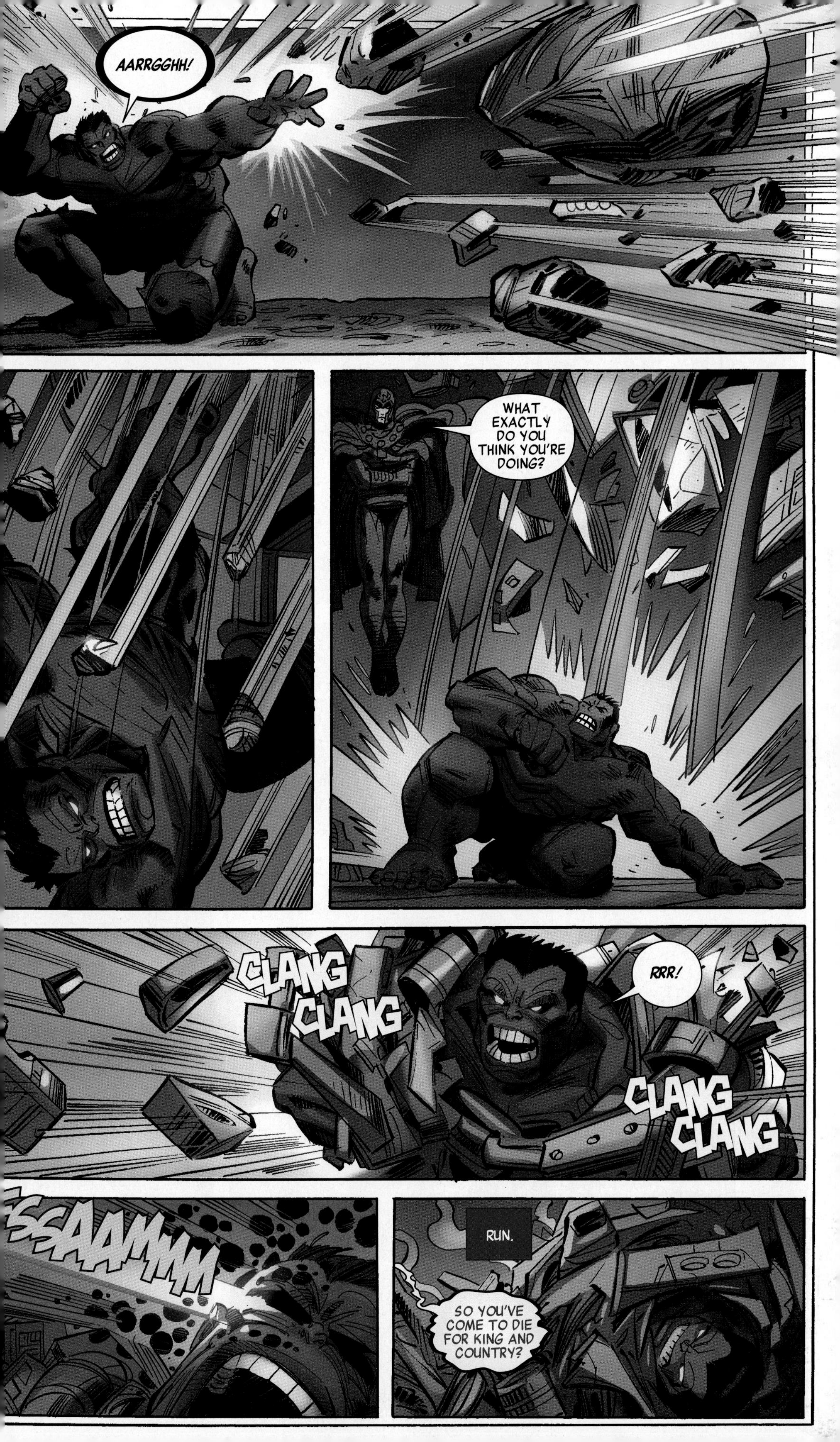
AARRGGHH!
WHAT EXACTLY DO YOU THINK YOU'RE DOING?
CLANG CLANG
RRR!
CLANG CLANG
SSAAMMMM
RUN.
SO YOU'VE COME TO DIE FOR KING AND COUNTRY?

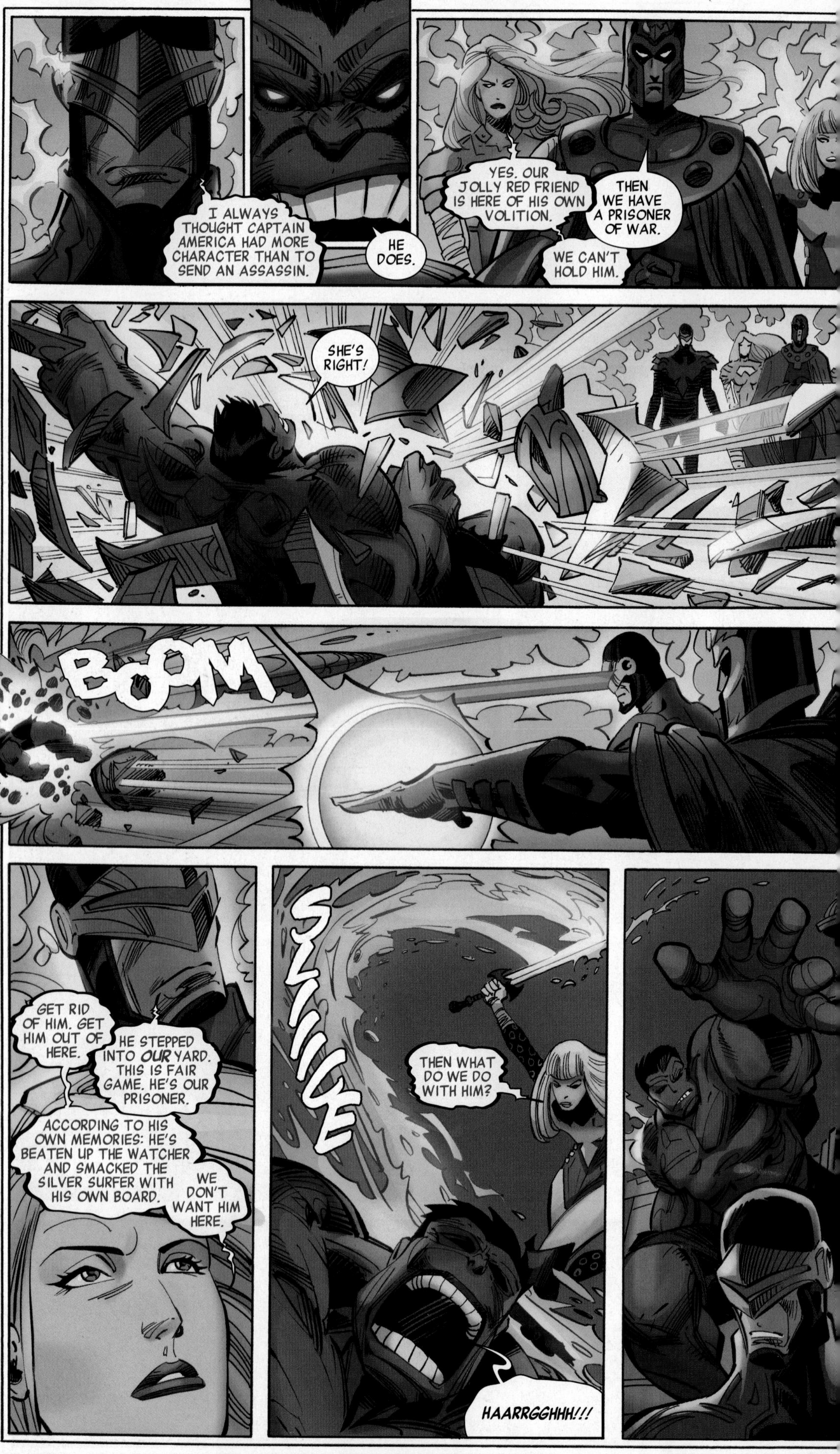
I ALWAYS THOUGHT CAPTAIN AMERICA HAD MORE CHARACTER THAN TO SEND AN ASSASSIN.
HE DOES.
YES. OUR JOLLY RED FRIEND IS HERE OF HIS OWN VOLITION.
THEN WE HAVE A PRISONER OF WAR.
WE CAN'T HOLD HIM.
SHE'S RIGHT!
BOOM
GET RID OF HIM. GET HIM OUT OF HERE.
HE STEPPED INTO OUR YARD. THIS IS FAIR GAME. HE'S OUR PRISONER.
ACCORDING TO HIS OWN MEMORIES: HE'S BEATEN UP THE WATCHER AND SMACKED THE SILVER SURFER WITH HIS OWN BOARD.
WE DON'T WANT HIM HERE.
SLIIIICE
THEN WHAT DO WE DO WITH HIM?
HAARRGGHHH!!!

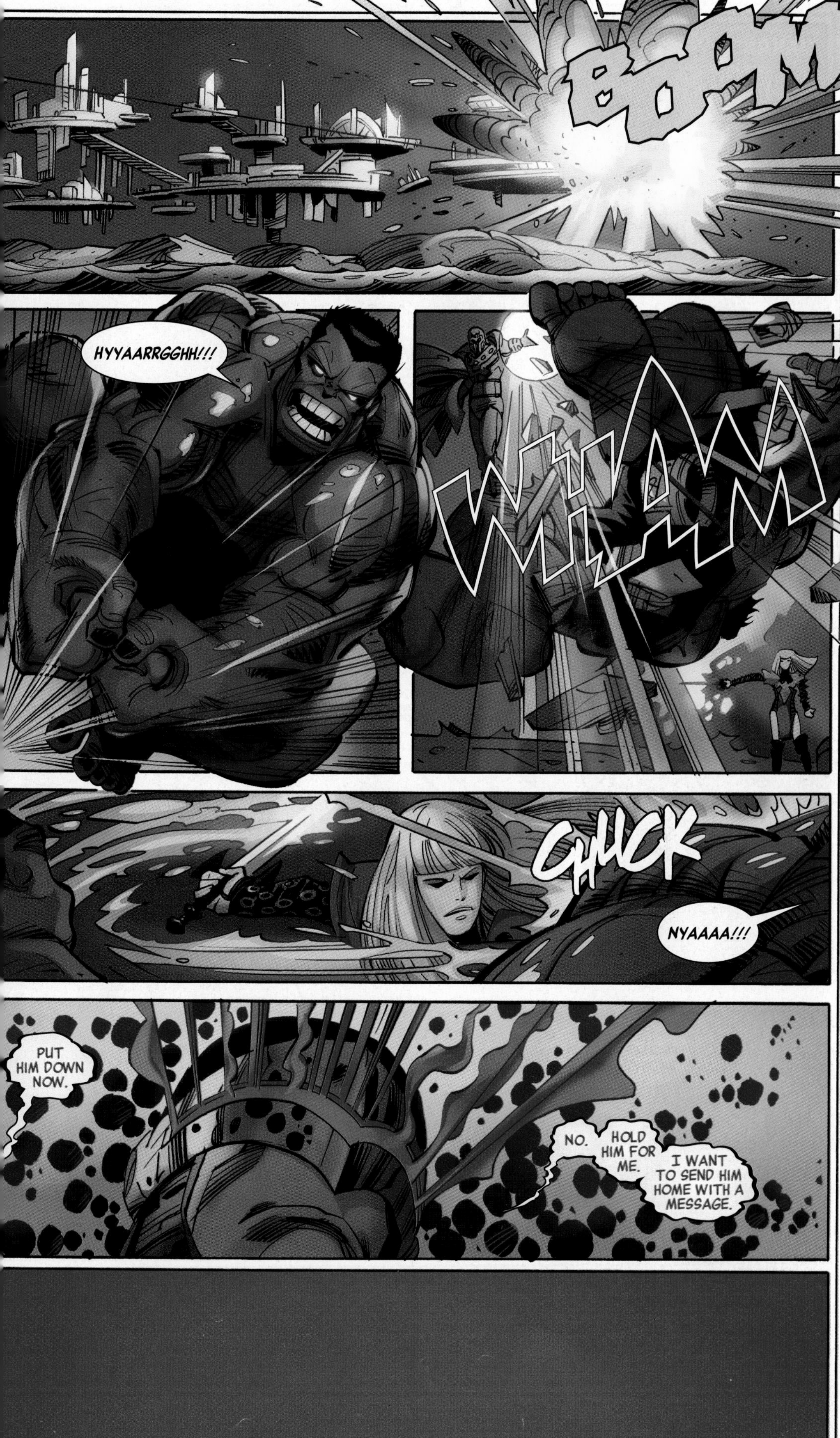
BOOM
HYYAARRGGHH!!!
WHAM
CHUCK
NYAAAA!!!
PUT HIM DOWN NOW.
NO.
HOLD HIM FOR ME.
I WANT TO SEND HIM HOME WITH A MESSAGE.

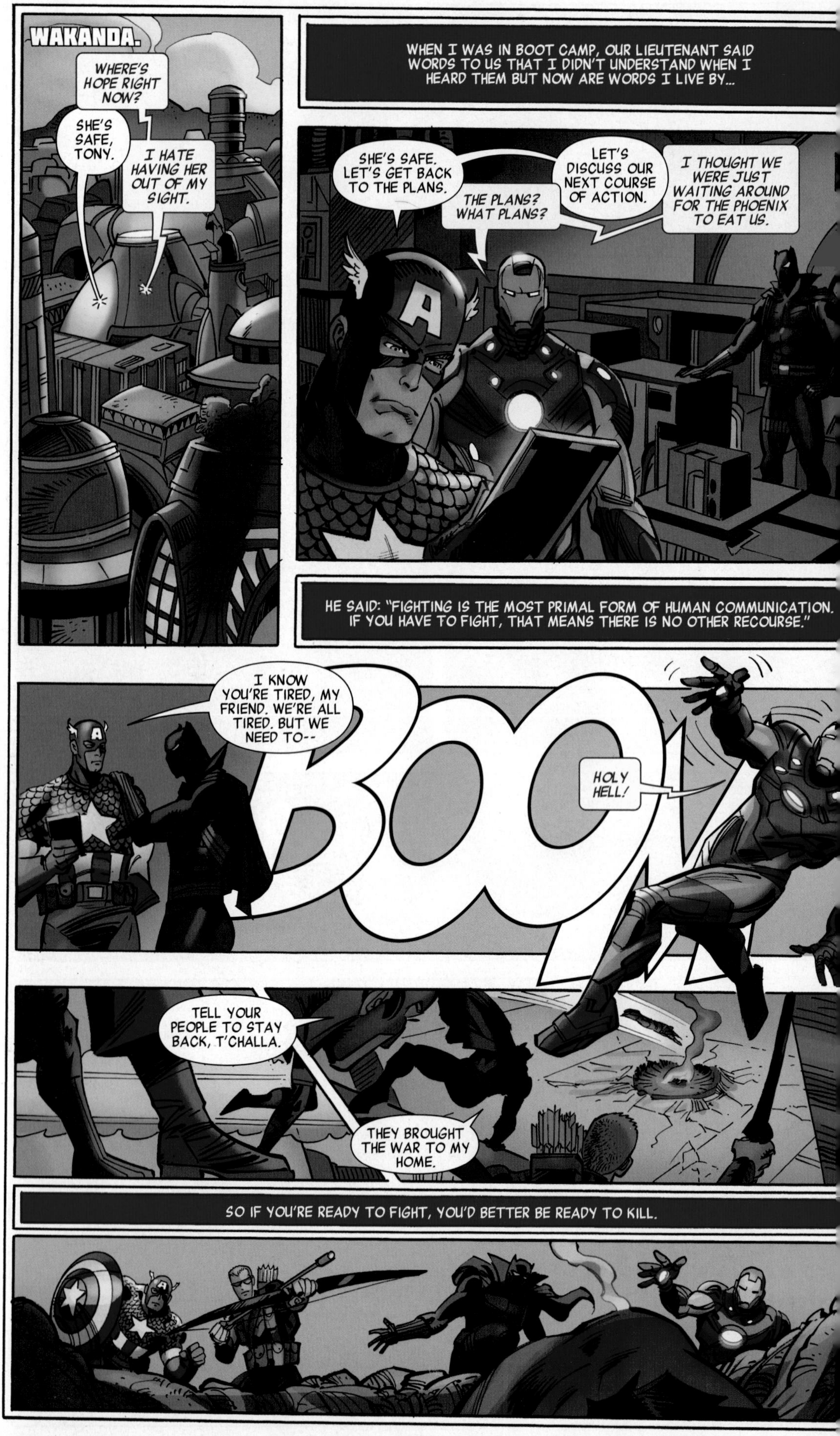
WAKANDA.
WHERE'S HOPE RIGHT NOW?
SHE'S SAFE, TONY.
I HATE HAVING HER OUT OF MY SIGHT.
WHEN I WAS IN BOOT CAMP, OUR LIEUTENANT SAID WORDS TO US THAT I DIDN'T UNDERSTAND WHEN I HEARD THEM BUT NOW ARE WORDS I LIVE BY...
SHE'S SAFE. LET'S GET BACK TO THE PLANS.
THE PLANS? WHAT PLANS?
LET'S DISCUSS OUR NEXT COURSE OF ACTION.
I THOUGHT WE WERE JUST WAITING AROUND FOR THE PHOENIX TO EAT US.
HE SAID: "FIGHTING IS THE MOST PRIMAL FORM OF HUMAN COMMUNICATION. IF YOU HAVE TO FIGHT, THAT MEANS THERE IS NO OTHER RECOURSE."
I KNOW YOU'RE TIRED, MY FRIEND. WE'RE ALL TIRED. BUT WE NEED TO--
BOOM
HOLY HELL!
TELL YOUR PEOPLE TO STAY BACK, T'CHALLA.
THEY BROUGHT THE WAR TO MY HOME.
SO IF YOU'RE READY TO FIGHT, YOU'D BETTER BE READY TO KILL.

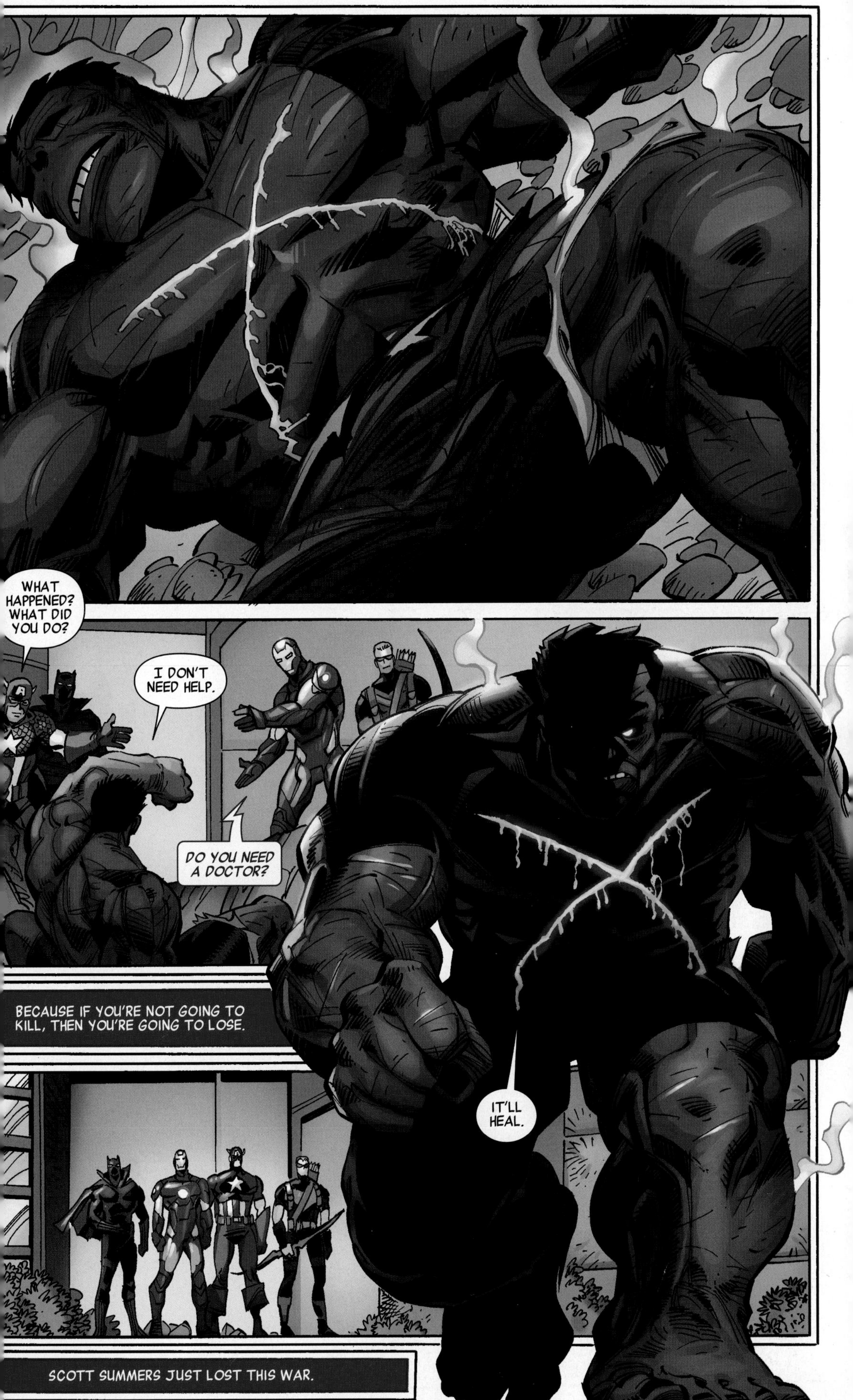

WHAT HAPPENED? WHAT DID YOU DO?
I DON'T NEED HELP.
DO YOU NEED A DOCTOR?
IT'LL HEAL.
BECAUSE IF YOU'RE NOT GOING TO KILL, THEN YOU'RE GOING TO LOSE.
SCOTT SUMMERS JUST LOST THIS WAR.

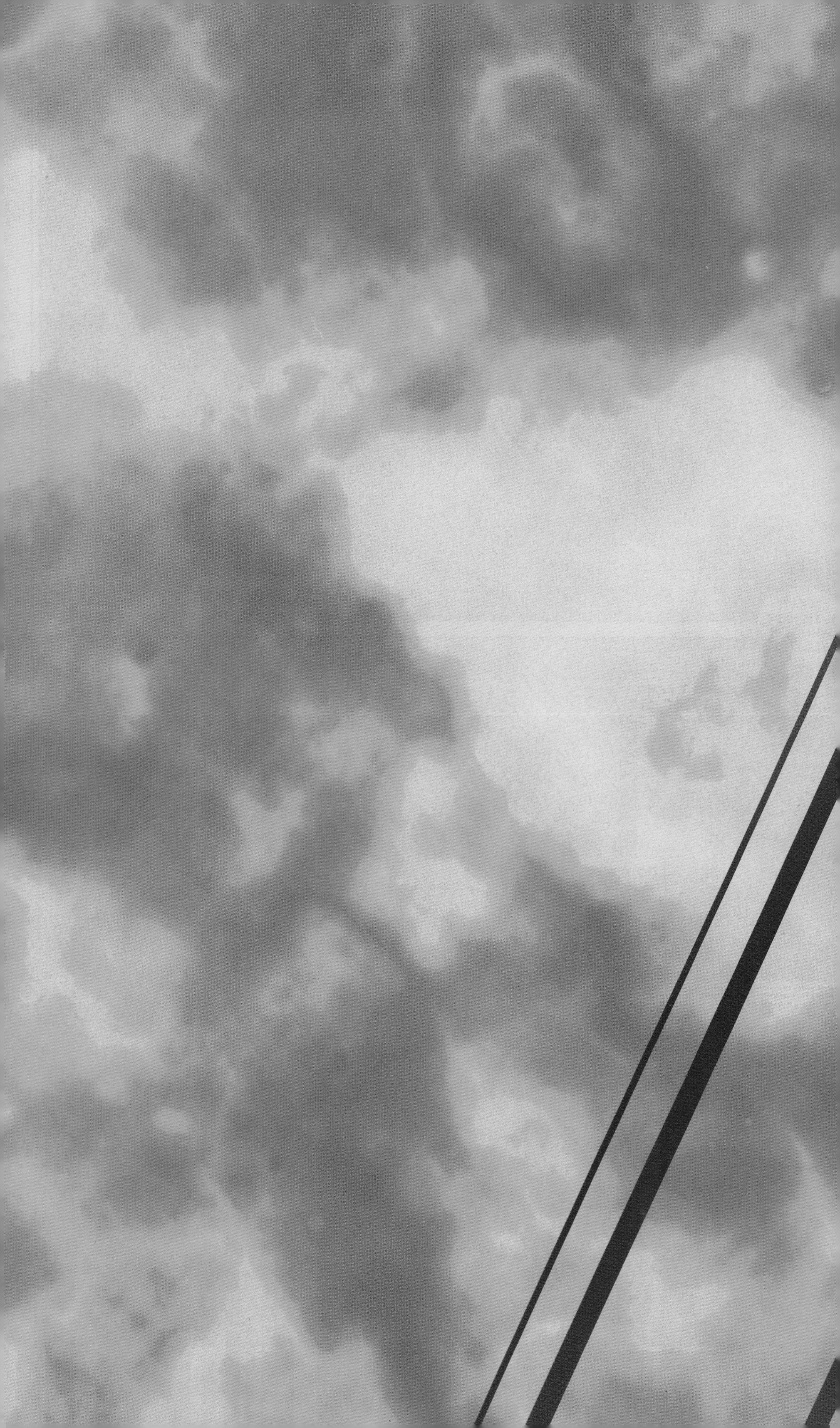

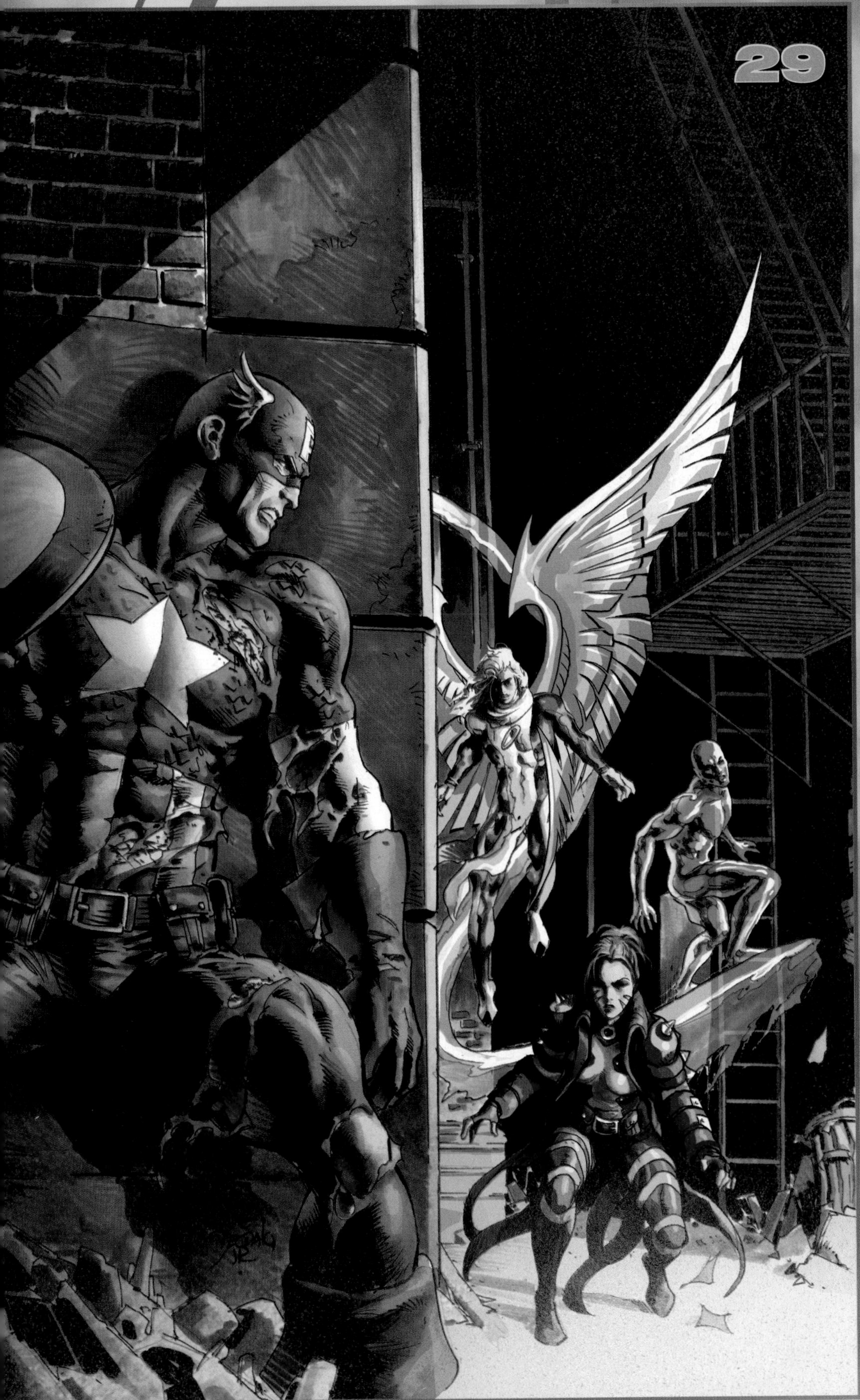
29

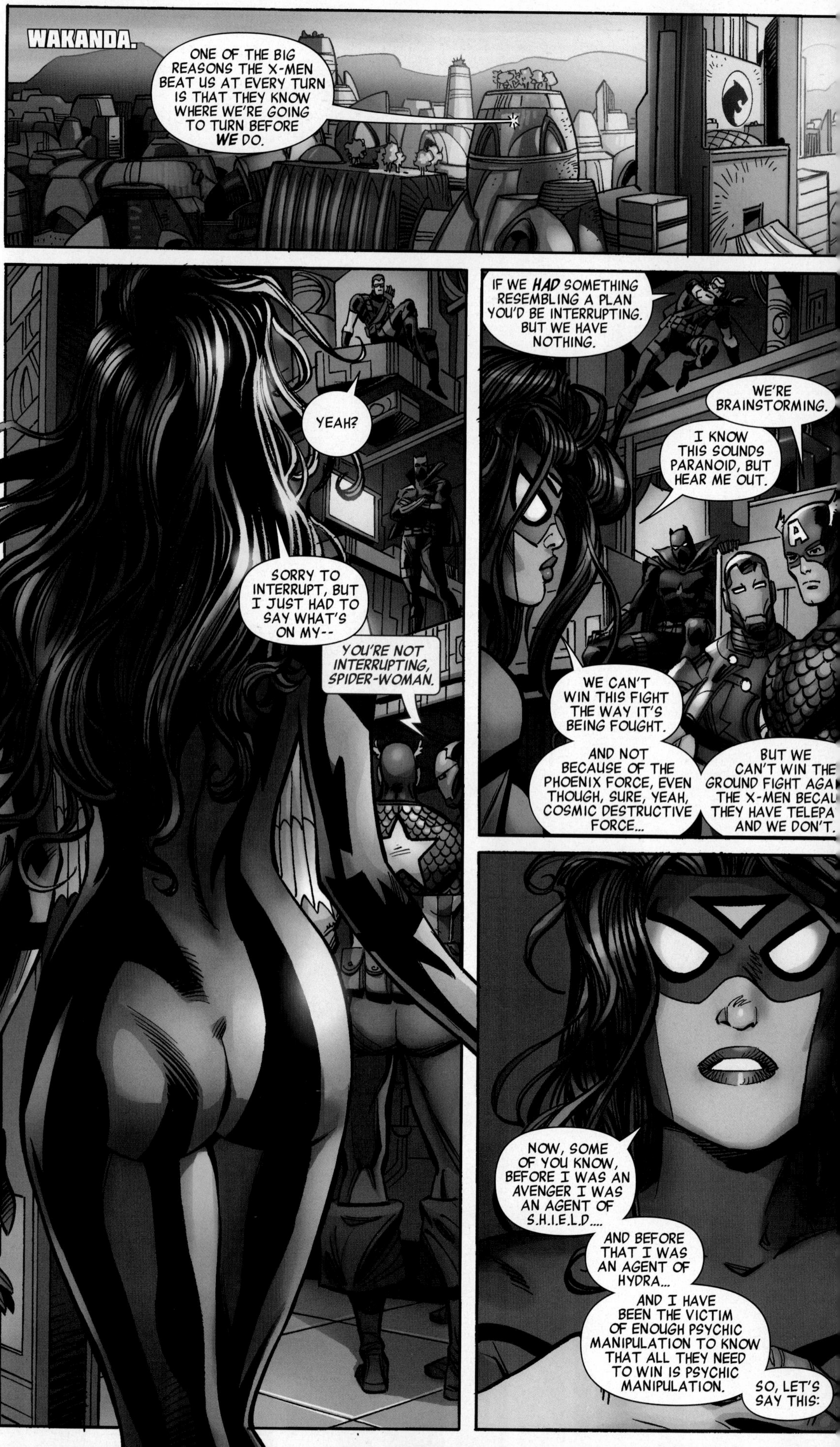

WAKANDA.
ONE OF THE BIG REASONS THE X-MEN BEAT US AT EVERY TURN IS THAT THEY KNOW WHERE WE'RE GOING TO TURN BEFORE WE DO.
YEAH?
SORRY TO INTERRUPT, BUT I JUST HAD TO SAY WHAT'S ON MY--
YOU'RE NOT INTERRUPTING, SPIDER-WOMAN.
IF WE HAD SOMETHING RESEMBLING A PLAN YOU'D BE INTERRUPTING. BUT WE HAVE NOTHING.
WE'RE BRAINSTORMING.
I KNOW THIS SOUNDS PARANOID, BUT HEAR ME OUT.
WE CAN'T WIN THIS FIGHT THE WAY IT'S BEING FOUGHT.
AND NOT BECAUSE OF THE PHOENIX FORCE, EVEN THOUGH, SURE, YEAH, COSMIC DESTRUCTIVE FORCE...
BUT WE CAN'T WIN THE GROUND FIGHT AGA THE X-MEN BECAU THEY HAVE TELEPA AND WE DON'T.
NOW, SOME OF YOU KNOW, BEFORE I WAS AN AVENGER I WAS AN AGENT OF S.H.I.E.L.D....
AND BEFORE THAT I WAS AN AGENT OF HYDRA...
AND I HAVE BEEN THE VICTIM OF ENOUGH PSYCHIC MANIPULATION TO KNOW THAT ALL THEY NEED TO WIN IS PSYCHIC MANIPULATION.
SO, LET'S SAY THIS:

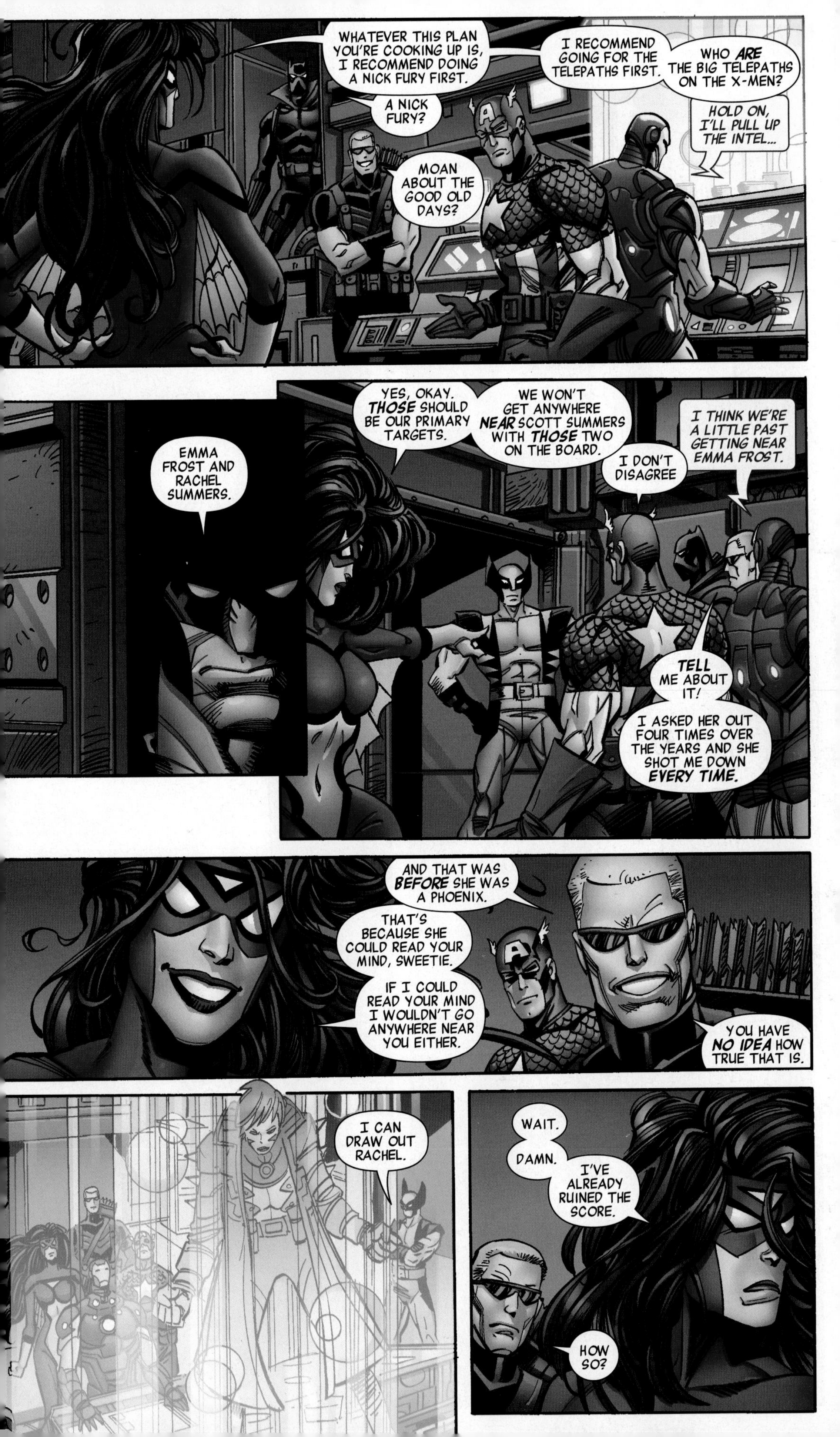

WHATEVER THIS PLAN YOU'RE COOKING UP IS, I RECOMMEND DOING A NICK FURY FIRST.
A NICK FURY?
MOAN ABOUT THE GOOD OLD DAYS?
I RECOMMEND GOING FOR THE TELEPATHS FIRST.
WHO ARE THE BIG TELEPATHS ON THE X-MEN?
HOLD ON, I'LL PULL UP THE INTEL...
EMMA FROST AND RACHEL SUMMERS.
YES, OKAY. THOSE SHOULD BE OUR PRIMARY TARGETS.
WE WON'T GET ANYWHERE NEAR SCOTT SUMMERS WITH THOSE TWO ON THE BOARD.
I DON'T DISAGREE
I THINK WE'RE A LITTLE PAST GETTING NEAR EMMA FROST.
TELL ME ABOUT IT!
I ASKED HER OUT FOUR TIMES OVER THE YEARS AND SHE SHOT ME DOWN EVERY TIME.
AND THAT WAS BEFORE SHE WAS A PHOENIX.
THAT'S BECAUSE SHE COULD READ YOUR MIND, SWEETIE.
IF I COULD READ YOUR MIND I WOULDN'T GO ANYWHERE NEAR YOU EITHER.
YOU HAVE NO IDEA HOW TRUE THAT IS.
I CAN DRAW OUT RACHEL.
WAIT.
DAMN.
I'VE ALREADY RUINED THE SCORE.
HOW SO?

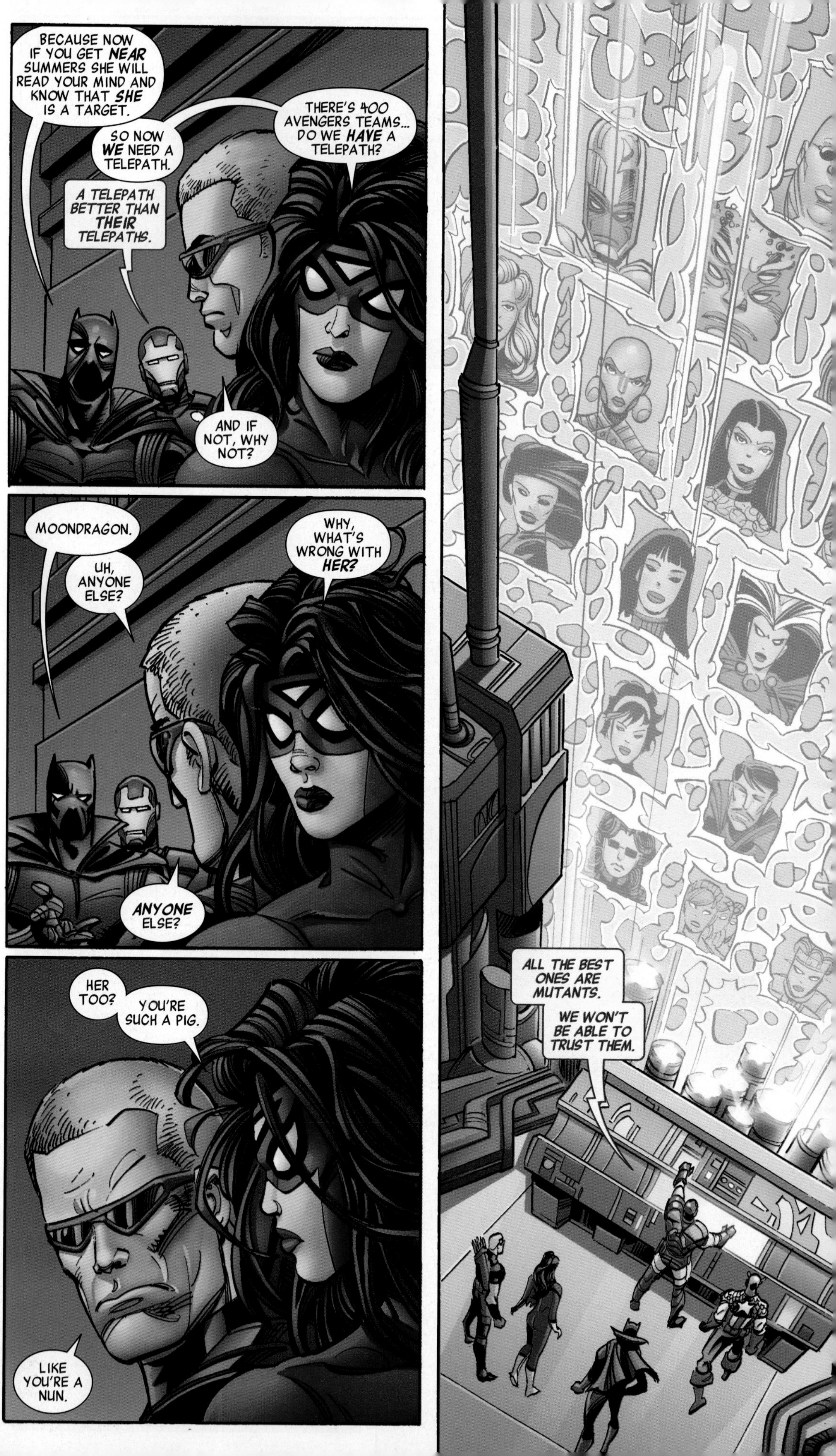
BECAUSE NOW IF YOU GET NEAR SUMMERS SHE WILL READ YOUR MIND AND KNOW THAT SHE IS A TARGET.
SO NOW WE NEED A TELEPATH.
A TELEPATH BETTER THAN THEIR TELEPATHS.
THERE'S 400 AVENGERS TEAMS... DO WE HAVE A TELEPATH?
AND IF NOT, WHY NOT?
MOONDRAGON.
UH, ANYONE ELSE?
WHY, WHAT'S WRONG WITH HER?
ANYONE ELSE?
HER TOO?
YOU'RE SUCH A PIG.
LIKE YOU'RE A NUN.
ALL THE BEST ONES ARE MUTANTS.
WE WON'T BE ABLE TO TRUST THEM.

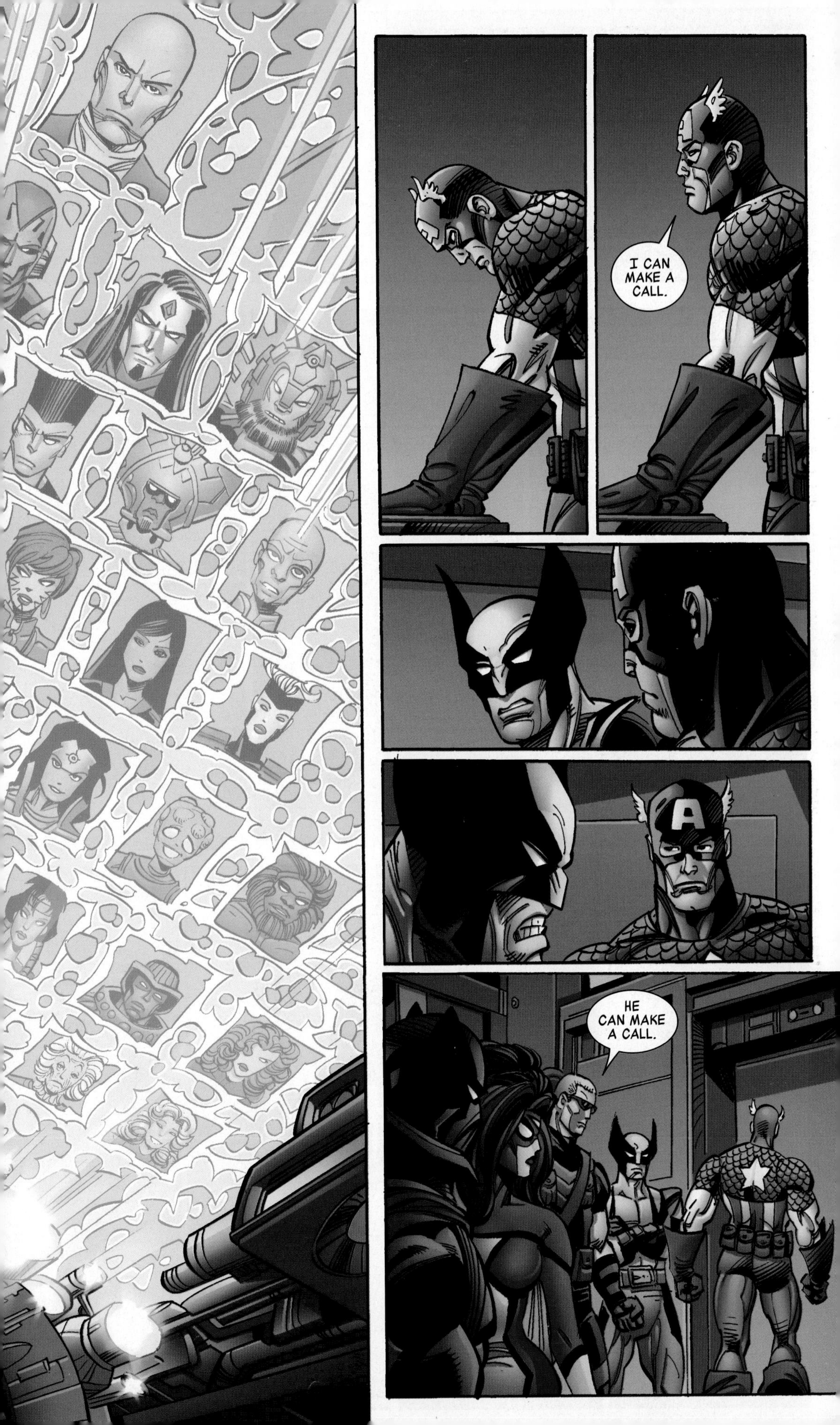
I CAN MAKE A CALL.
HE CAN MAKE A CALL.

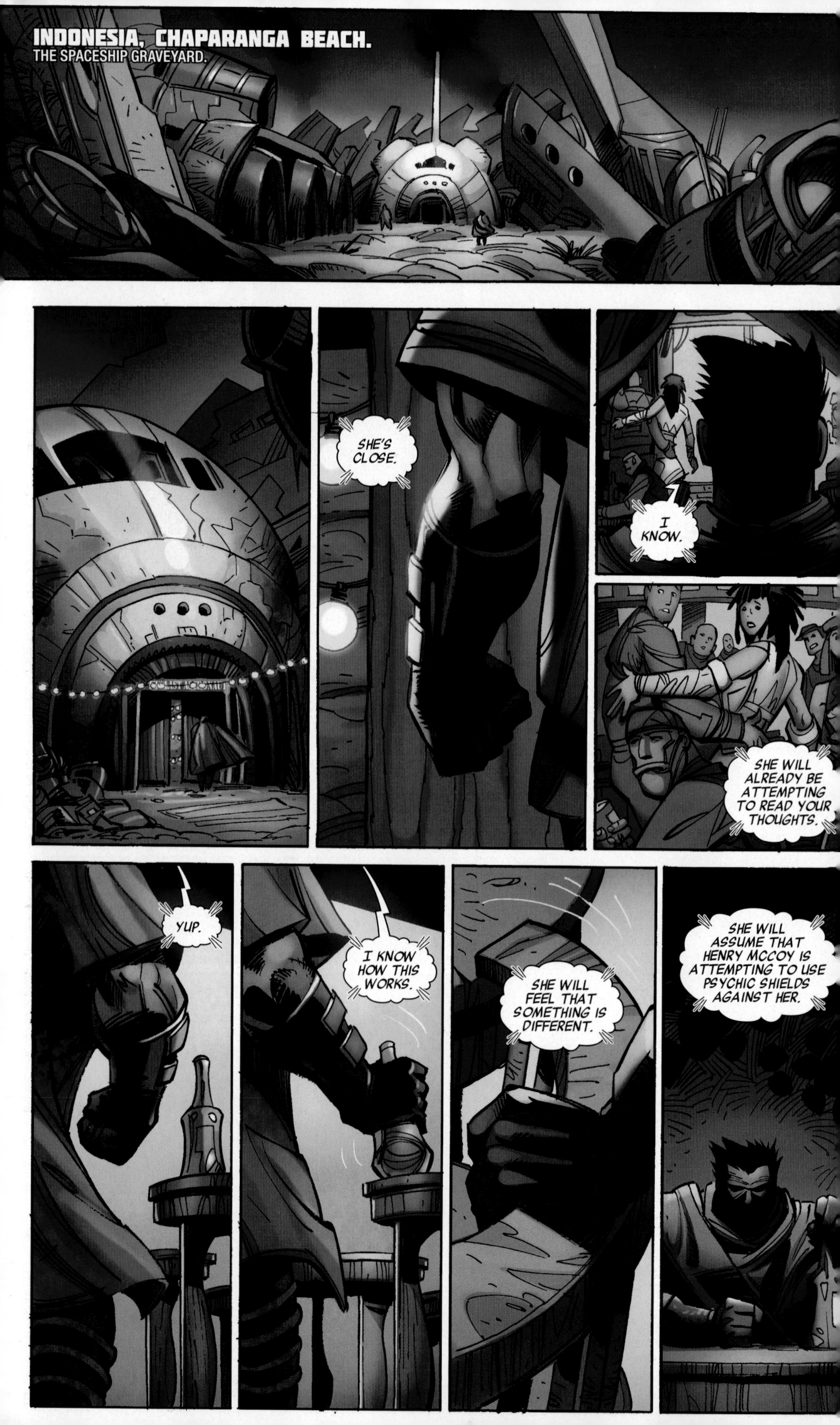
INDONESIA, CHAPARANGA BEACH.
THE SPACESHIP GRAVEYARD.
SHE'S CLOSE.
I KNOW.
SHE WILL ALREADY BE ATTEMPTING TO READ YOUR THOUGHTS.
YUP.
I KNOW HOW THIS WORKS.
SHE WILL FEEL THAT SOMETHING IS DIFFERENT.
SHE WILL ASSUME THAT HENRY MCCOY IS ATTEMPTING TO USE PSYCHIC SHIELDS AGAINST HER.

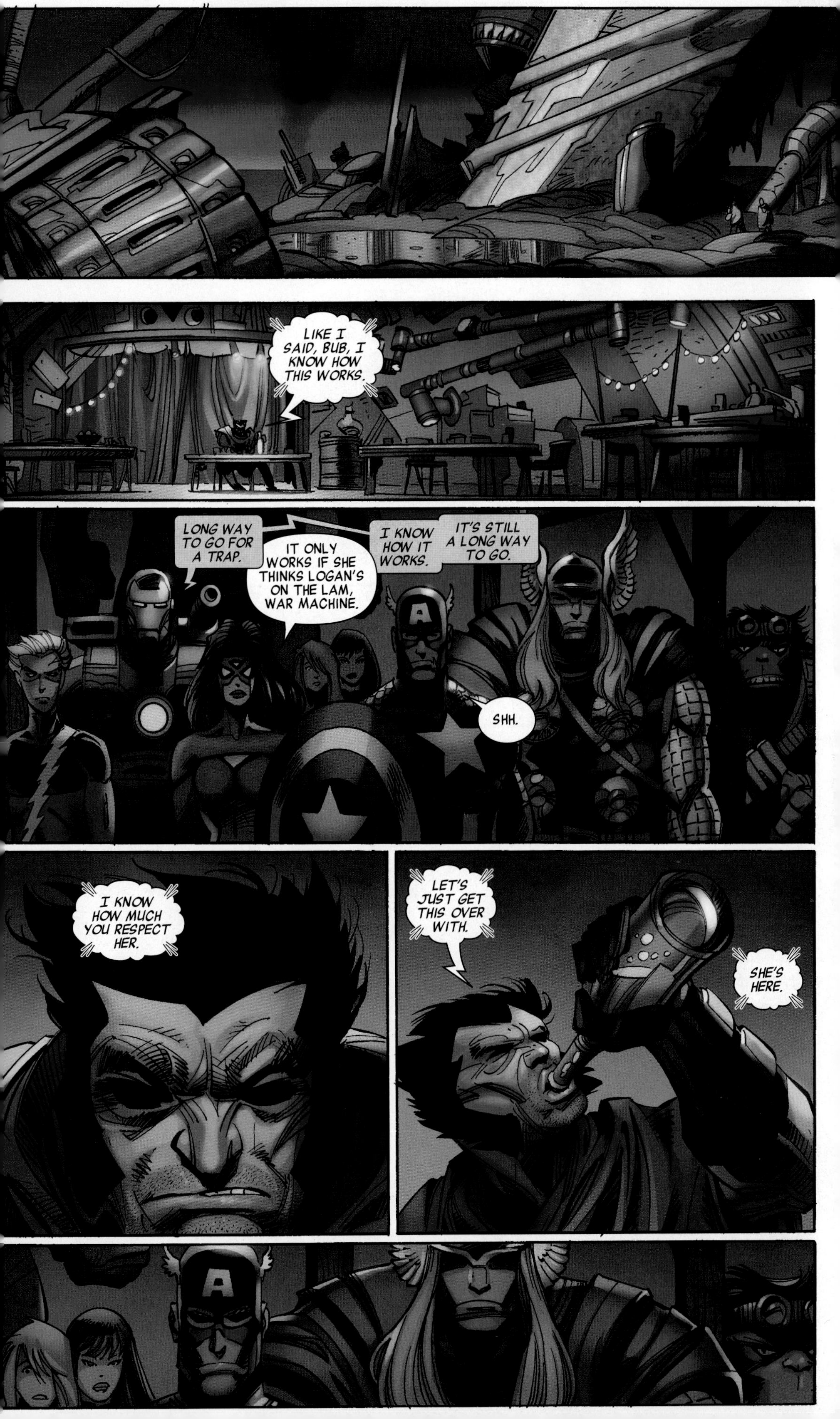
LIKE I SAID, BUB, I KNOW HOW THIS WORKS.
LONG WAY TO GO FOR A TRAP.
IT ONLY WORKS IF SHE THINKS LOGAN'S ON THE LAM, WAR MACHINE.
I KNOW HOW IT WORKS.
IT'S STILL A LONG WAY TO GO.
SHH.
I KNOW HOW MUCH YOU RESPECT HER.
LET'S JUST GET THIS OVER WITH.
SHE'S HERE.

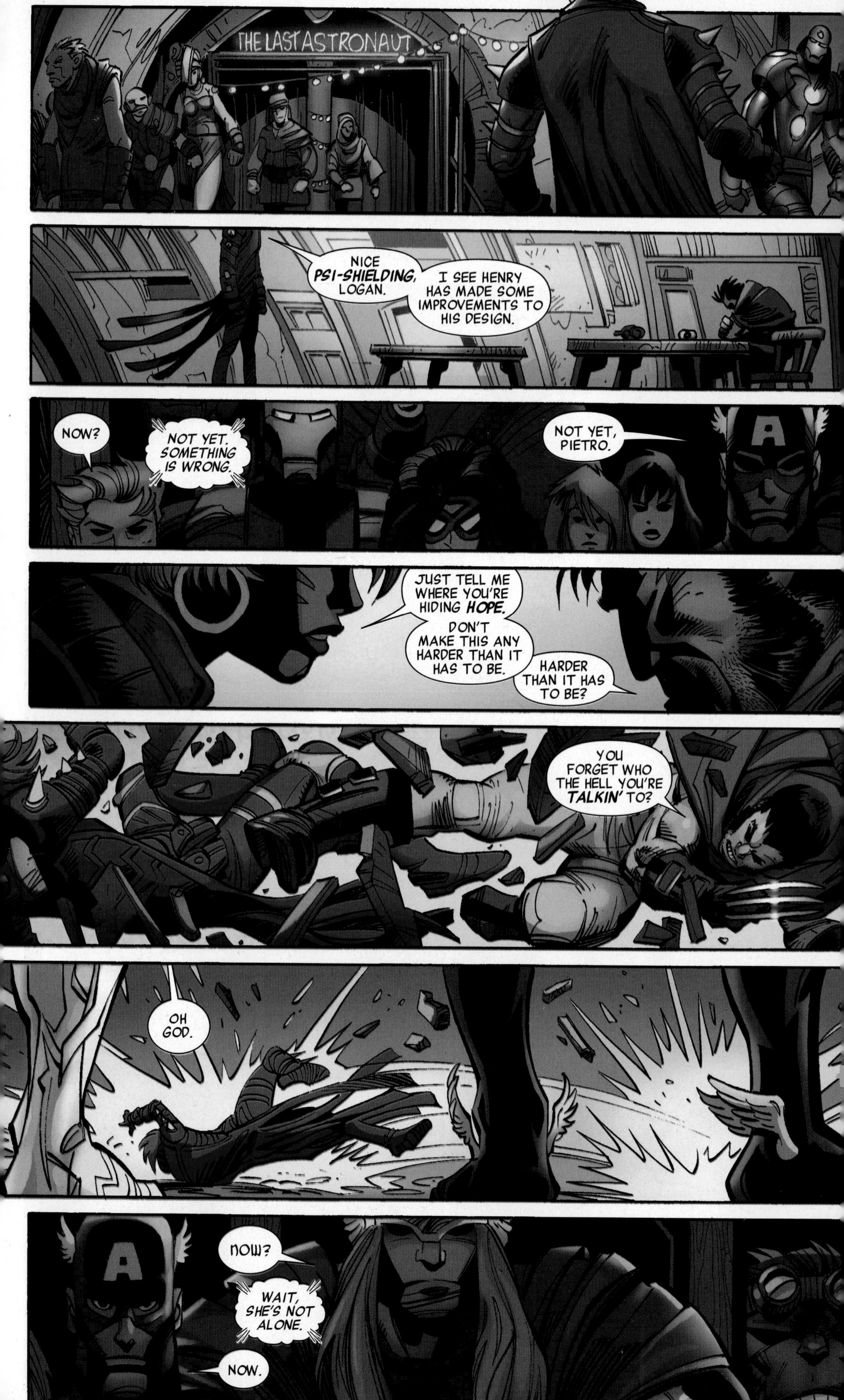
THE LAST ASTRONAUT
NICE PSI-SHIELDING, LOGAN.
I SEE HENRY HAS MADE SOME IMPROVEMENTS TO HIS DESIGN.
NOW?
NOT YET. SOMETHING IS WRONG.
NOT YET, PIETRO.
JUST TELL ME WHERE YOU'RE HIDING HOPE.
DON'T MAKE THIS ANY HARDER THAN IT HAS TO BE.
HARDER THAN IT HAS TO BE?
YOU FORGET WHO THE HELL YOU'RE TALKIN' TO?
OH GOD.
NOW?
WAIT, SHE'S NOT ALONE.
NOW.

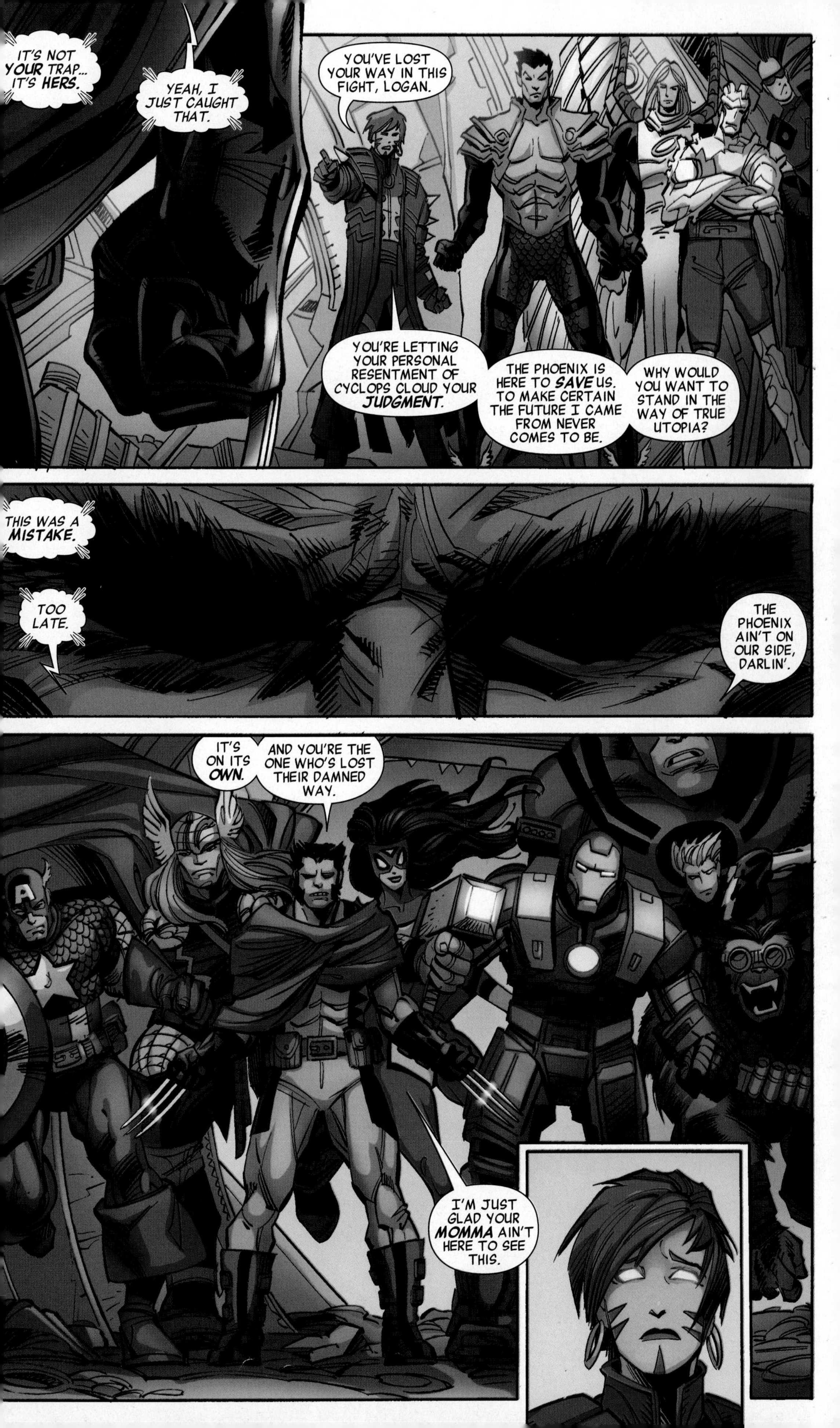
IT'S NOT YOUR TRAP... IT'S HERS.
YEAH, I JUST CAUGHT THAT.
YOU'VE LOST YOUR WAY IN THIS FIGHT, LOGAN.
YOU'RE LETTING YOUR PERSONAL RESENTMENT OF CYCLOPS CLOUD YOUR JUDGMENT.
THE PHOENIX IS HERE TO SAVE US. TO MAKE CERTAIN THE FUTURE I CAME FROM NEVER COMES TO BE.
WHY WOULD YOU WANT TO STAND IN THE WAY OF TRUE UTOPIA?
THIS WAS A MISTAKE.
TOO LATE.
THE PHOENIX AIN'T ON OUR SIDE, DARLIN'.
IT'S ON ITS OWN.
AND YOU'RE THE ONE WHO'S LOST THEIR DAMNED WAY.
I'M JUST GLAD YOUR MOMMA AIN'T HERE TO SEE THIS.

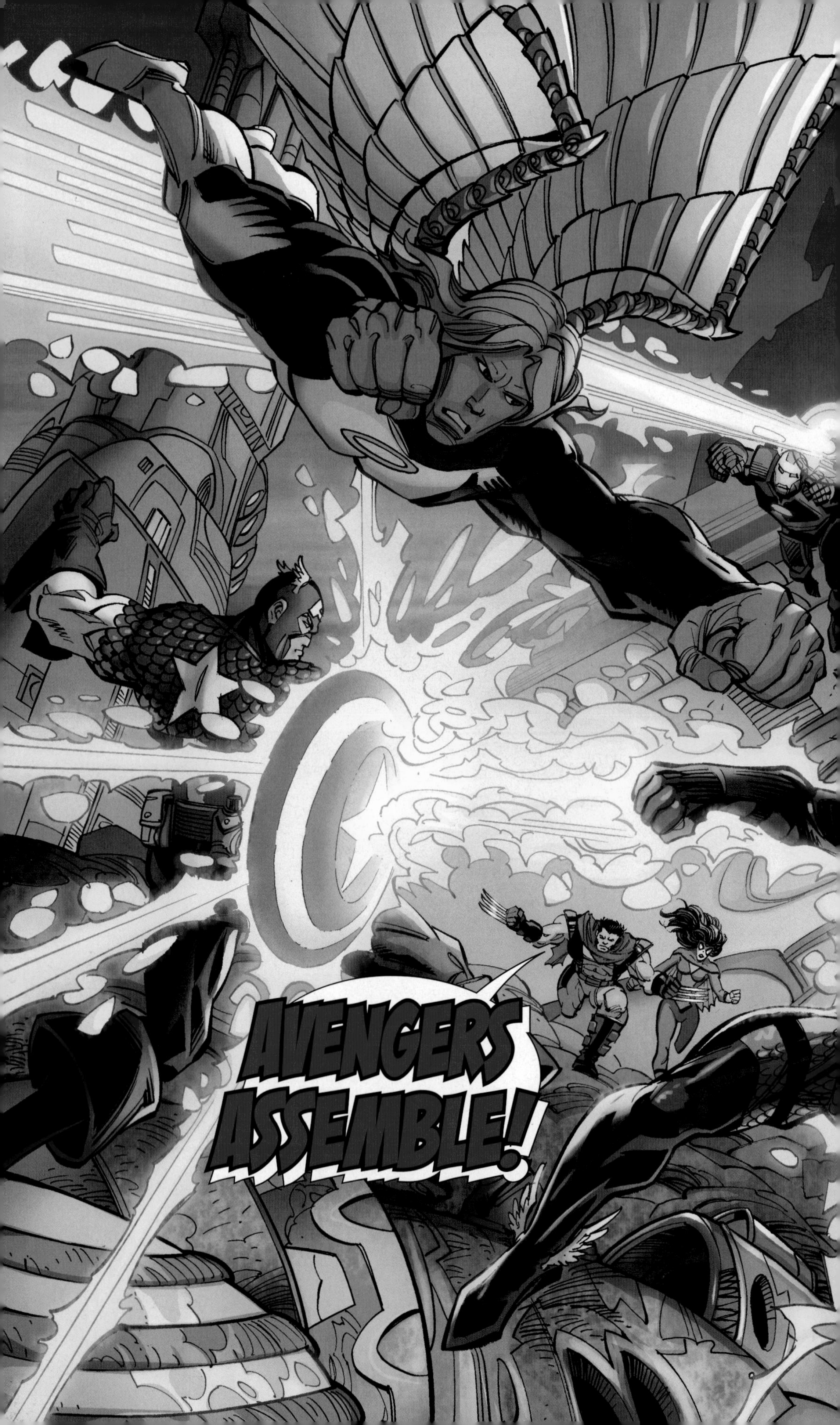
AVENGERS ASSEMBLE!

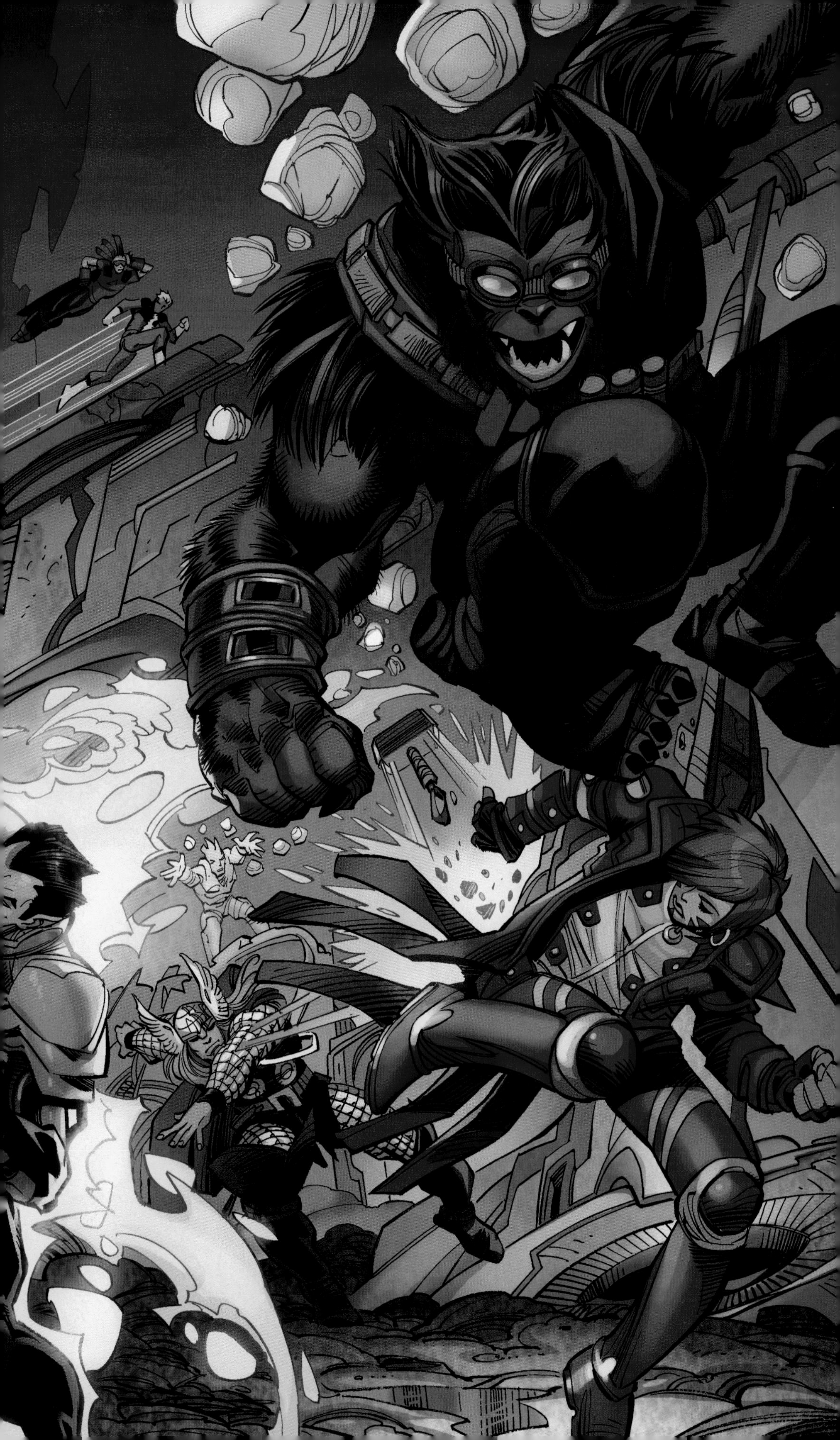

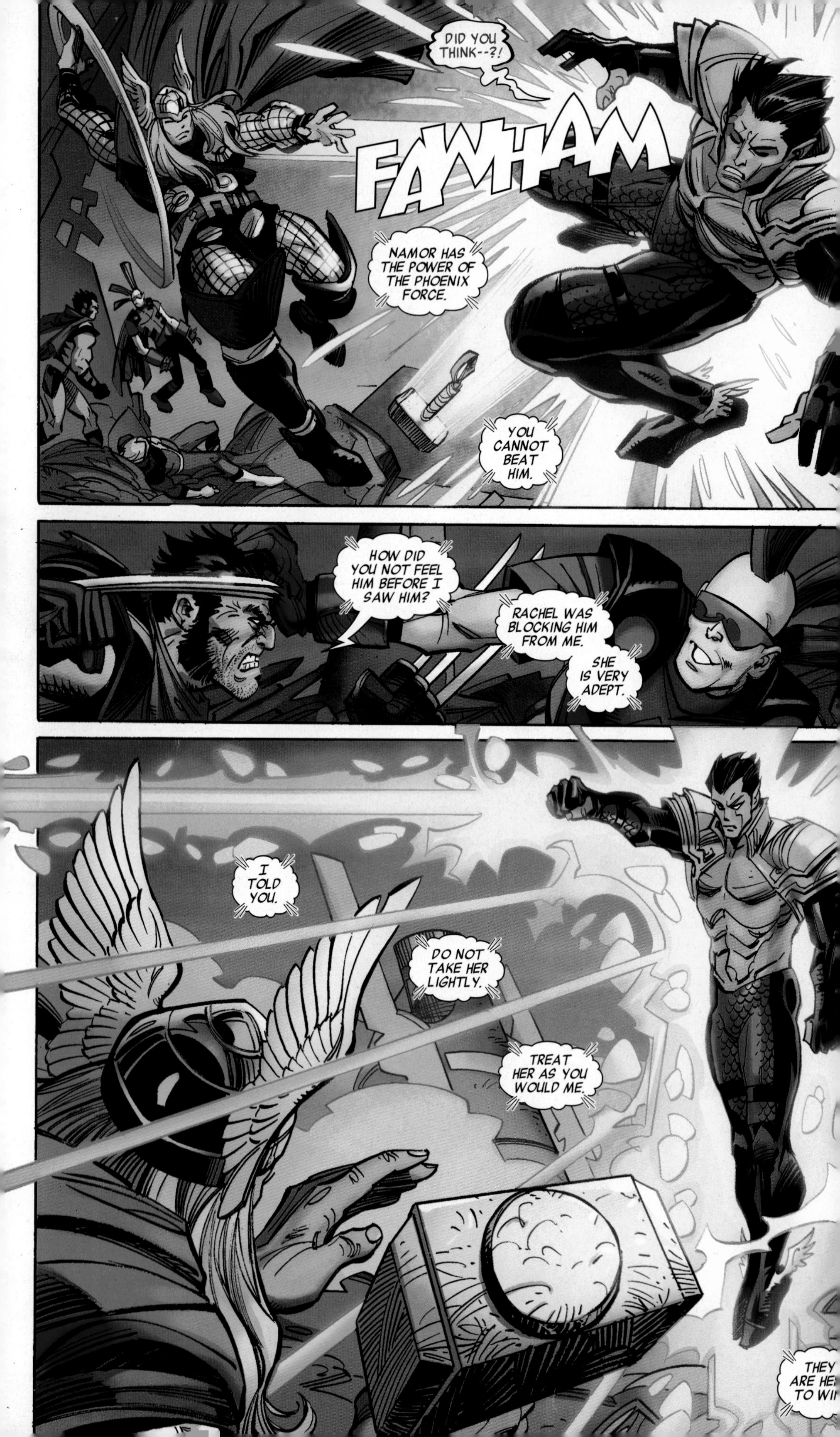

DID YOU THINK--?!
FAWHAM
NAMOR HAS THE POWER OF THE PHOENIX FORCE.
YOU CANNOT BEAT HIM.
HOW DID YOU NOT FEEL HIM BEFORE I SAW HIM?
RACHEL WAS BLOCKING HIM FROM ME.
SHE IS VERY ADEPT.
I TOLD YOU.
DO NOT TAKE HER LIGHTLY.
TREAT HER AS YOU WOULD ME.

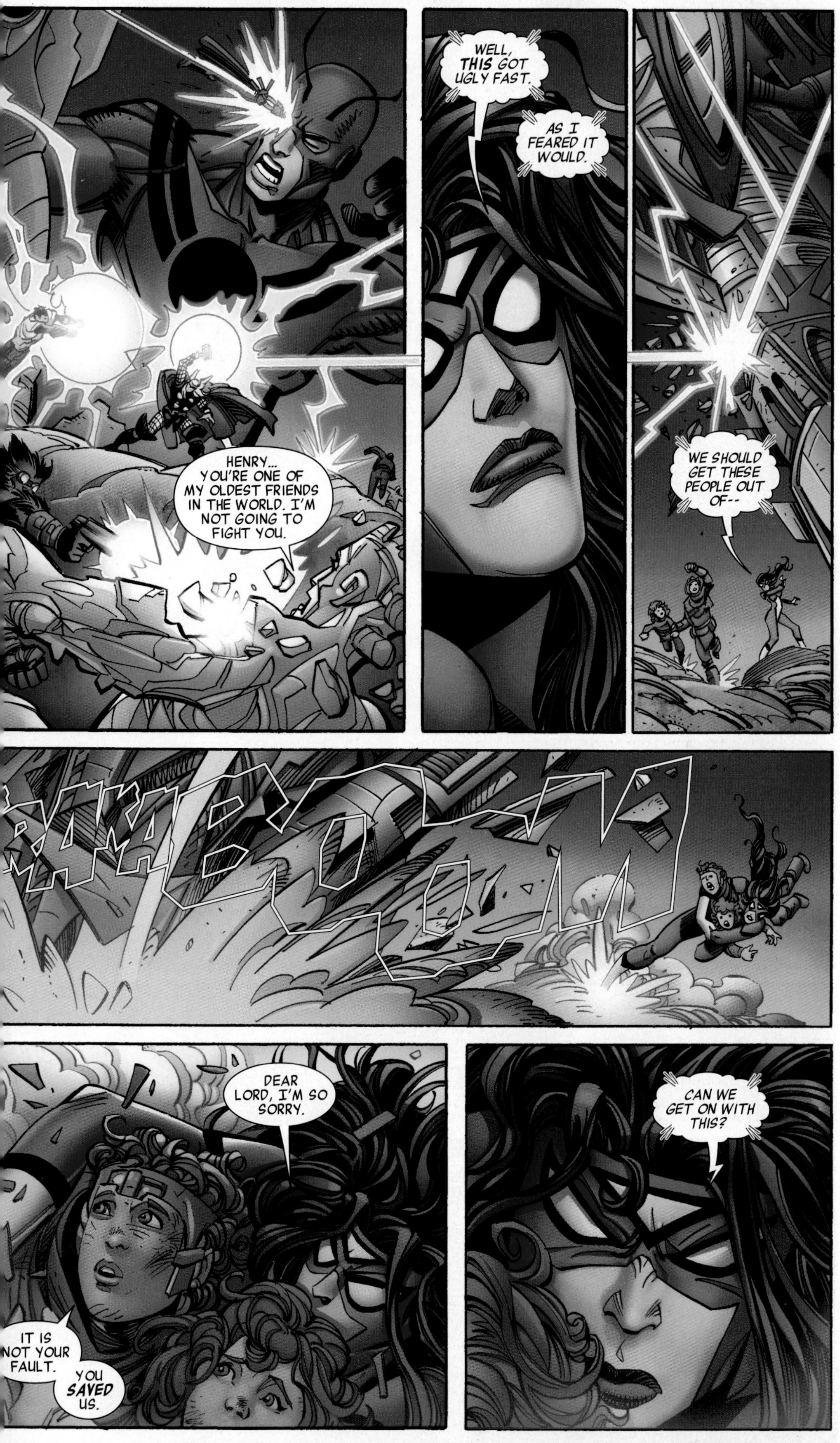
HENRY... YOU'RE ONE OF MY OLDEST FRIENDS IN THE WORLD. I'M NOT GOING TO FIGHT YOU.
WELL, THIS GOT UGLY FAST.
AS I FEARED IT WOULD.
WE SHOULD GET THESE PEOPLE OUT OF--
KRAKABOOM
DEAR LORD, I'M SO SORRY.
IT IS NOT YOUR FAULT.
YOU SAVED US.
CAN WE GET ON WITH THIS?

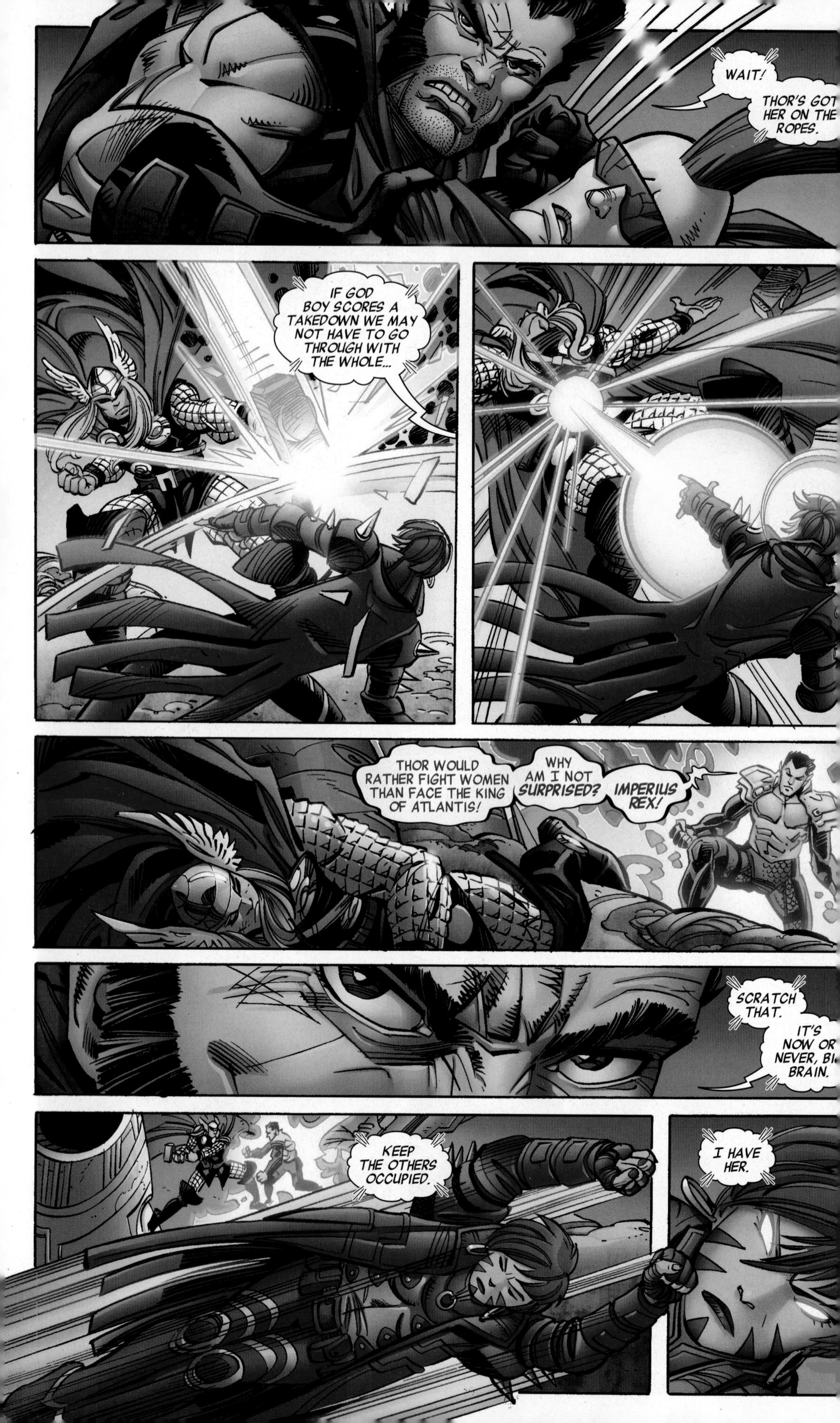
WAIT!
THOR'S GOT HER ON THE ROPES.
IF GOD BOY SCORES A TAKEDOWN WE MAY NOT HAVE TO GO THROUGH WITH THE WHOLE...
THOR WOULD RATHER FIGHT WOMEN THAN FACE THE KING OF ATLANTIS!
WHY AM I NOT SURPRISED?
IMPERIUS REX!
SCRATCH THAT.
IT'S NOW OR NEVER, BI BRAIN.
KEEP THE OTHERS OCCUPIED.
I HAVE HER.

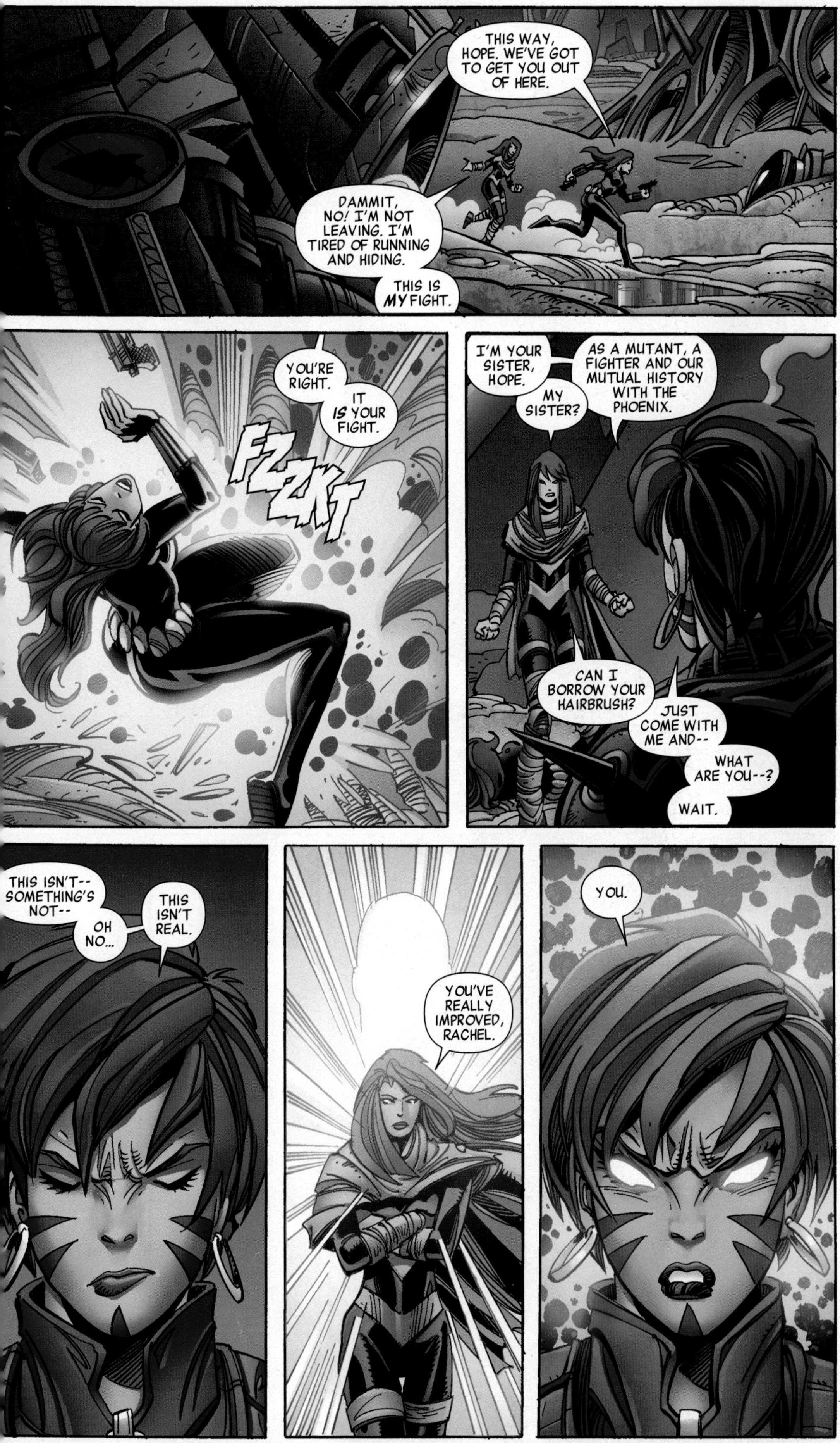
THIS WAY, HOPE. WE'VE GOT TO GET YOU OUT OF HERE.
DAMMIT, NO! I'M NOT LEAVING. I'M TIRED OF RUNNING AND HIDING.
THIS IS MY FIGHT.
YOU'RE RIGHT.
IT IS YOUR FIGHT.
FZZKT
I'M YOUR SISTER, HOPE.
AS A MUTANT, A FIGHTER AND OUR MUTUAL HISTORY WITH THE PHOENIX.
MY SISTER?
CAN I BORROW YOUR HAIRBRUSH?
JUST COME WITH ME AND--
WHAT ARE YOU--?
WAIT.
THIS ISN'T-- SOMETHING'S NOT--
OH NO...
THIS ISN'T REAL.
YOU'VE REALLY IMPROVED, RACHEL.
YOU.

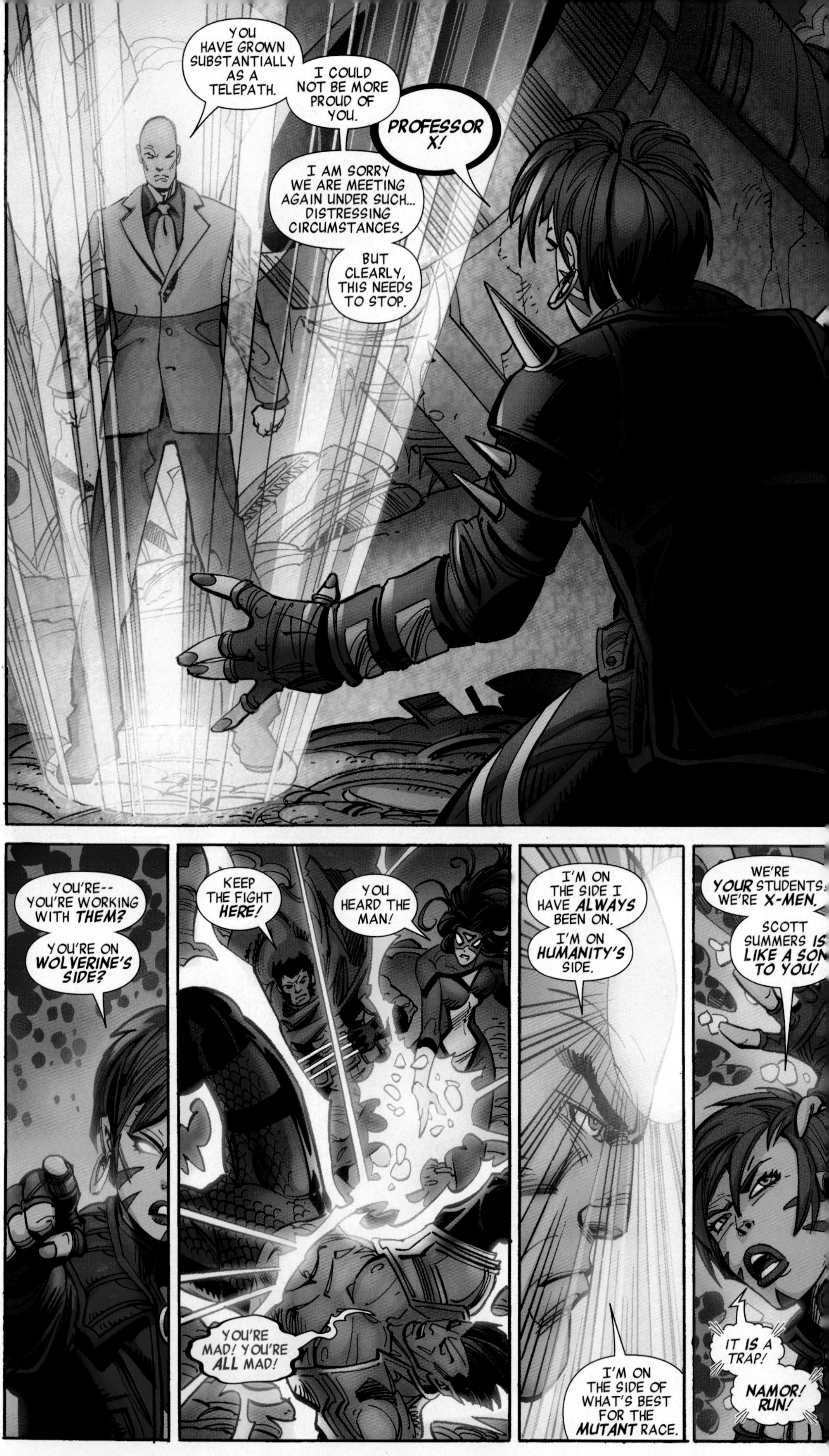
YOU HAVE GROWN SUBSTANTIALLY AS A TELEPATH.
I COULD NOT BE MORE PROUD OF YOU.
PROFESSOR X!
I AM SORRY WE ARE MEETING AGAIN UNDER SUCH... DISTRESSING CIRCUMSTANCES.
BUT CLEARLY, THIS NEEDS TO STOP.
YOU'RE-- YOU'RE WORKING WITH THEM?
YOU'RE ON WOLVERINE'S SIDE?
KEEP THE FIGHT HERE!
YOU HEARD THE MAN!
YOU'RE MAD! YOU'RE ALL MAD!
I'M ON THE SIDE I HAVE ALWAYS BEEN ON.
I'M ON HUMANITY'S SIDE.
I'M ON THE SIDE OF WHAT'S BEST FOR THE MUTANT RACE.
WE'RE YOUR STUDENTS. WE'RE X-MEN.
SCOTT SUMMERS IS LIKE A SON TO YOU!
IT IS A TRAP!
NAMOR! RUN!

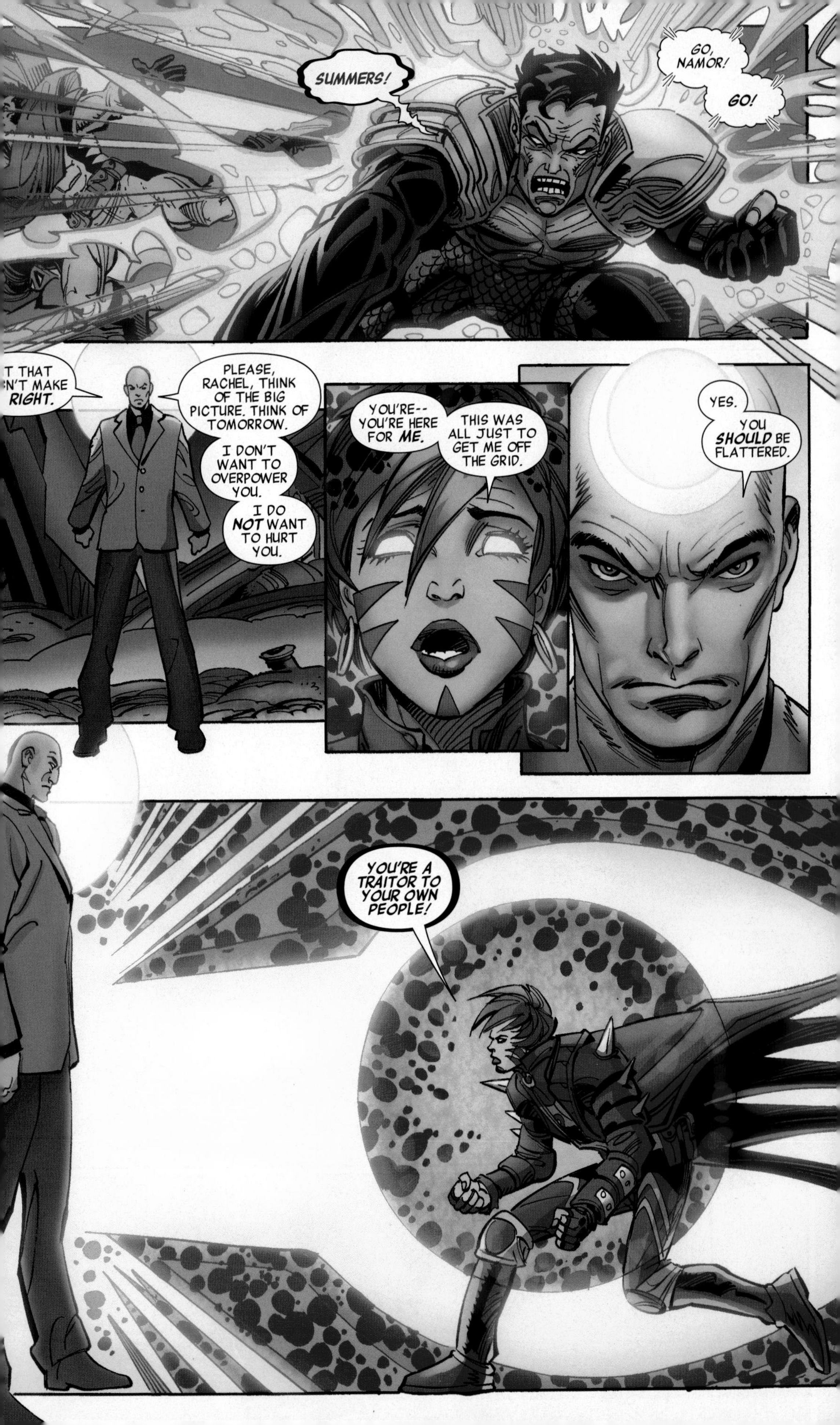
SUMMERS!
GO, NAMOR!
GO!
T THAT
N'T MAKE
RIGHT.
PLEASE, RACHEL, THINK OF THE BIG PICTURE. THINK OF TOMORROW.
I DON'T WANT TO OVERPOWER YOU.
I DO NOT WANT TO HURT YOU.
YOU'RE-- YOU'RE HERE FOR ME.
THIS WAS ALL JUST TO GET ME OFF THE GRID.
YES.
YOU SHOULD BE FLATTERED.
YOU'RE A TRAITOR TO YOUR OWN PEOPLE!

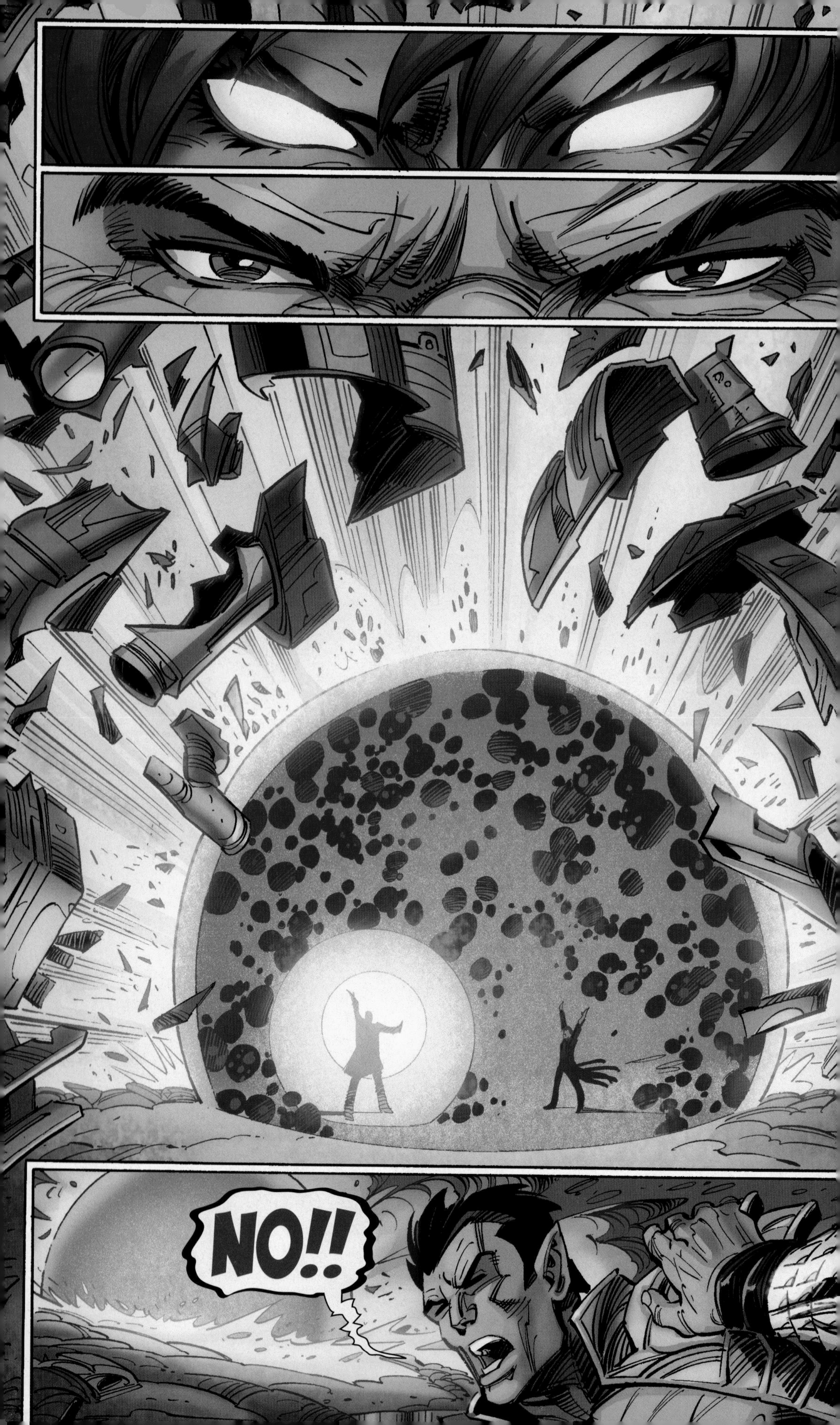
NO!!

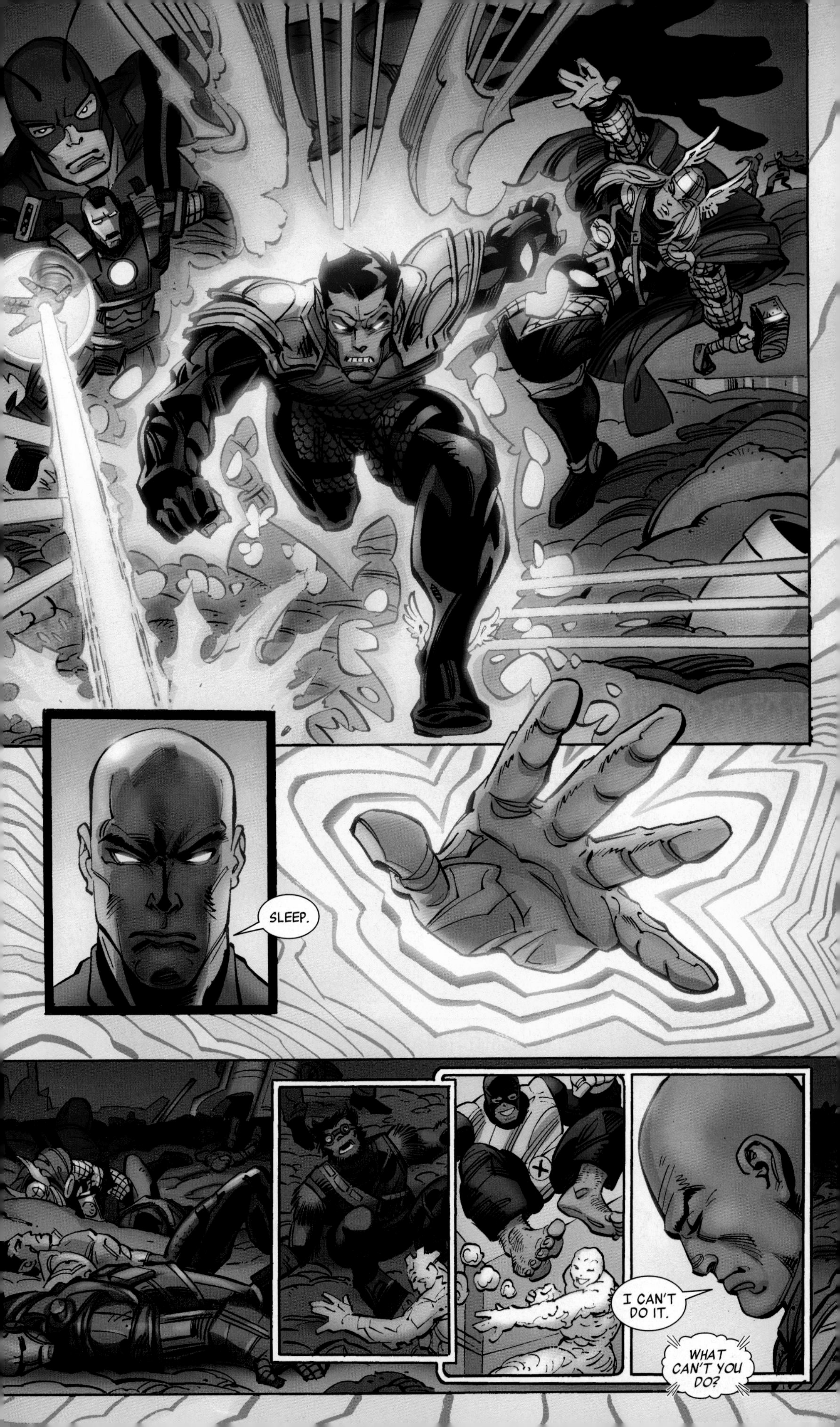
SLEEP.
I CAN'T DO IT.
WHAT CAN'T YOU DO?

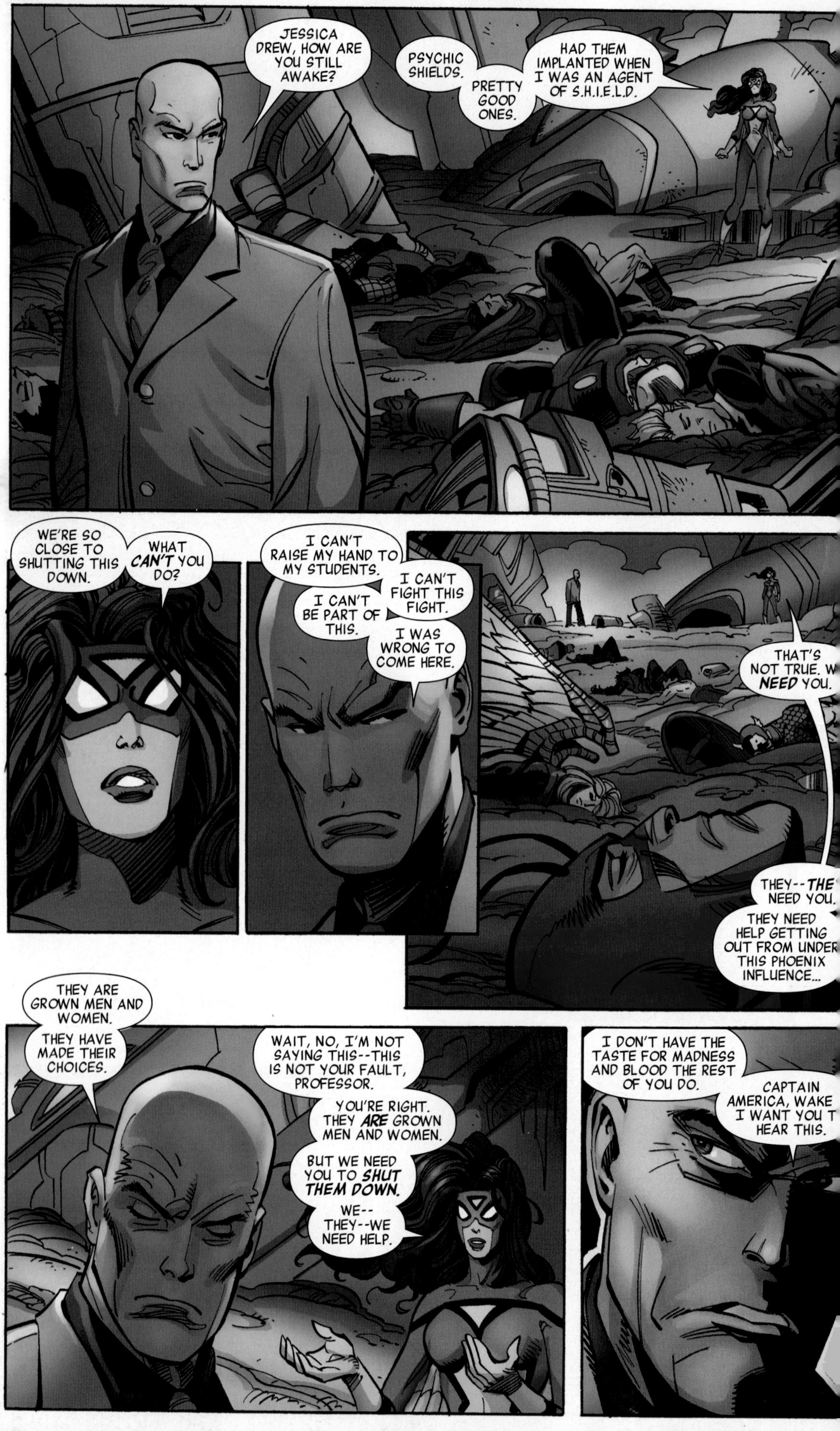
JESSICA DREW, HOW ARE YOU STILL AWAKE?
PSYCHIC SHIELDS.
PRETTY GOOD ONES.
HAD THEM IMPLANTED WHEN I WAS AN AGENT OF S.H.I.E.L.D.
WE'RE SO CLOSE TO SHUTTING THIS DOWN.
WHAT CAN'T YOU DO?
I CAN'T RAISE MY HAND TO MY STUDENTS.
I CAN'T BE PART OF THIS.
I CAN'T FIGHT THIS FIGHT.
I WAS WRONG TO COME HERE.
THAT'S NOT TRUE. W NEED YOU.
THEY--THE NEED YOU.
THEY NEED HELP GETTING OUT FROM UNDER THIS PHOENIX INFLUENCE...
THEY ARE GROWN MEN AND WOMEN.
THEY HAVE MADE THEIR CHOICES.
WAIT, NO, I'M NOT SAYING THIS--THIS IS NOT YOUR FAULT, PROFESSOR.
YOU'RE RIGHT. THEY ARE GROWN MEN AND WOMEN.
BUT WE NEED YOU TO SHUT THEM DOWN.
WE-- THEY--WE NEED HELP.
I DON'T HAVE THE TASTE FOR MADNESS AND BLOOD THE REST OF YOU DO.
CAPTAIN AMERICA, WAKE I WANT YOU T HEAR THIS.

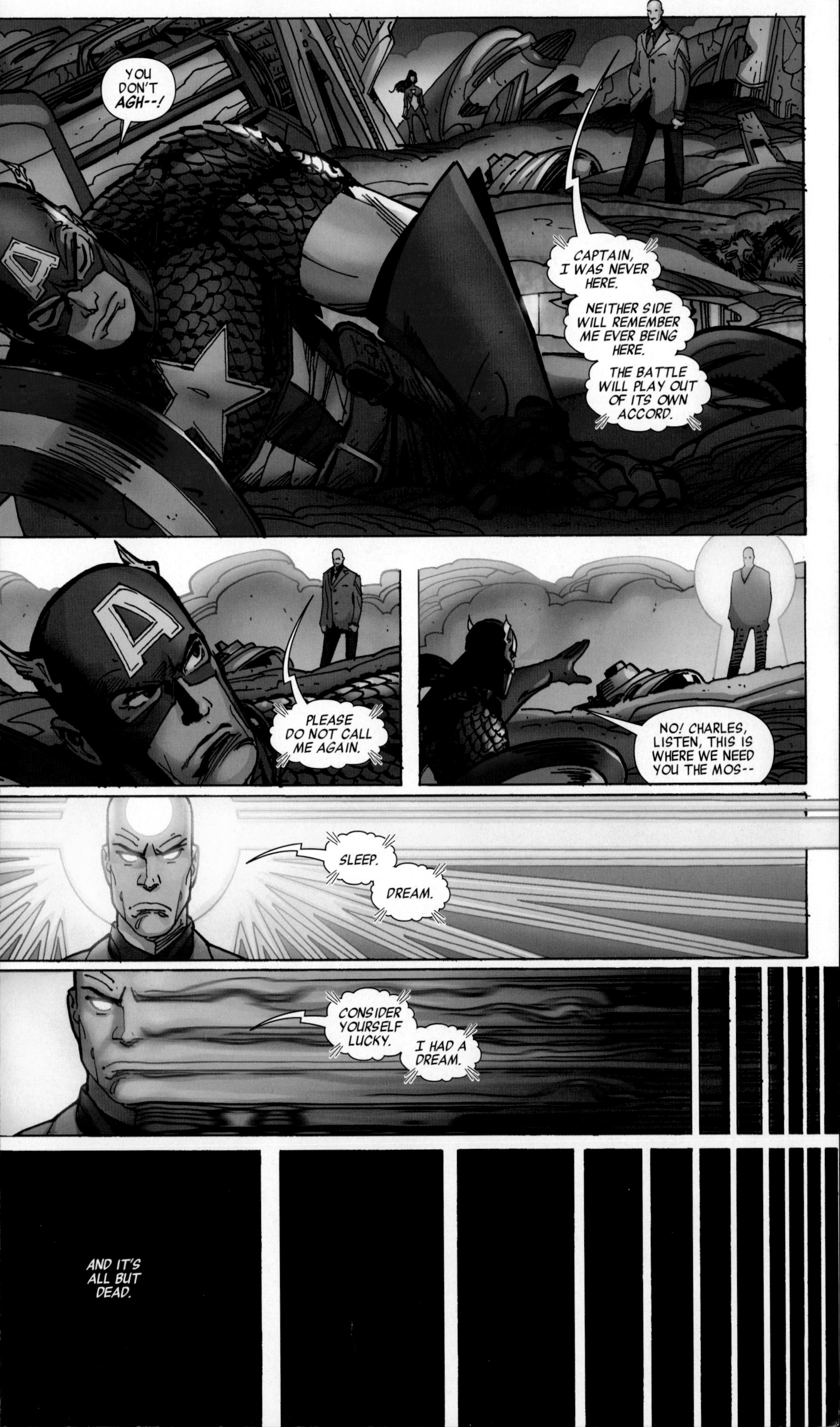
YOU DON'T AGH--!
CAPTAIN, I WAS NEVER HERE.
NEITHER SIDE WILL REMEMBER ME EVER BEING HERE.
THE BATTLE WILL PLAY OUT OF ITS OWN ACCORD.
PLEASE DO NOT CALL ME AGAIN.
NO! CHARLES, LISTEN, THIS IS WHERE WE NEED YOU THE MOS--
SLEEP.
DREAM.
CONSIDER YOURSELF LUCKY.
I HAD A DREAM.
AND IT'S ALL BUT DEAD.

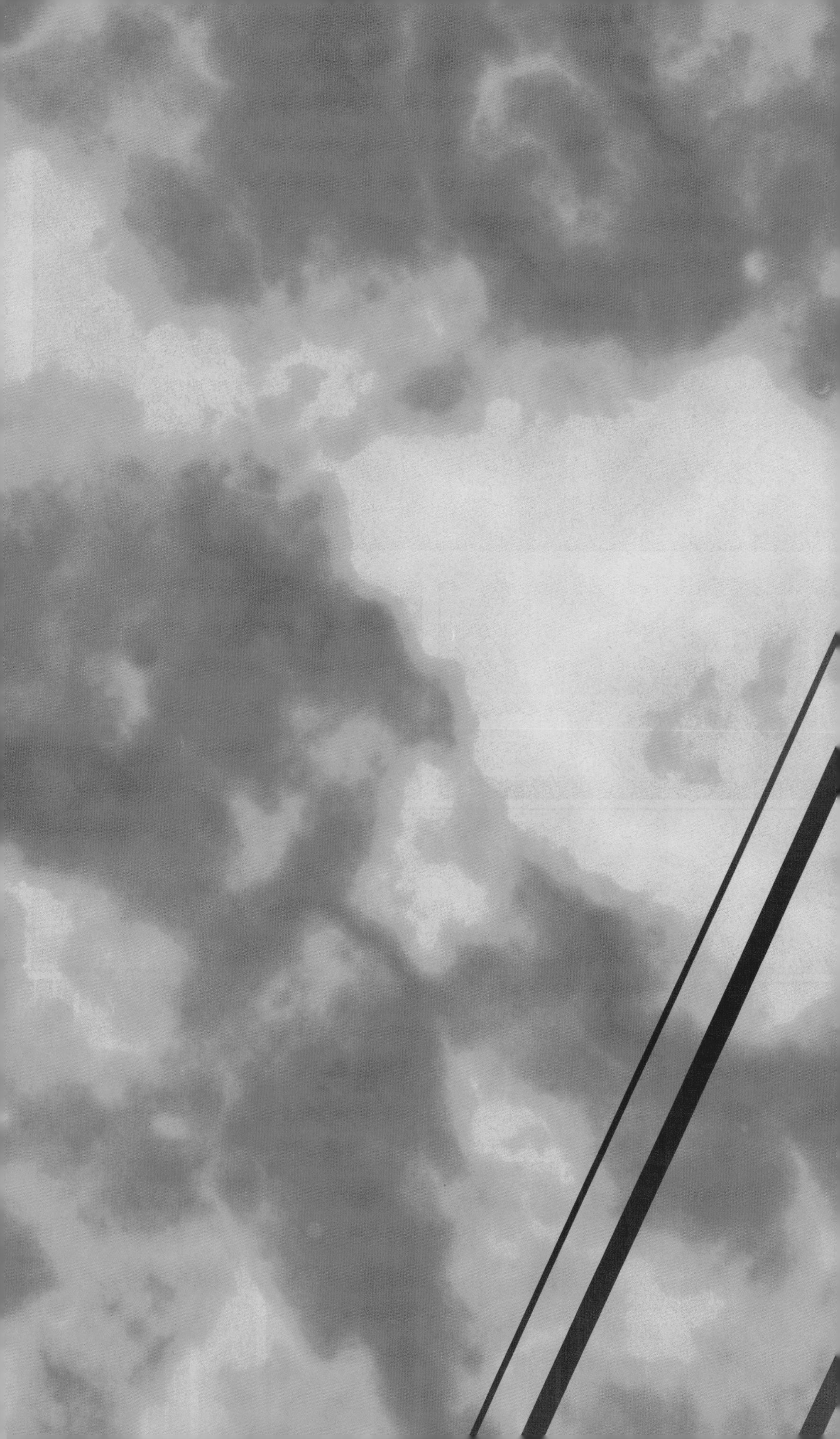

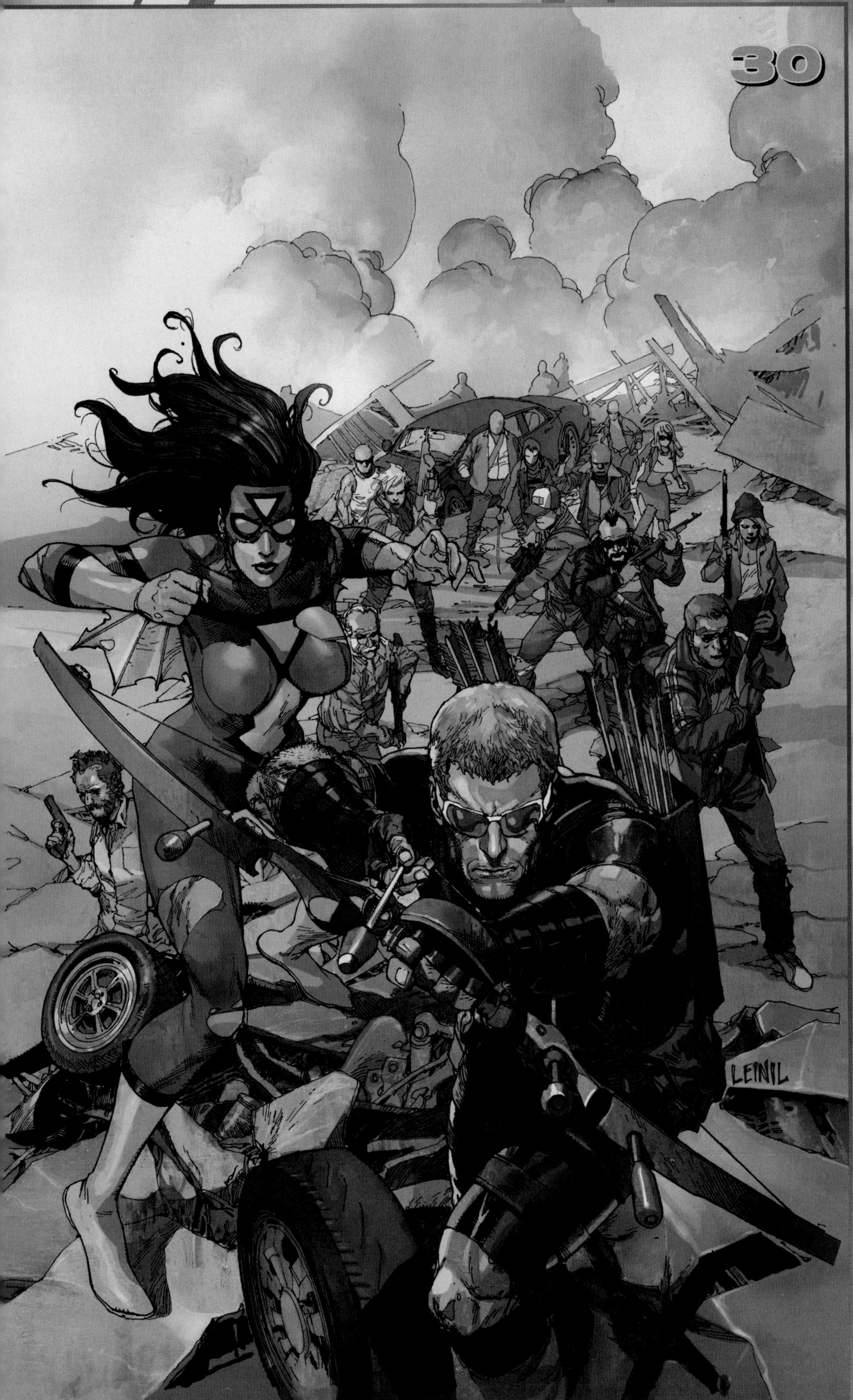
30
LEINIL

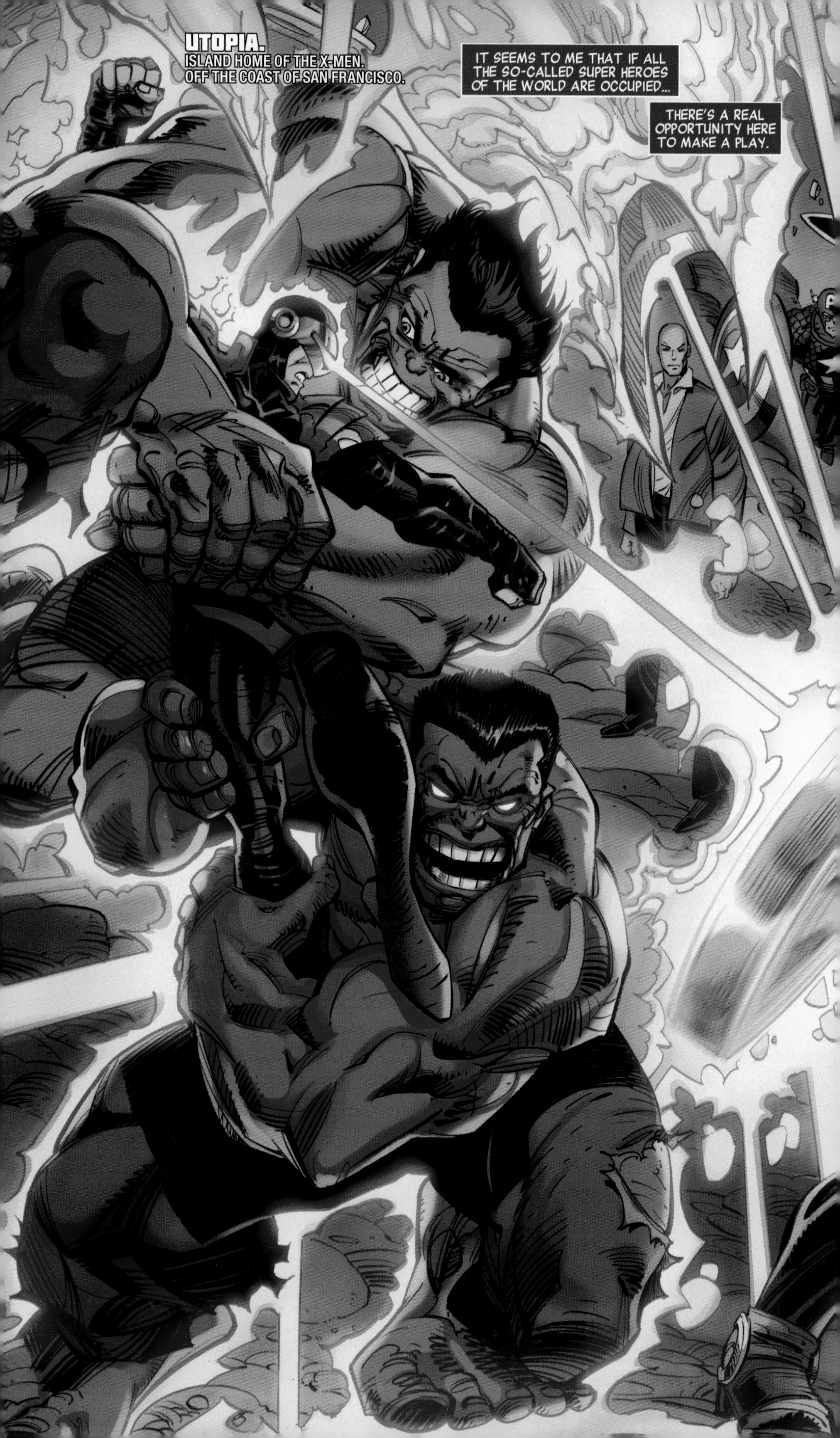
UTOPIA.
ISLAND HOME OF THE X-MEN.
OFF THE COAST OF SAN FRANCISCO.
IT SEEMS TO ME THAT IF ALL THE SO-CALLED SUPER HEROES OF THE WORLD ARE OCCUPIED...
THERE'S A REAL OPPORTUNITY HERE TO MAKE A PLAY.

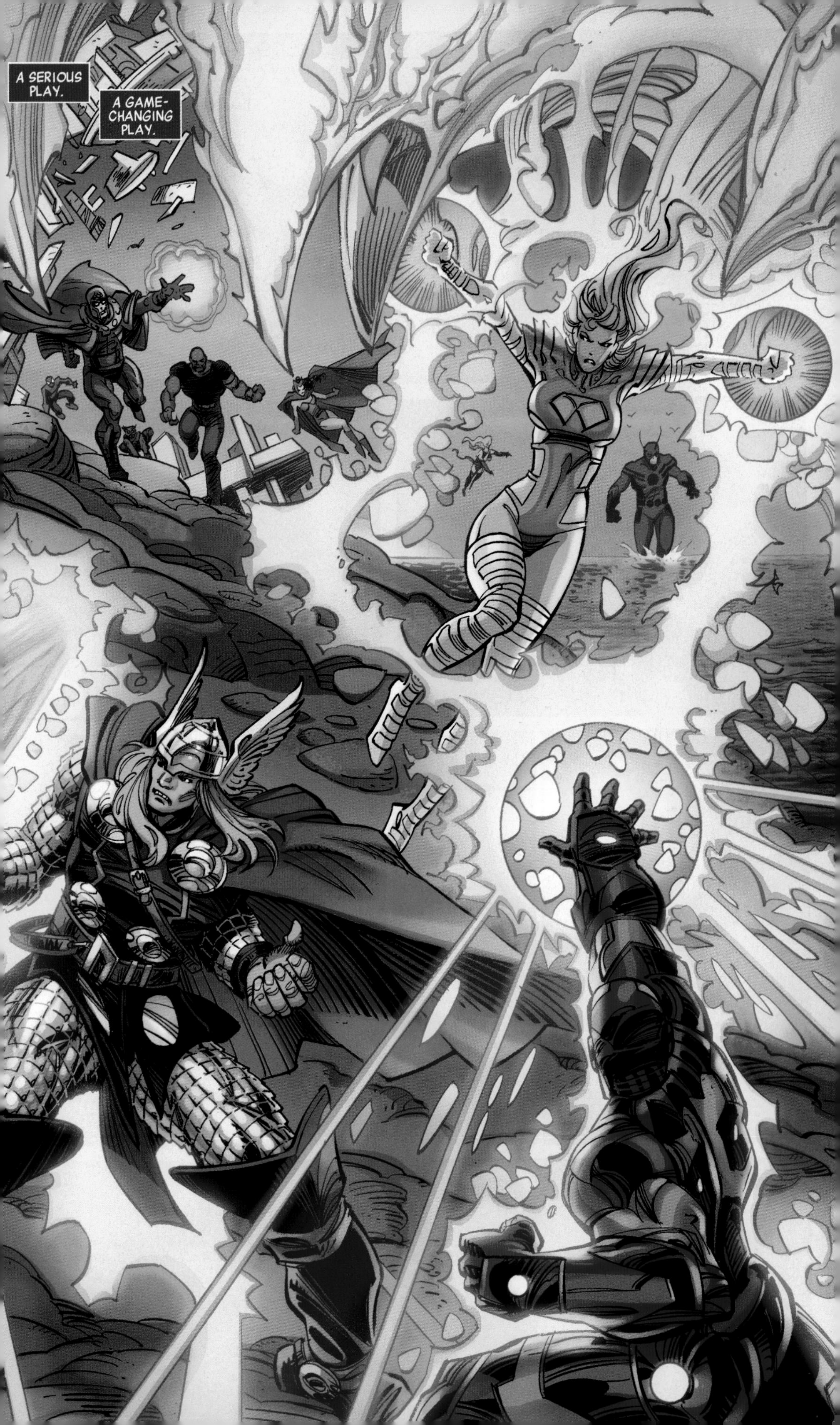
A SERIOUS PLAY.
A GAME-CHANGING PLAY.

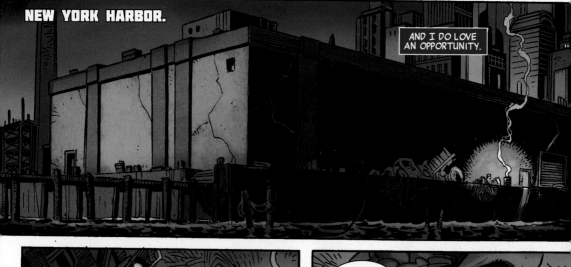

NEW YORK HARBOR.

AND I DO LOVE AN OPPORTUNITY.

NORTH CONCOURSE SECURE.

AGAIN. AS ALWAYS.

OKAY, DON'T ANSWER ME.

I GET PAID EITHER WAY.

GKKSS!

SHICK

THE OUTER PERIMETER IS SECURE, MASTER.

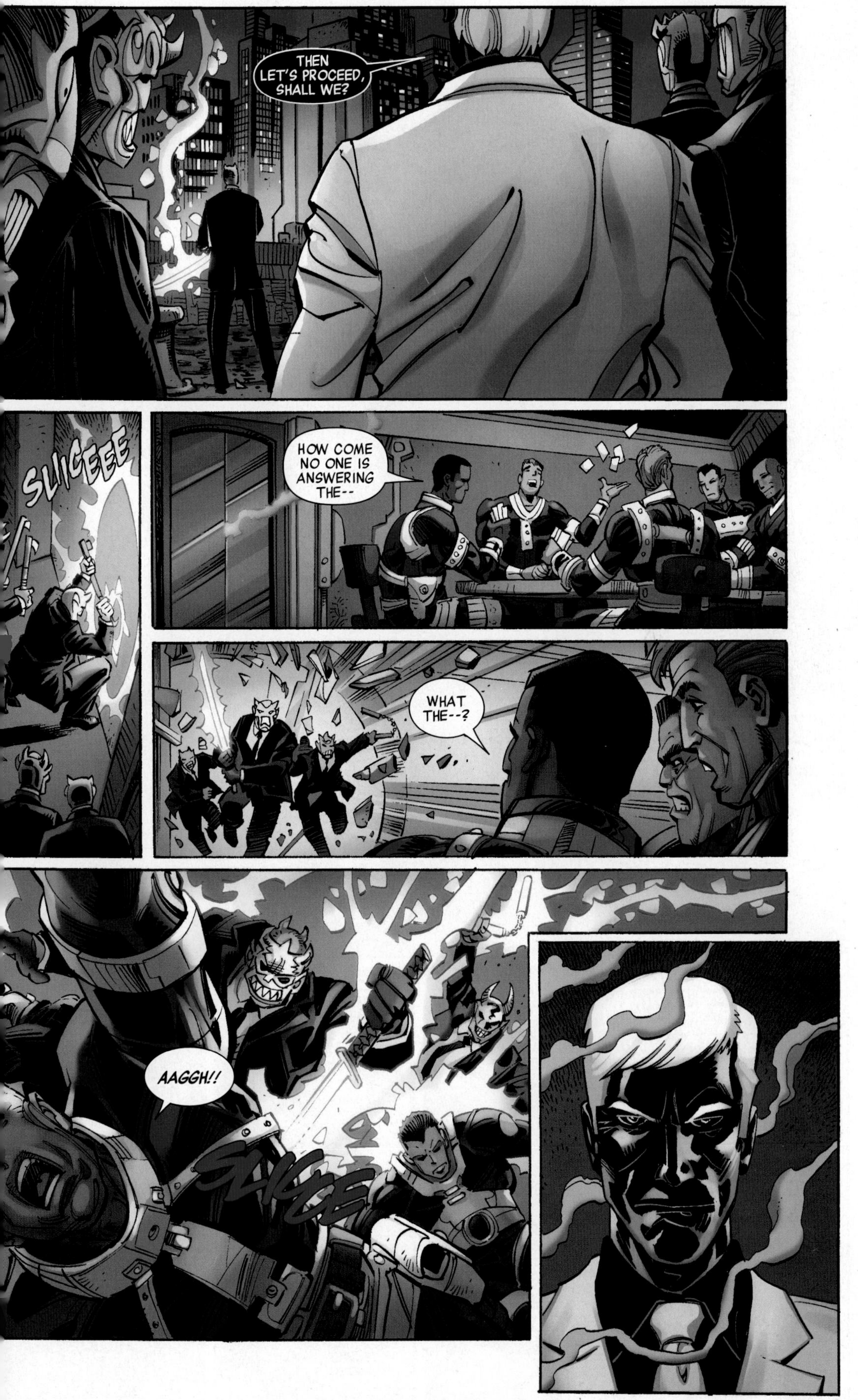
THEN LET'S PROCEED, SHALL WE?
SLICEEE
HOW COME NO ONE IS ANSWERING THE--
WHAT THE--?
AAGGH!!
SLICE

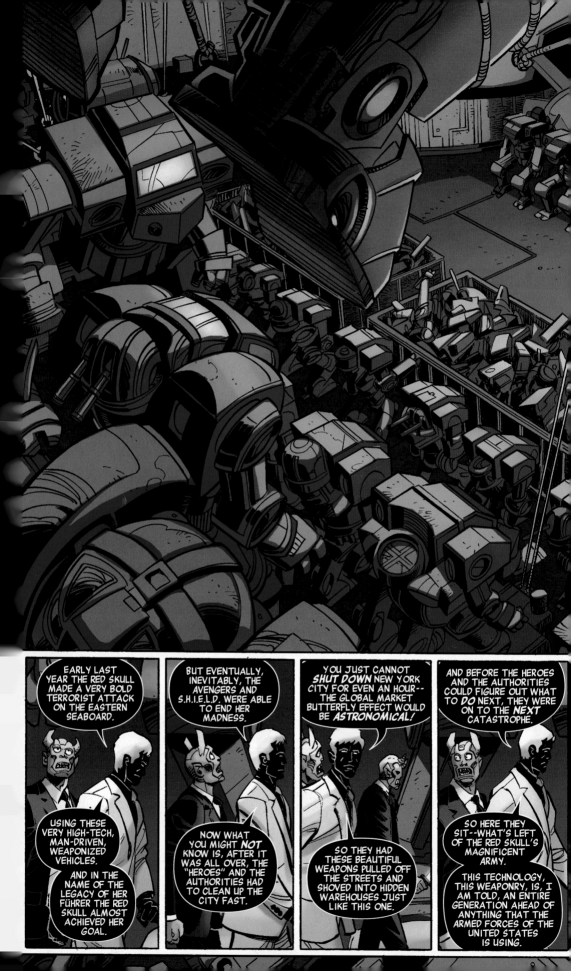

EARLY LAST YEAR THE RED SKULL MADE A VERY BOLD TERRORIST ATTACK ON THE EASTERN SEABOARD.

USING THESE VERY HIGH-TECH, MAN-DRIVEN, WEAPONIZED VEHICLES.

AND IN THE NAME OF THE LEGACY OF HER FÜHRER THE RED SKULL ALMOST ACHIEVED HER GOAL.

BUT EVENTUALLY, INEVITABLY, THE AVENGERS AND S.H.I.E.L.D. WERE ABLE TO END HER MADNESS.

NOW WHAT YOU MIGHT NOT KNOW IS, AFTER IT WAS ALL OVER, THE "HEROES" AND THE AUTHORITIES HAD TO CLEAN UP THE CITY FAST.

YOU JUST CANNOT SHUT DOWN NEW YORK CITY FOR EVEN AN HOUR-- THE GLOBAL MARKET BUTTERFLY EFFECT WOULD BE ASTRONOMICAL!

SO THEY HAD THESE BEAUTIFUL WEAPONS PULLED OFF THE STREETS AND SHOVED INTO HIDDEN WAREHOUSES JUST LIKE THIS ONE.

AND BEFORE THE HEROES AND THE AUTHORITIES COULD FIGURE OUT WHAT TO DO NEXT, THEY WERE ON TO THE NEXT CATASTROPHE.

SO HERE THEY SIT--WHAT'S LEFT OF THE RED SKULL'S MAGNIFICENT ARMY.

THIS TECHNOLOGY, THIS WEAPONRY, IS, I AM TOLD, AN ENTIRE GENERATION AHEAD OF ANYTHING THAT THE ARMED FORCES OF THE UNITED STATES IS USING.

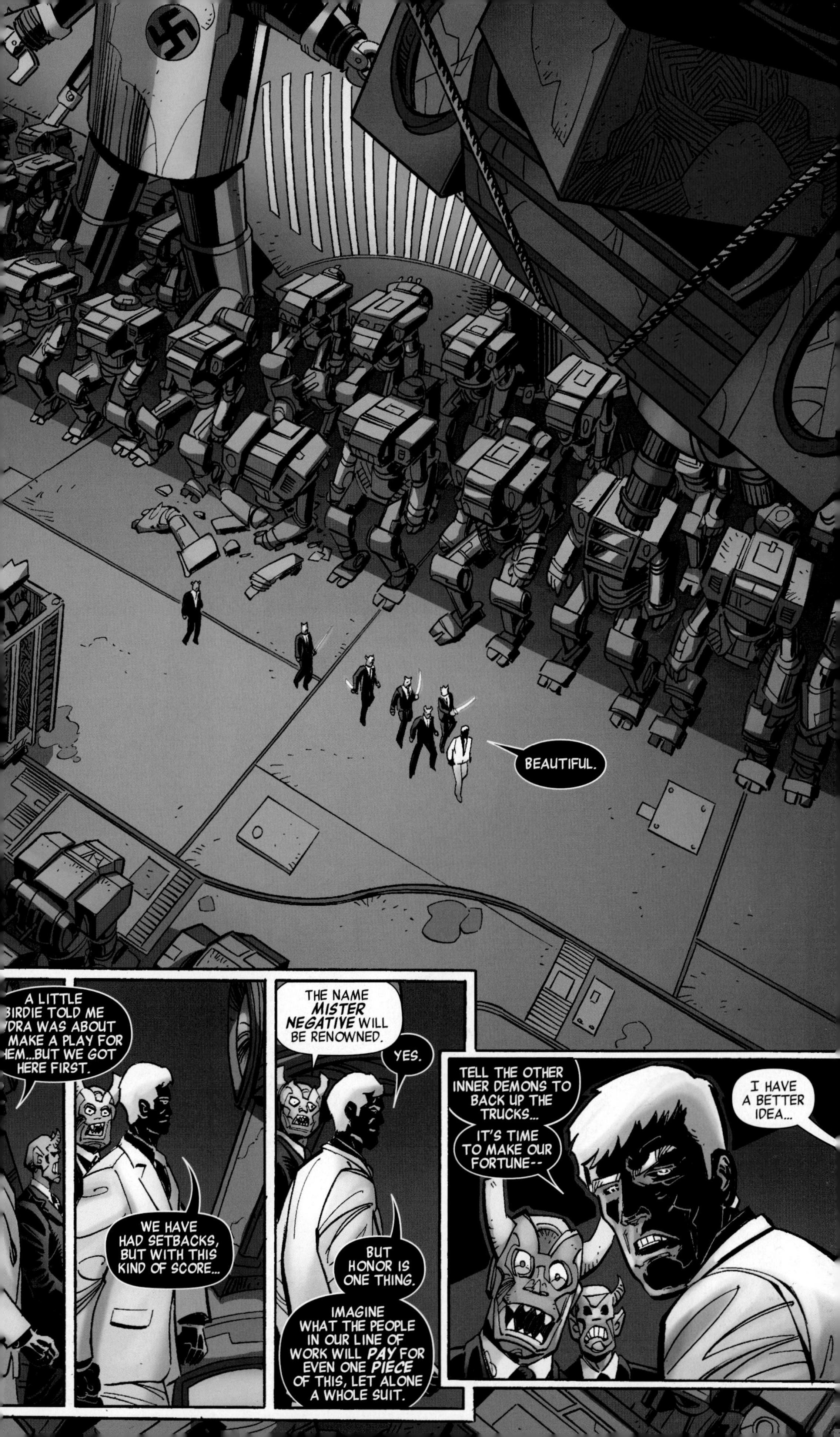
BEAUTIFUL.
A LITTLE BIRDIE TOLD ME YDRA WAS ABOUT MAKE A PLAY FOR HEM...BUT WE GOT HERE FIRST.
WE HAVE HAD SETBACKS, BUT WITH THIS KIND OF SCORE...
THE NAME MISTER NEGATIVE WILL BE RENOWNED.
YES.
BUT HONOR IS ONE THING.
IMAGINE WHAT THE PEOPLE IN OUR LINE OF WORK WILL PAY FOR EVEN ONE PIECE OF THIS, LET ALONE A WHOLE SUIT.
TELL THE OTHER INNER DEMONS TO BACK UP THE TRUCKS...
IT'S TIME TO MAKE OUR FORTUNE--
I HAVE A BETTER IDEA...

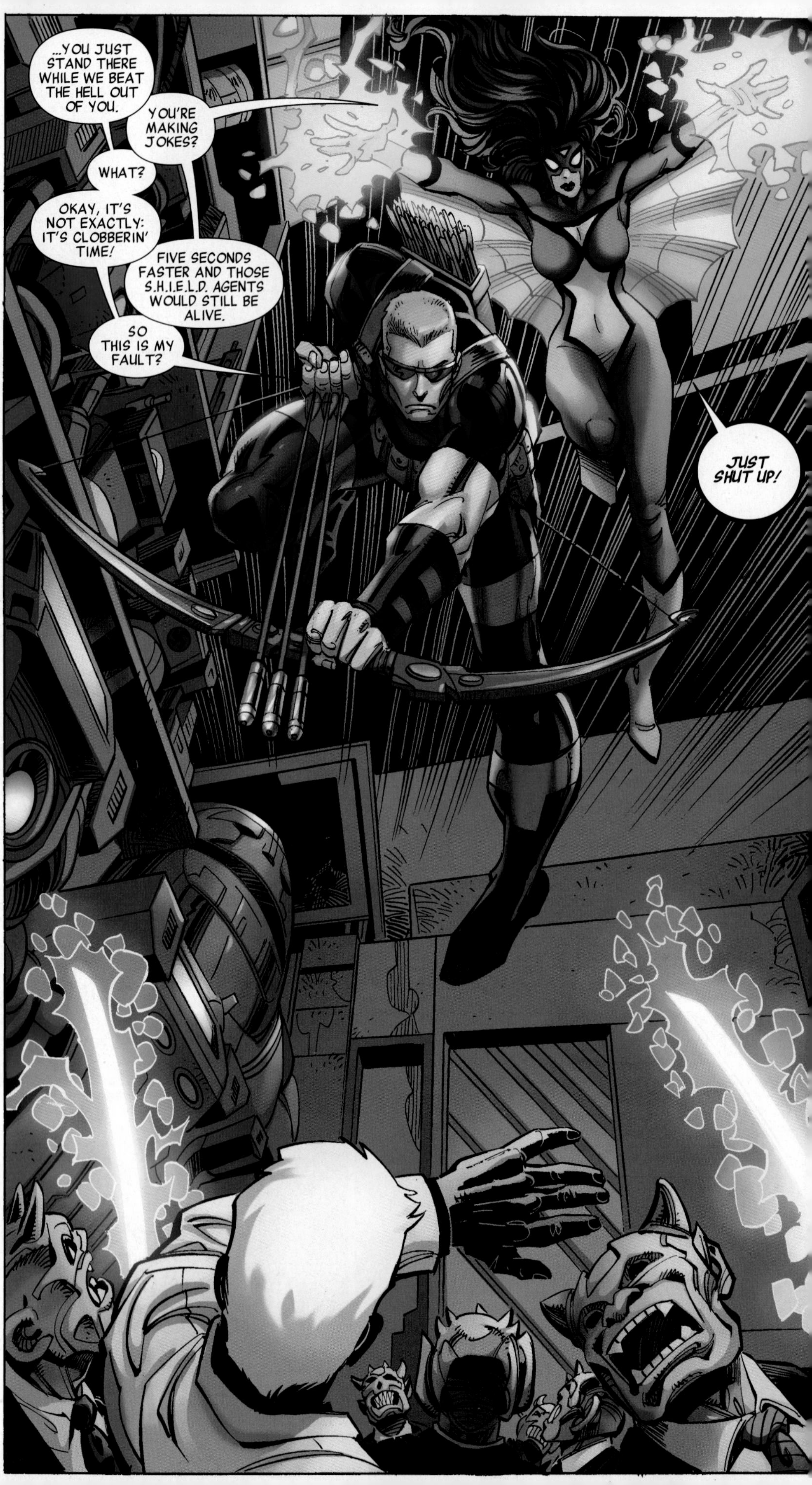
...YOU JUST STAND THERE WHILE WE BEAT THE HELL OUT OF YOU.
YOU'RE MAKING JOKES?
WHAT?
OKAY, IT'S NOT EXACTLY: IT'S CLOBBERIN' TIME!
FIVE SECONDS FASTER AND THOSE S.H.I.E.L.D. AGENTS WOULD STILL BE ALIVE.
SO THIS IS MY FAULT?
JUST SHUT UP!

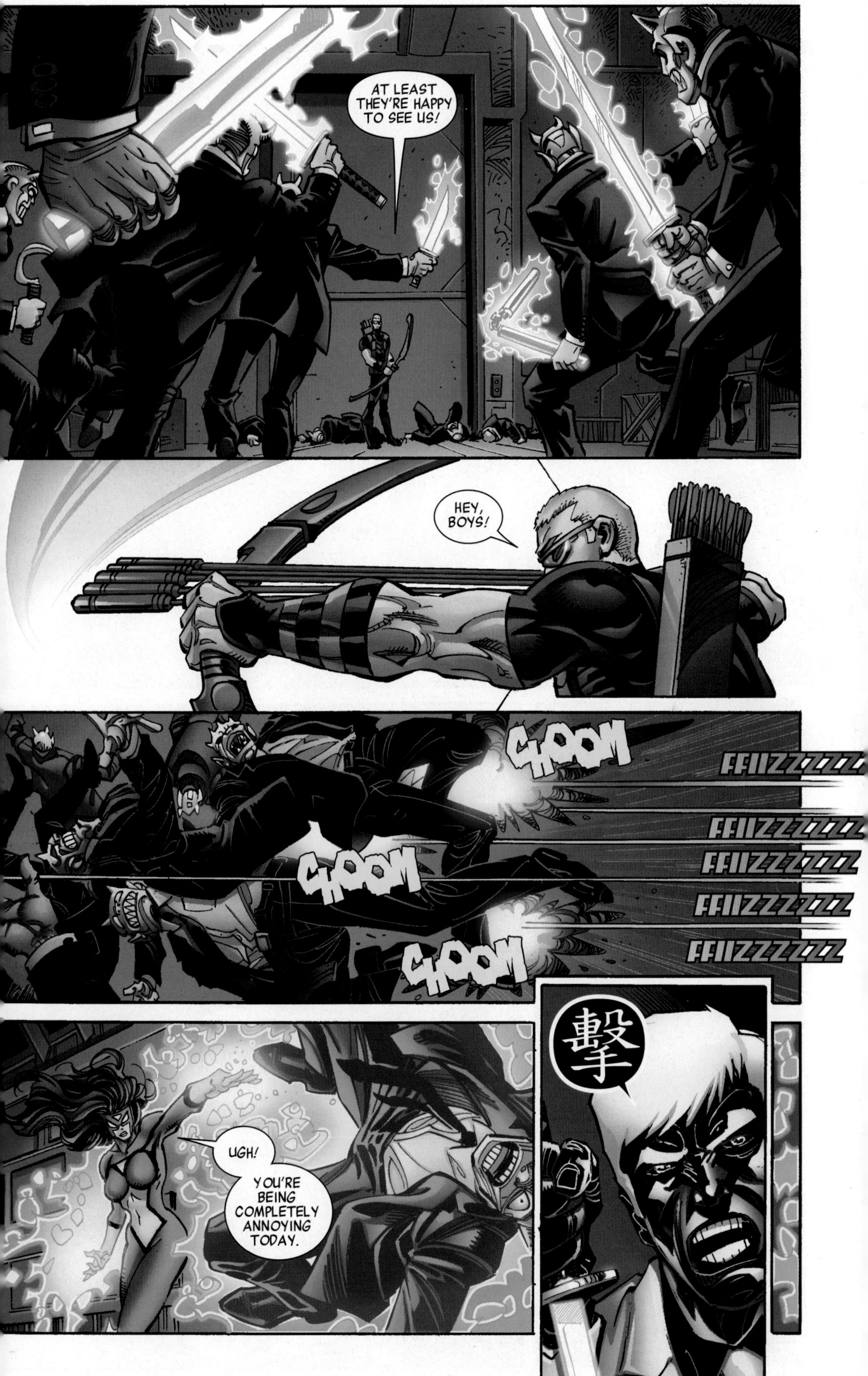
AT LEAST THEY'RE HAPPY TO SEE US!
HEY, BOYS!
CHOOM
FFIIZZZZZZZ
FFIIZZZZZZZ
CHOOM
FFIIZZZZZZZ
FFIIZZZZZZZ
CHOOM
FFIIZZZZZZZ
擊
UGH!
YOU'RE BEING COMPLETELY ANNOYING TODAY.

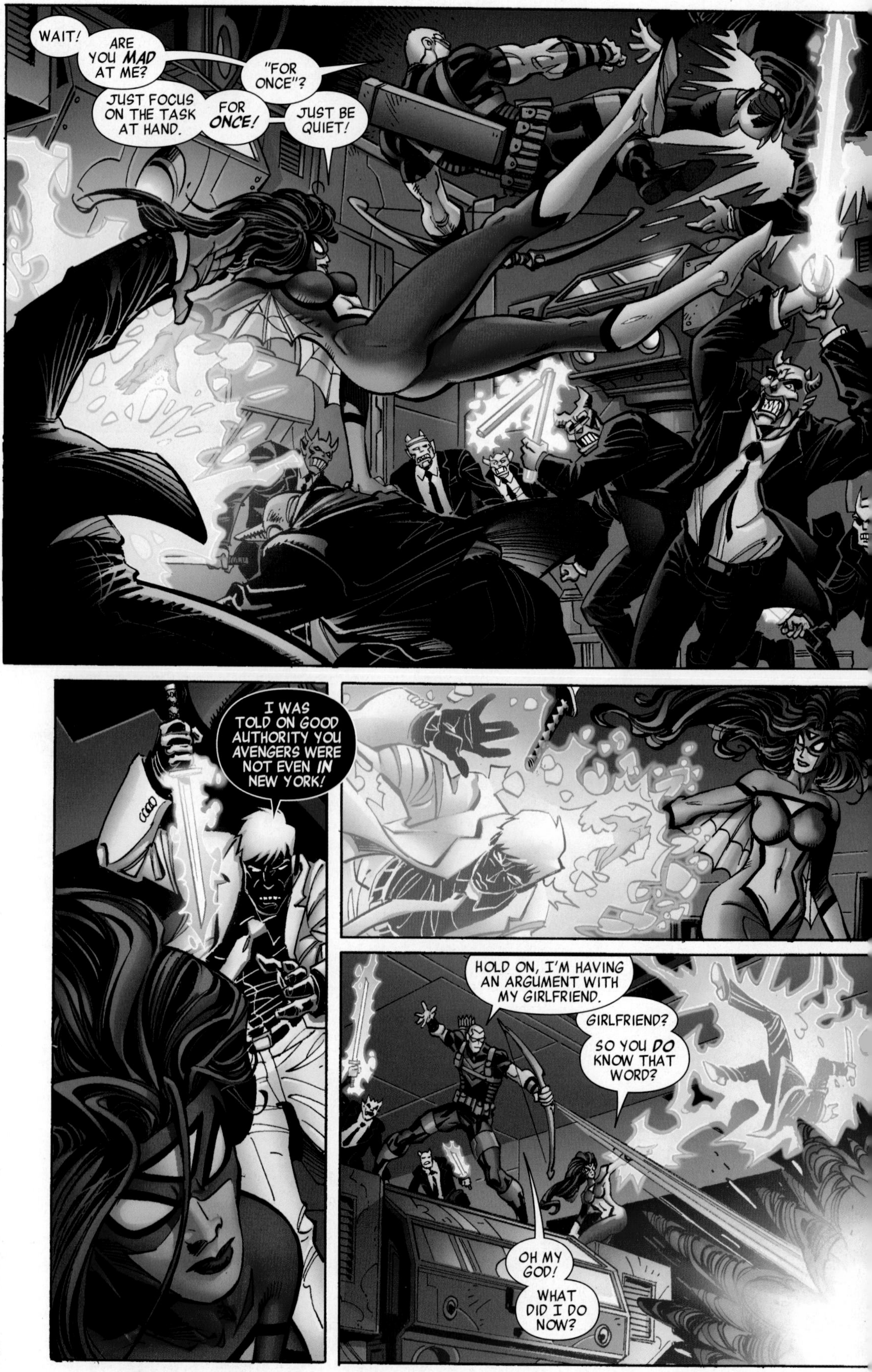
WAIT!
ARE YOU MAD AT ME?
"FOR ONCE"?
JUST FOCUS ON THE TASK AT HAND.
FOR ONCE!
JUST BE QUIET!
I WAS TOLD ON GOOD AUTHORITY YOU AVENGERS WERE NOT EVEN IN NEW YORK!
HOLD ON, I'M HAVING AN ARGUMENT WITH MY GIRLFRIEND.
GIRLFRIEND?
SO YOU DO KNOW THAT WORD?
OH MY GOD!
WHAT DID I DO NOW?

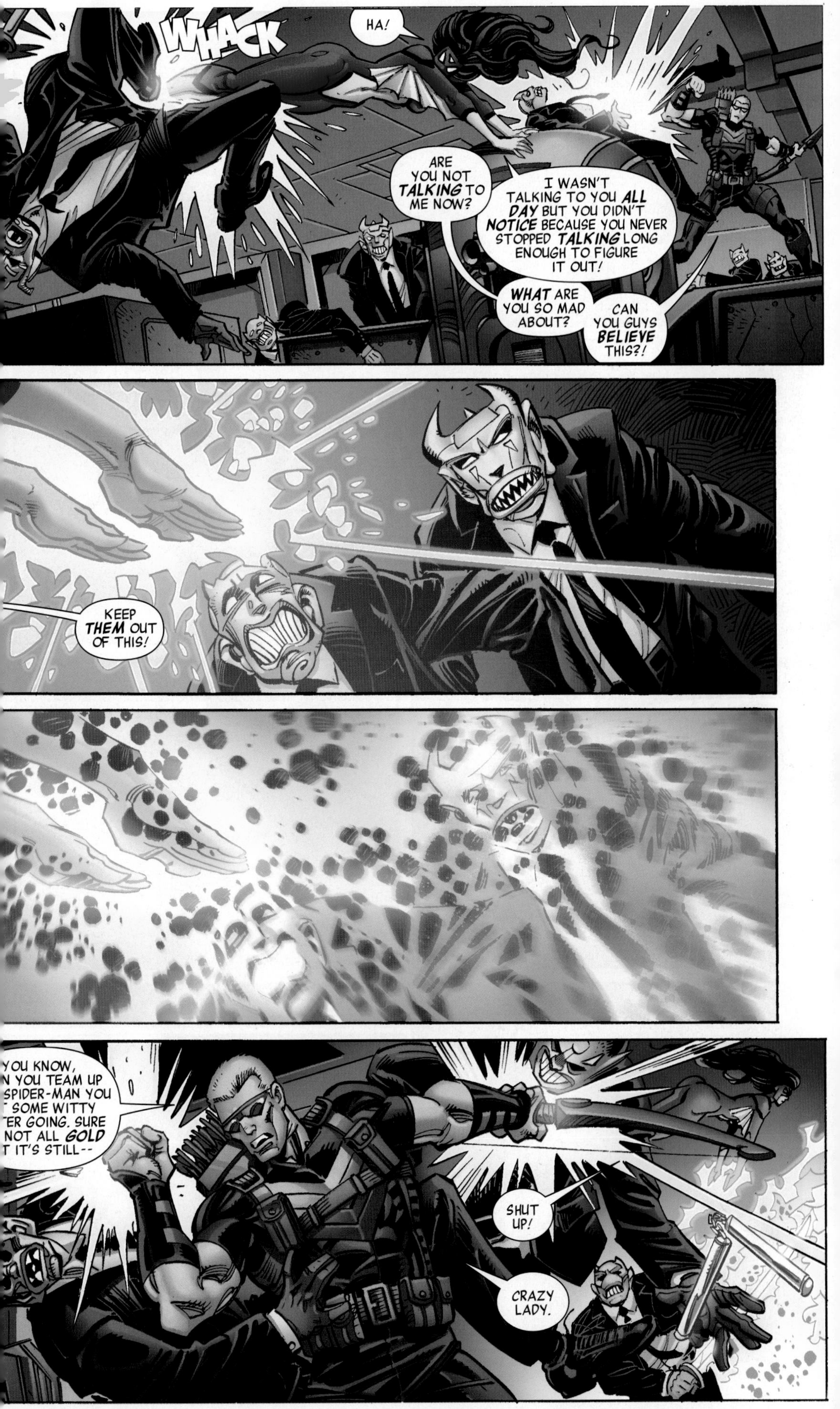
WHACK
HA!
ARE YOU NOT TALKING TO ME NOW?
I WASN'T TALKING TO YOU ALL DAY BUT YOU DIDN'T NOTICE BECAUSE YOU NEVER STOPPED TALKING LONG ENOUGH TO FIGURE IT OUT!
WHAT ARE YOU SO MAD ABOUT?
CAN YOU GUYS BELIEVE THIS?!
KEEP THEM OUT OF THIS!
YOU KNOW, N YOU TEAM UP SPIDER-MAN YOU T SOME WITTY TER GOING. SURE NOT ALL GOLD T IT'S STILL--
SHUT UP!
CRAZY LADY.

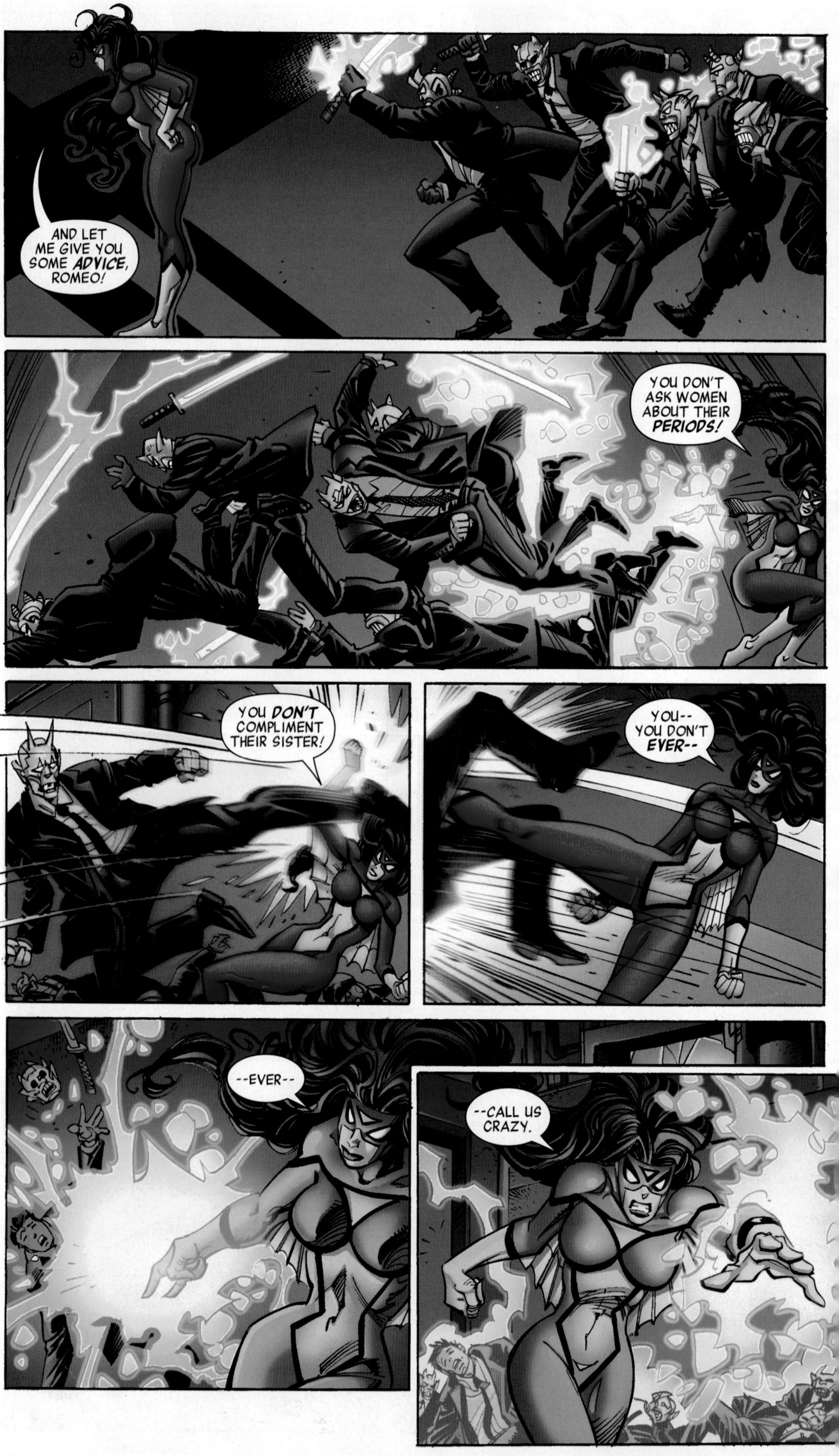
AND LET ME GIVE YOU SOME ADVICE, ROMEO!
YOU DON'T ASK WOMEN ABOUT THEIR PERIODS!
YOU DON'T COMPLIMENT THEIR SISTER!
YOU-- YOU DON'T EVER--
--EVER--
--CALL US CRAZY.

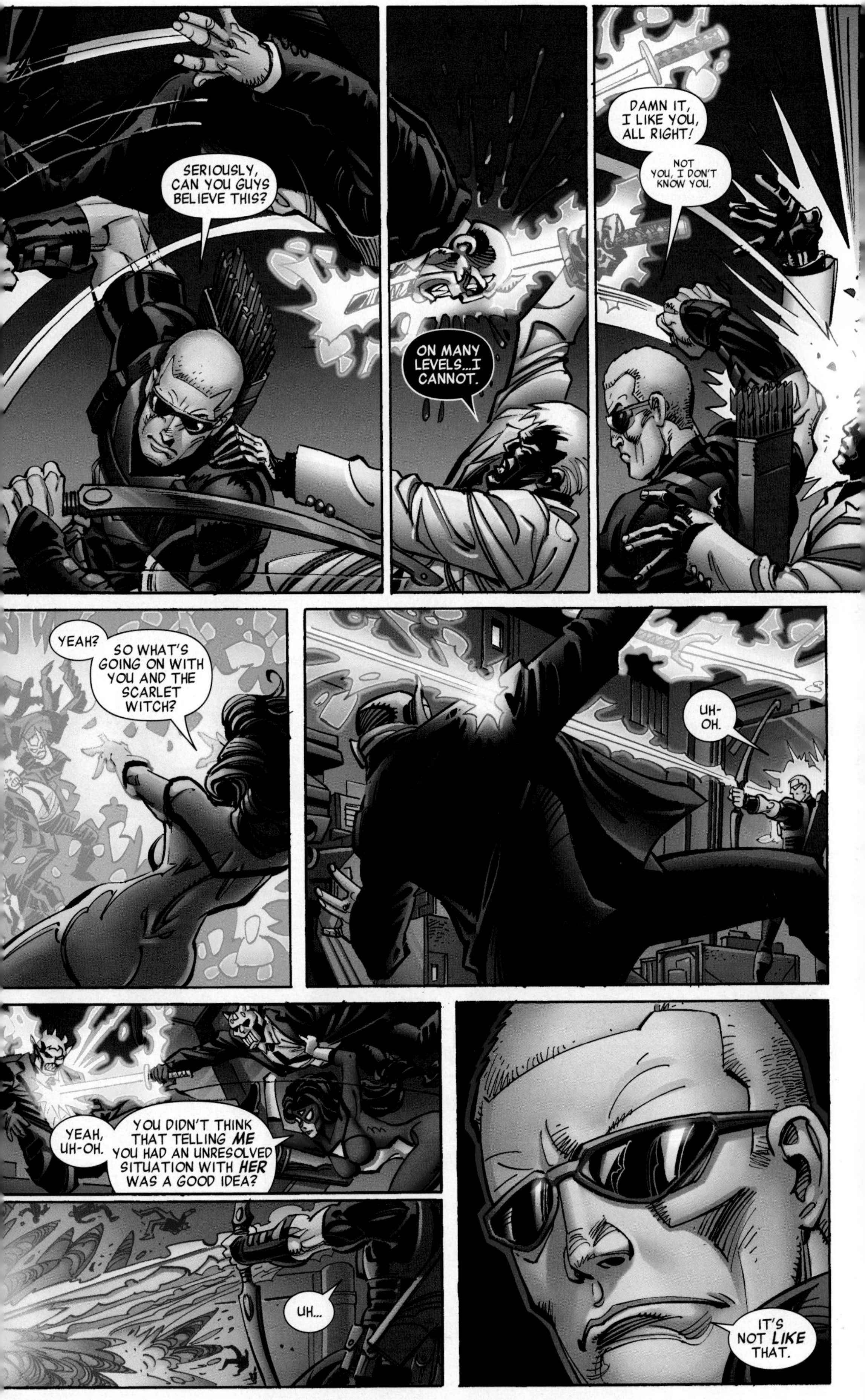
SERIOUSLY, CAN YOU GUYS BELIEVE THIS?
ON MANY LEVELS...I CANNOT.
DAMN IT, I LIKE YOU, ALL RIGHT!
NOT YOU, I DON'T KNOW YOU.
YEAH?
SO WHAT'S GOING ON WITH YOU AND THE SCARLET WITCH?
UH-OH.
YEAH, UH-OH.
YOU DIDN'T THINK THAT TELLING ME YOU HAD AN UNRESOLVED SITUATION WITH HER WAS A GOOD IDEA?
UH...
IT'S NOT LIKE THAT.

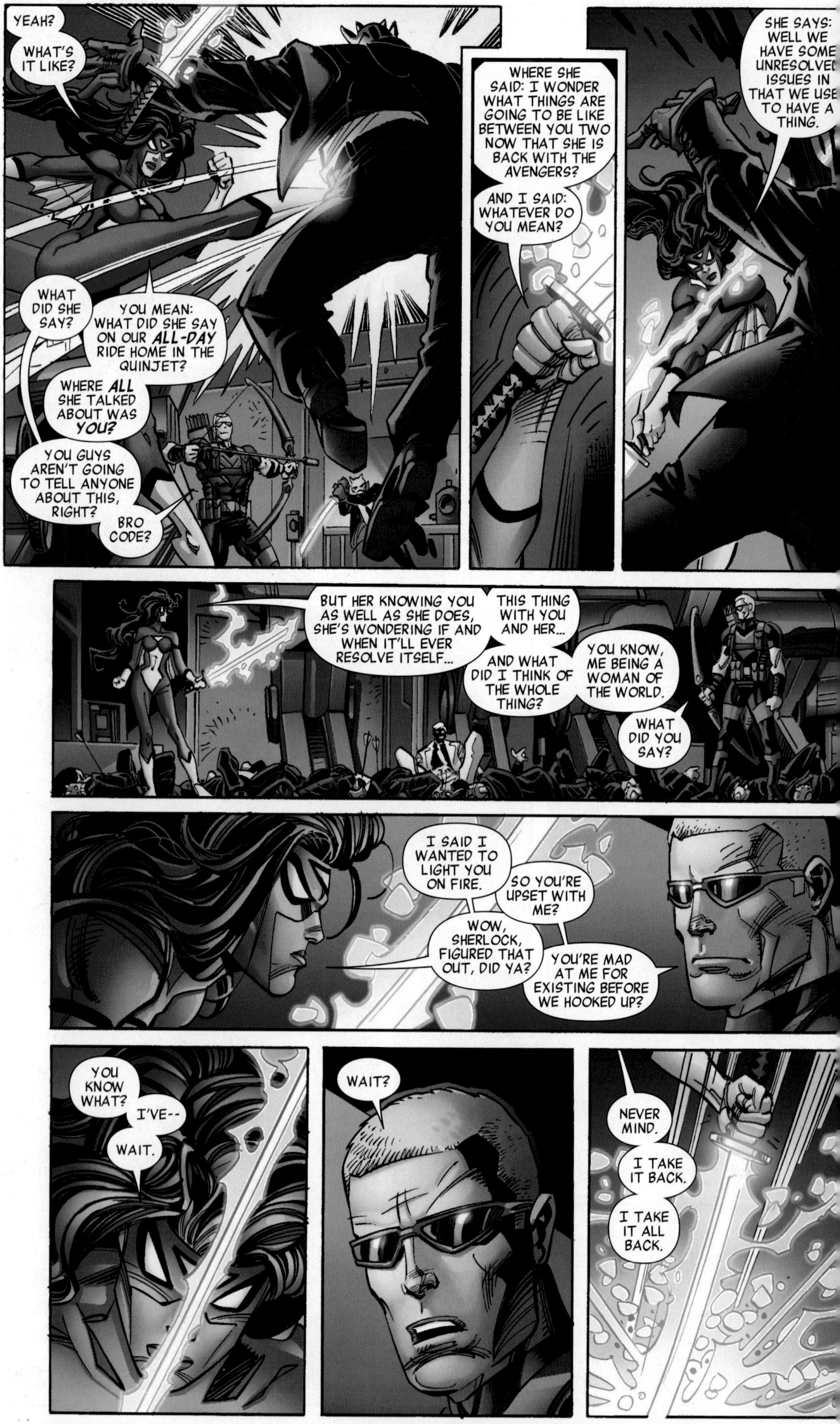
YEAH?
WHAT'S IT LIKE?
WHAT DID SHE SAY?
YOU MEAN: WHAT DID SHE SAY ON OUR ALL-DAY RIDE HOME IN THE QUINJET?
WHERE ALL SHE TALKED ABOUT WAS YOU?
YOU GUYS AREN'T GOING TO TELL ANYONE ABOUT THIS, RIGHT?
BRO CODE?
WHERE SHE SAID: I WONDER WHAT THINGS ARE GOING TO BE LIKE BETWEEN YOU TWO NOW THAT SHE IS BACK WITH THE AVENGERS?
AND I SAID: WHATEVER DO YOU MEAN?
SHE SAYS: WELL WE HAVE SOME UNRESOLVED ISSUES IN THAT WE USE TO HAVE A THING.
BUT HER KNOWING YOU AS WELL AS SHE DOES, SHE'S WONDERING IF AND WHEN IT'LL EVER RESOLVE ITSELF...
THIS THING WITH YOU AND HER...
AND WHAT DID I THINK OF THE WHOLE THING?
YOU KNOW, ME BEING A WOMAN OF THE WORLD.
WHAT DID YOU SAY?
I SAID I WANTED TO LIGHT YOU ON FIRE.
SO YOU'RE UPSET WITH ME?
WOW, SHERLOCK, FIGURED THAT OUT, DID YA?
YOU'RE MAD AT ME FOR EXISTING BEFORE WE HOOKED UP?
YOU KNOW WHAT?
I'VE--
WAIT.
WAIT?
NEVER MIND.
I TAKE IT BACK.
I TAKE IT ALL BACK.

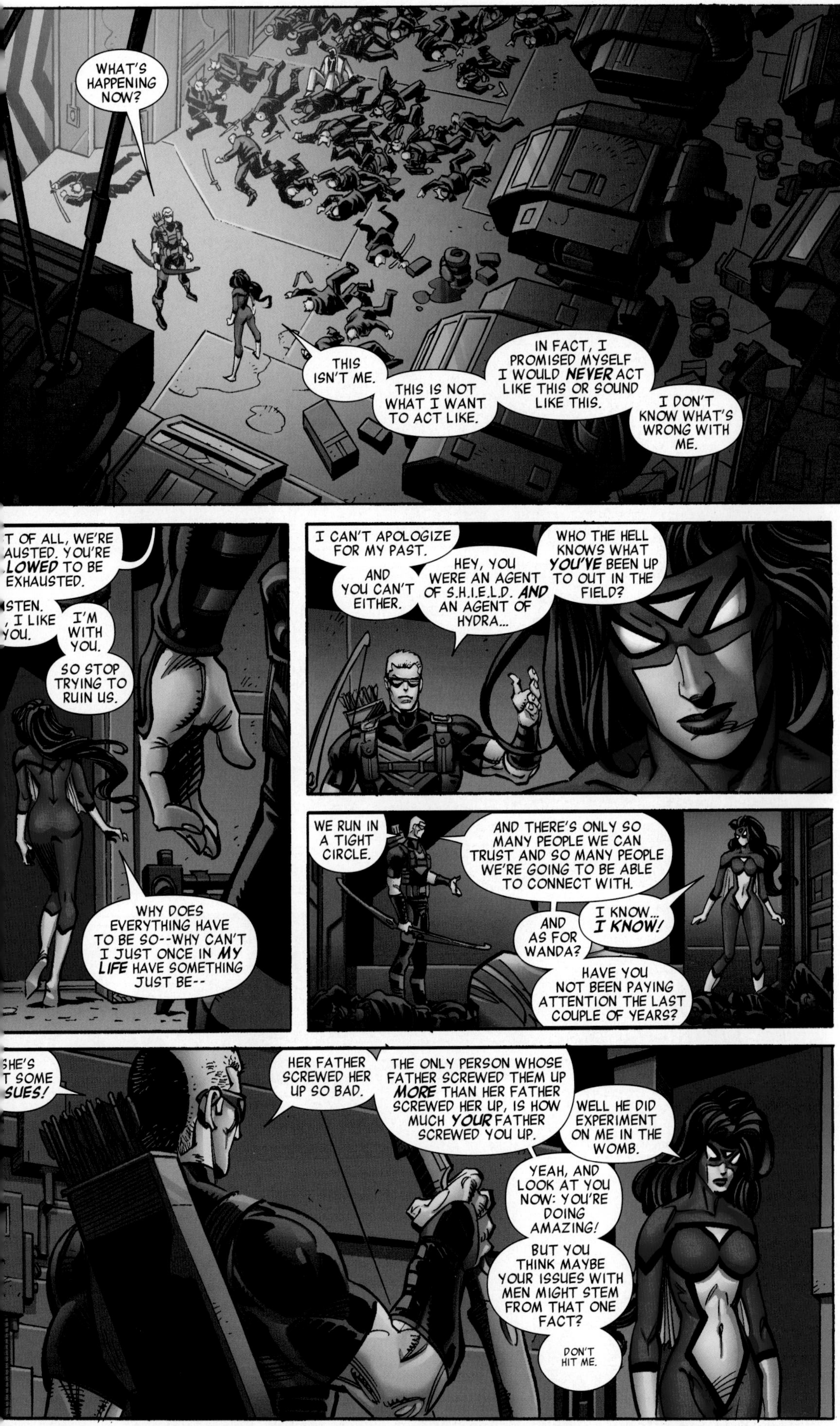
WHAT'S HAPPENING NOW?
THIS ISN'T ME.
THIS IS NOT WHAT I WANT TO ACT LIKE.
IN FACT, I PROMISED MYSELF I WOULD NEVER ACT LIKE THIS OR SOUND LIKE THIS.
I DON'T KNOW WHAT'S WRONG WITH ME.
T OF ALL, WE'RE AUSTED. YOU'RE LOWED TO BE EXHAUSTED.
STEN. , I LIKE YOU.
I'M WITH YOU.
SO STOP TRYING TO RUIN US.
WHY DOES EVERYTHING HAVE TO BE SO--WHY CAN'T I JUST ONCE IN MY LIFE HAVE SOMETHING JUST BE--
I CAN'T APOLOGIZE FOR MY PAST.
AND YOU CAN'T EITHER.
HEY, YOU WERE AN AGENT OF S.H.I.E.L.D. AND AN AGENT OF HYDRA...
WHO THE HELL KNOWS WHAT YOU'VE BEEN UP TO OUT IN THE FIELD?
WE RUN IN A TIGHT CIRCLE.
AND THERE'S ONLY SO MANY PEOPLE WE CAN TRUST AND SO MANY PEOPLE WE'RE GOING TO BE ABLE TO CONNECT WITH.
AND AS FOR WANDA?
I KNOW... I KNOW!
HAVE YOU NOT BEEN PAYING ATTENTION THE LAST COUPLE OF YEARS?
SHE'S T SOME SUES!
HER FATHER SCREWED HER UP SO BAD.
THE ONLY PERSON WHOSE FATHER SCREWED THEM UP MORE THAN HER FATHER SCREWED HER UP, IS HOW MUCH YOUR FATHER SCREWED YOU UP.
WELL HE DID EXPERIMENT ON ME IN THE WOMB.
YEAH, AND LOOK AT YOU NOW: YOU'RE DOING AMAZING!
BUT YOU THINK MAYBE YOUR ISSUES WITH MEN MIGHT STEM FROM THAT ONE FACT?
DON'T HIT ME.

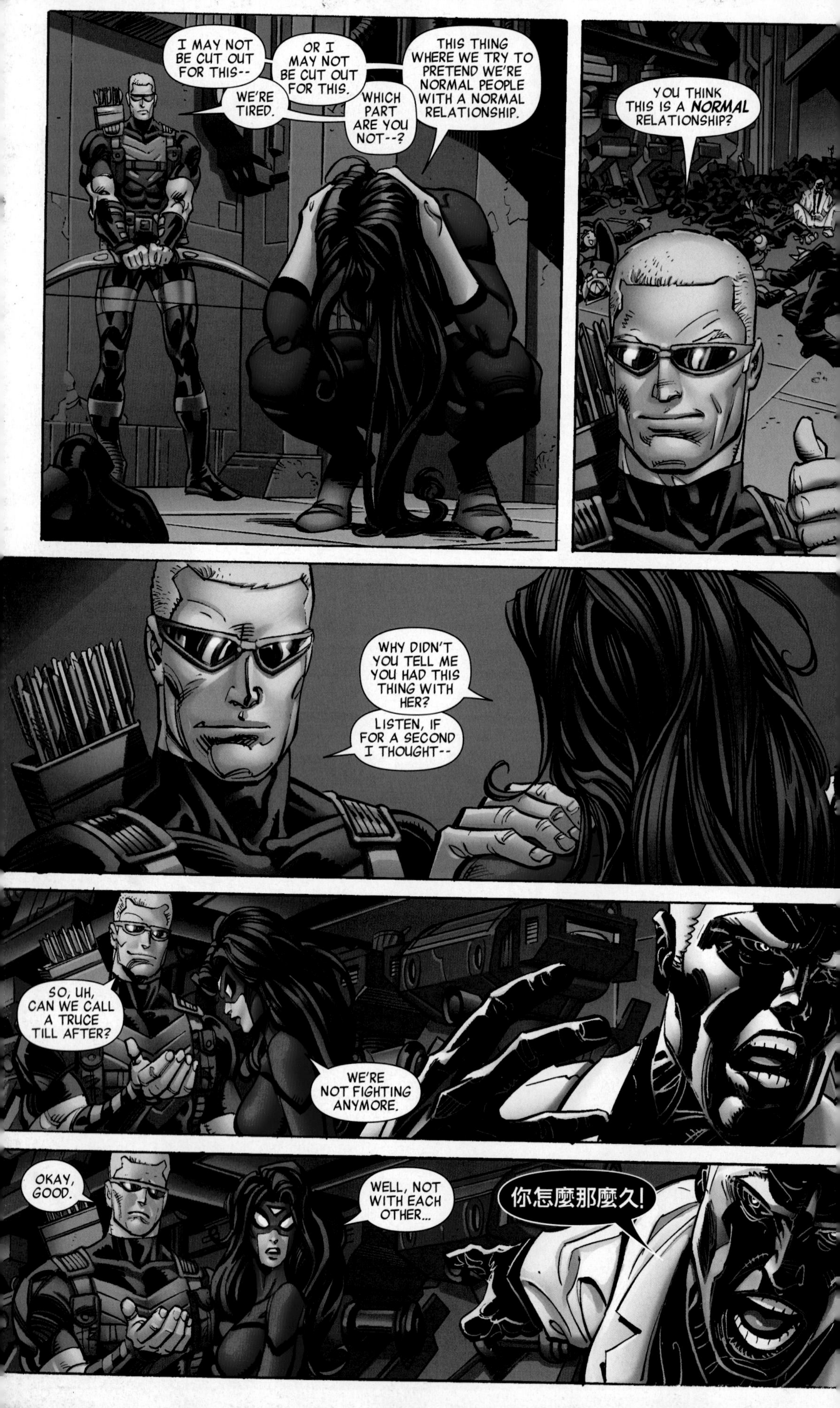

I MAY NOT BE CUT OUT FOR THIS--
OR I MAY NOT BE CUT OUT FOR THIS.
THIS THING WHERE WE TRY TO PRETEND WE'RE NORMAL PEOPLE WITH A NORMAL RELATIONSHIP.
WE'RE TIRED.
WHICH PART ARE YOU NOT--?
YOU THINK THIS IS A **NORMAL** RELATIONSHIP?
WHY DIDN'T YOU TELL ME YOU HAD THIS THING WITH HER?
LISTEN, IF FOR A SECOND I THOUGHT--
SO, UH, CAN WE CALL A TRUCE TILL AFTER?
WE'RE NOT FIGHTING ANYMORE.
OKAY, GOOD.
WELL, NOT WITH EACH OTHER...
你怎麼那麼久!

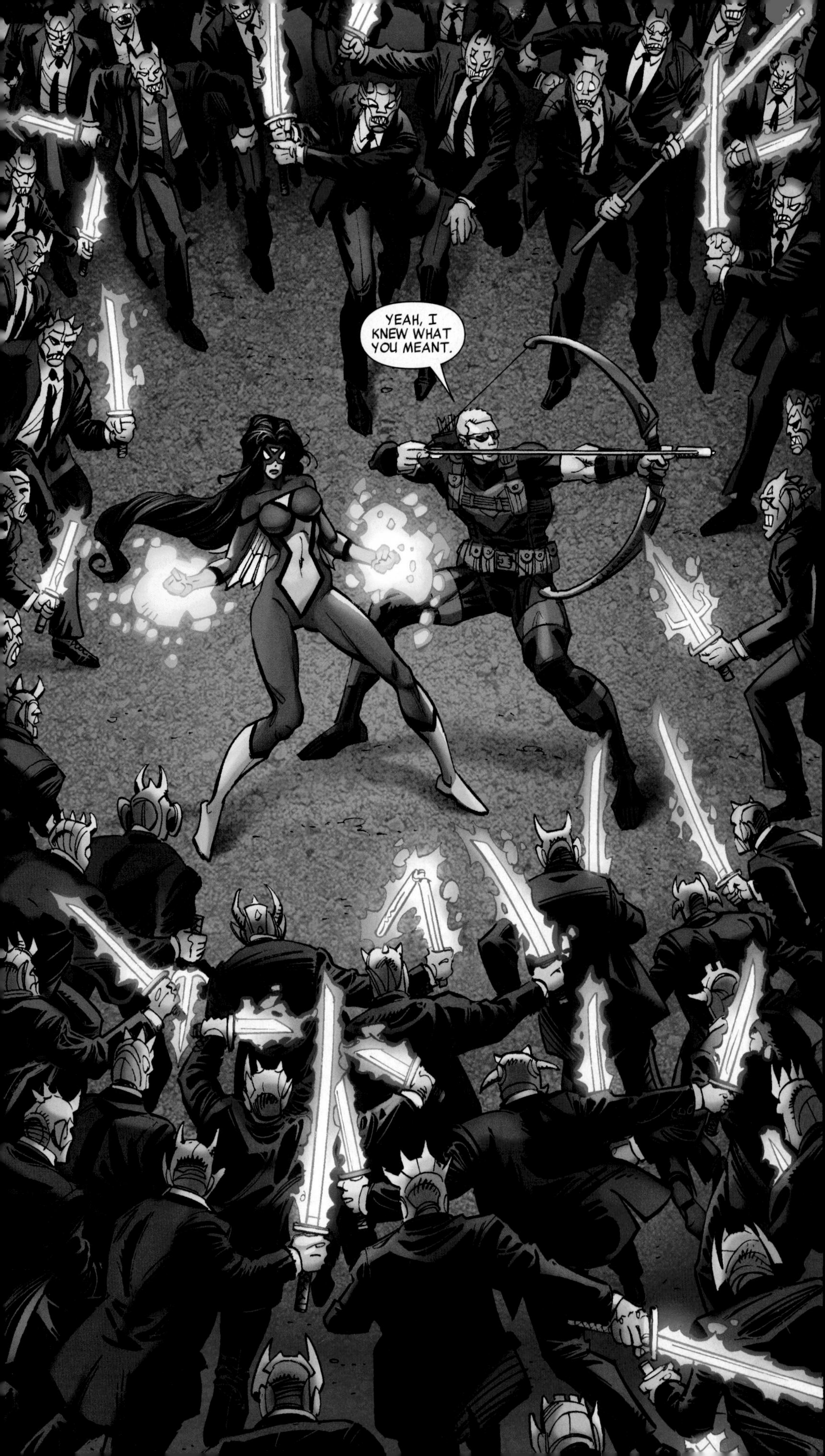
YEAH, I KNEW WHAT YOU MEANT.

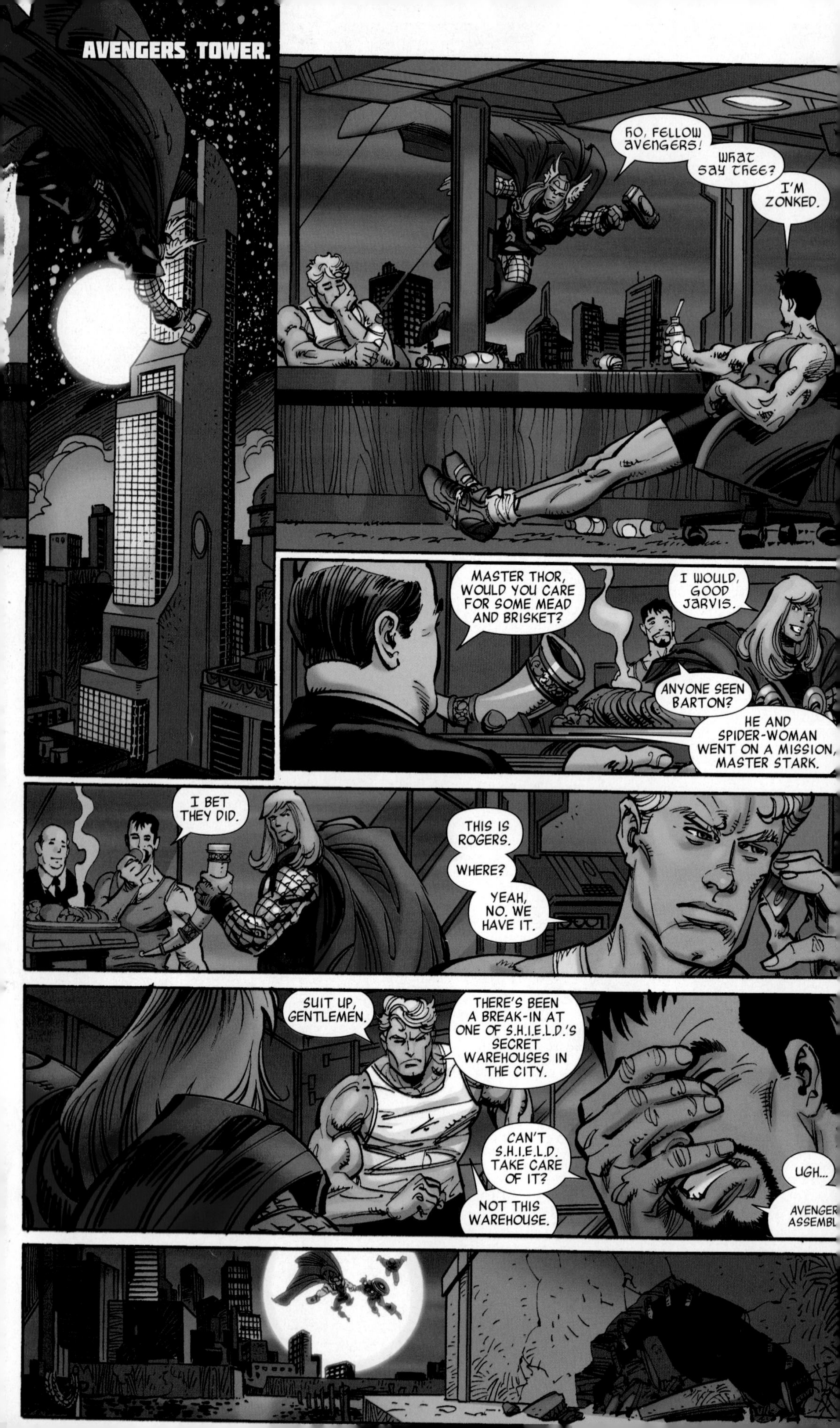
AVENGERS TOWER.
HO, FELLOW AVENGERS!
WHAT SAY THEE?
I'M ZONKED.
MASTER THOR, WOULD YOU CARE FOR SOME MEAD AND BRISKET?
I WOULD, GOOD JARVIS.
ANYONE SEEN BARTON?
HE AND SPIDER-WOMAN WENT ON A MISSION, MASTER STARK.
I BET THEY DID.
THIS IS ROGERS.
WHERE?
YEAH, NO. WE HAVE IT.
SUIT UP, GENTLEMEN.
THERE'S BEEN A BREAK-IN AT ONE OF S.H.I.E.L.D.'S SECRET WAREHOUSES IN THE CITY.
CAN'T S.H.I.E.L.D. TAKE CARE OF IT?
NOT THIS WAREHOUSE.
UGH...

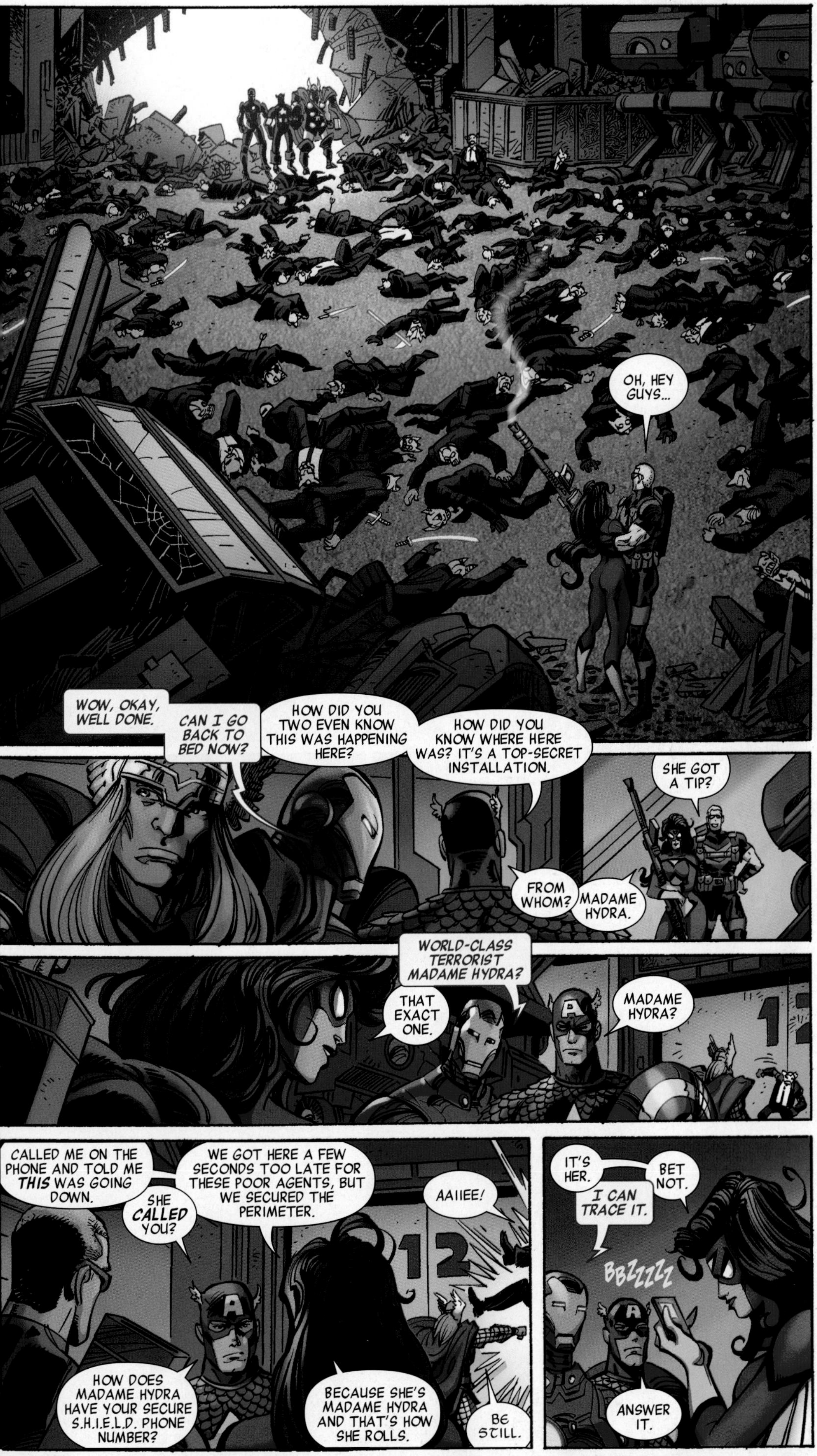
OH, HEY GUYS...
WOW, OKAY, WELL DONE.
CAN I GO BACK TO BED NOW?
HOW DID YOU TWO EVEN KNOW THIS WAS HAPPENING HERE?
HOW DID YOU KNOW WHERE HERE WAS? IT'S A TOP-SECRET INSTALLATION.
SHE GOT A TIP?
FROM WHOM?
MADAME HYDRA.
WORLD-CLASS TERRORIST MADAME HYDRA?
THAT EXACT ONE.
MADAME HYDRA?
CALLED ME ON THE PHONE AND TOLD ME THIS WAS GOING DOWN.
SHE CALLED YOU?
WE GOT HERE A FEW SECONDS TOO LATE FOR THESE POOR AGENTS, BUT WE SECURED THE PERIMETER.
AAIIEE!
HOW DOES MADAME HYDRA HAVE YOUR SECURE S.H.I.E.L.D. PHONE NUMBER?
BECAUSE SHE'S MADAME HYDRA AND THAT'S HOW SHE ROLLS.
BE STILL.
IT'S HER.
BET NOT.
I CAN TRACE IT.
BBZZZZZ
ANSWER IT.

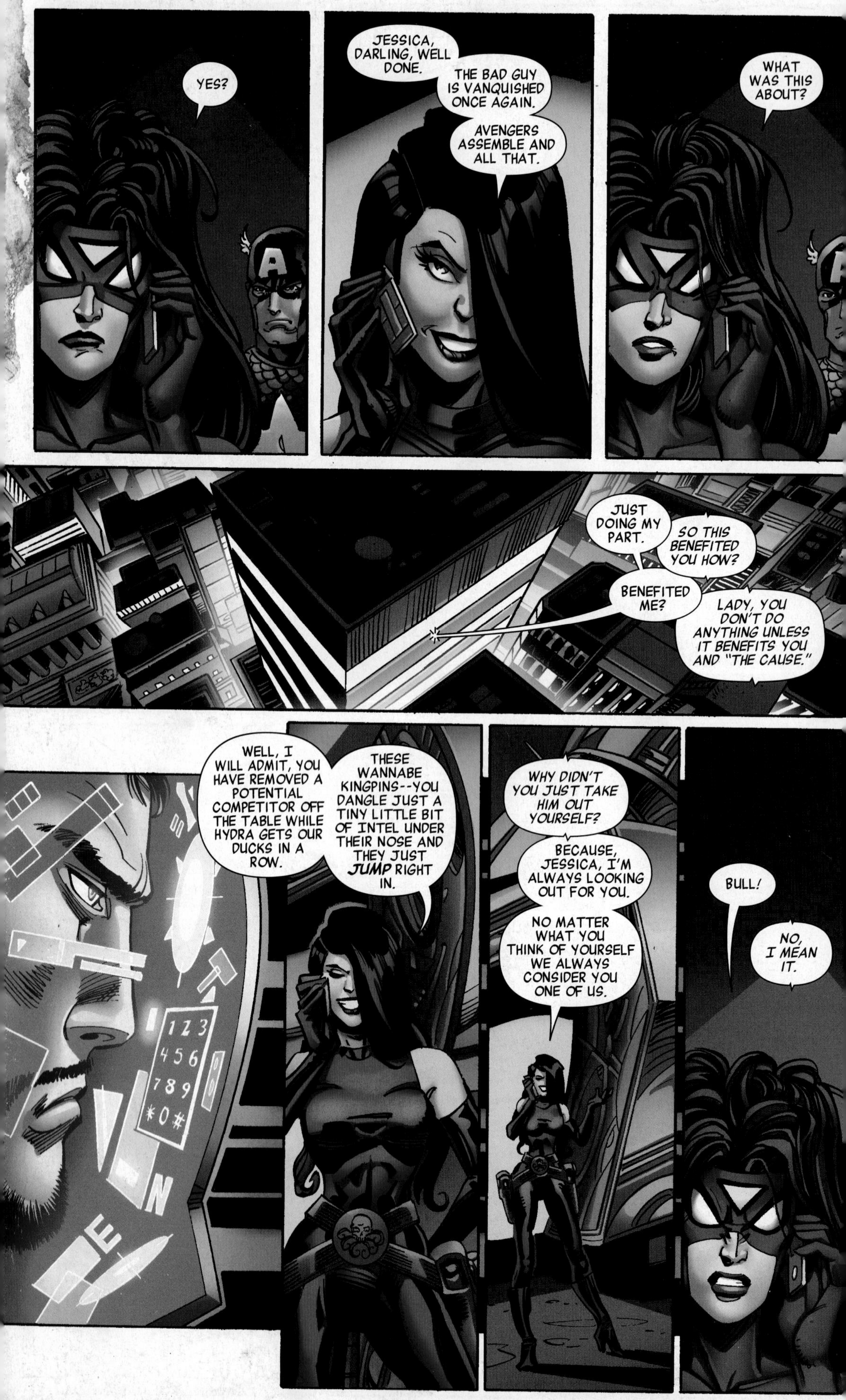
YES?
JESSICA, DARLING, WELL DONE.
THE BAD GUY IS VANQUISHED ONCE AGAIN.
AVENGERS ASSEMBLE AND ALL THAT.
WHAT WAS THIS ABOUT?
JUST DOING MY PART.
SO THIS BENEFITED YOU HOW?
BENEFITED ME?
LADY, YOU DON'T DO ANYTHING UNLESS IT BENEFITS YOU AND "THE CAUSE."
WELL, I WILL ADMIT, YOU HAVE REMOVED A POTENTIAL COMPETITOR OFF THE TABLE WHILE HYDRA GETS OUR DUCKS IN A ROW.
THESE WANNABE KINGPINS--YOU DANGLE JUST A TINY LITTLE BIT OF INTEL UNDER THEIR NOSE AND THEY JUST **JUMP** RIGHT IN.
WHY DIDN'T YOU JUST TAKE HIM OUT YOURSELF?
BECAUSE, JESSICA, I'M ALWAYS LOOKING OUT FOR YOU.
NO MATTER WHAT YOU THINK OF YOURSELF WE ALWAYS CONSIDER YOU ONE OF US.
BULL!
NO, I MEAN IT.

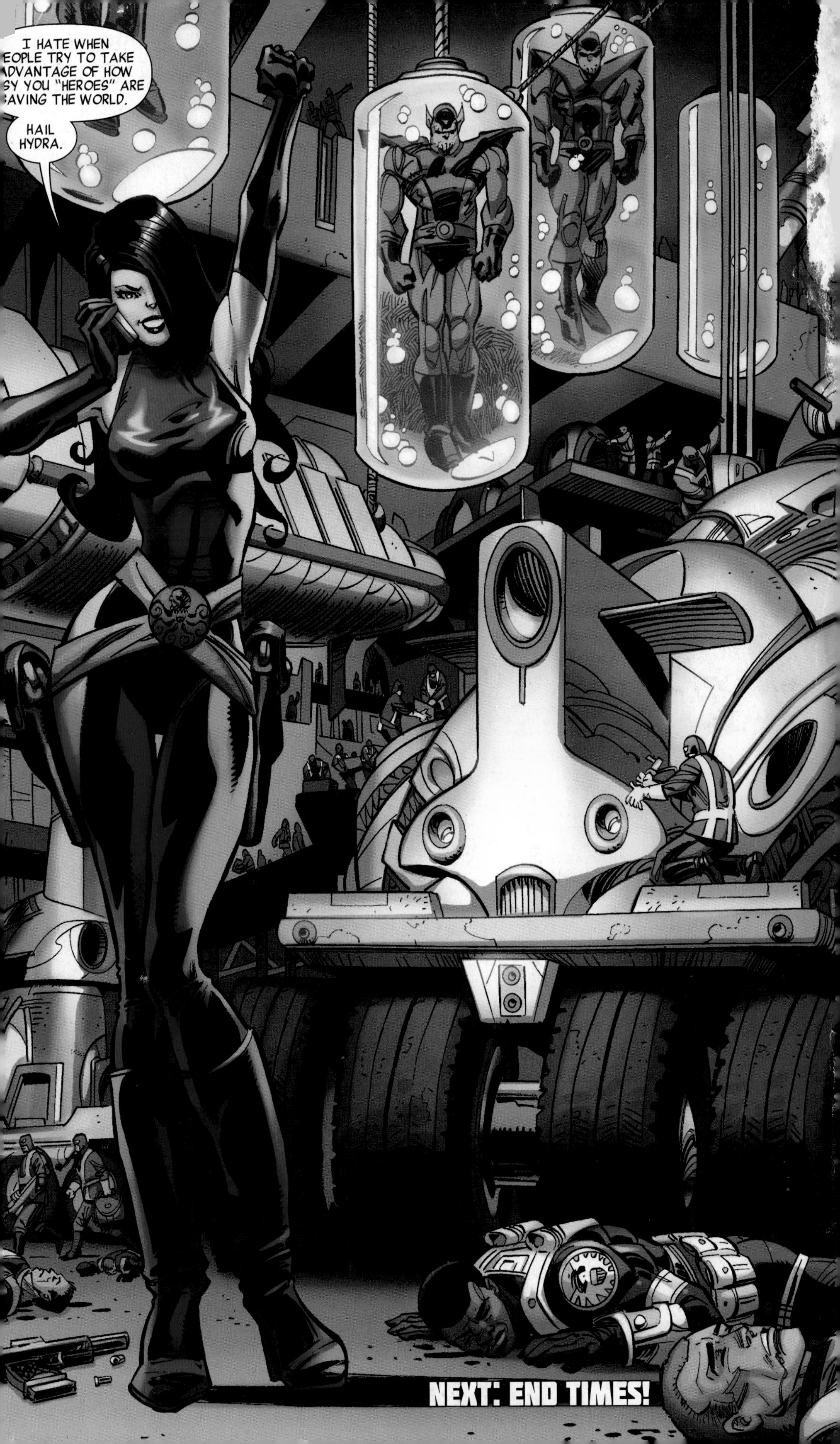
I HATE WHEN
EOPLE TRY TO TAKE
DVANTAGE OF HOW
SY YOU "HEROES" ARE
AVING THE WORLD.
HAIL
HYDRA.
NEXT: END TIMES!

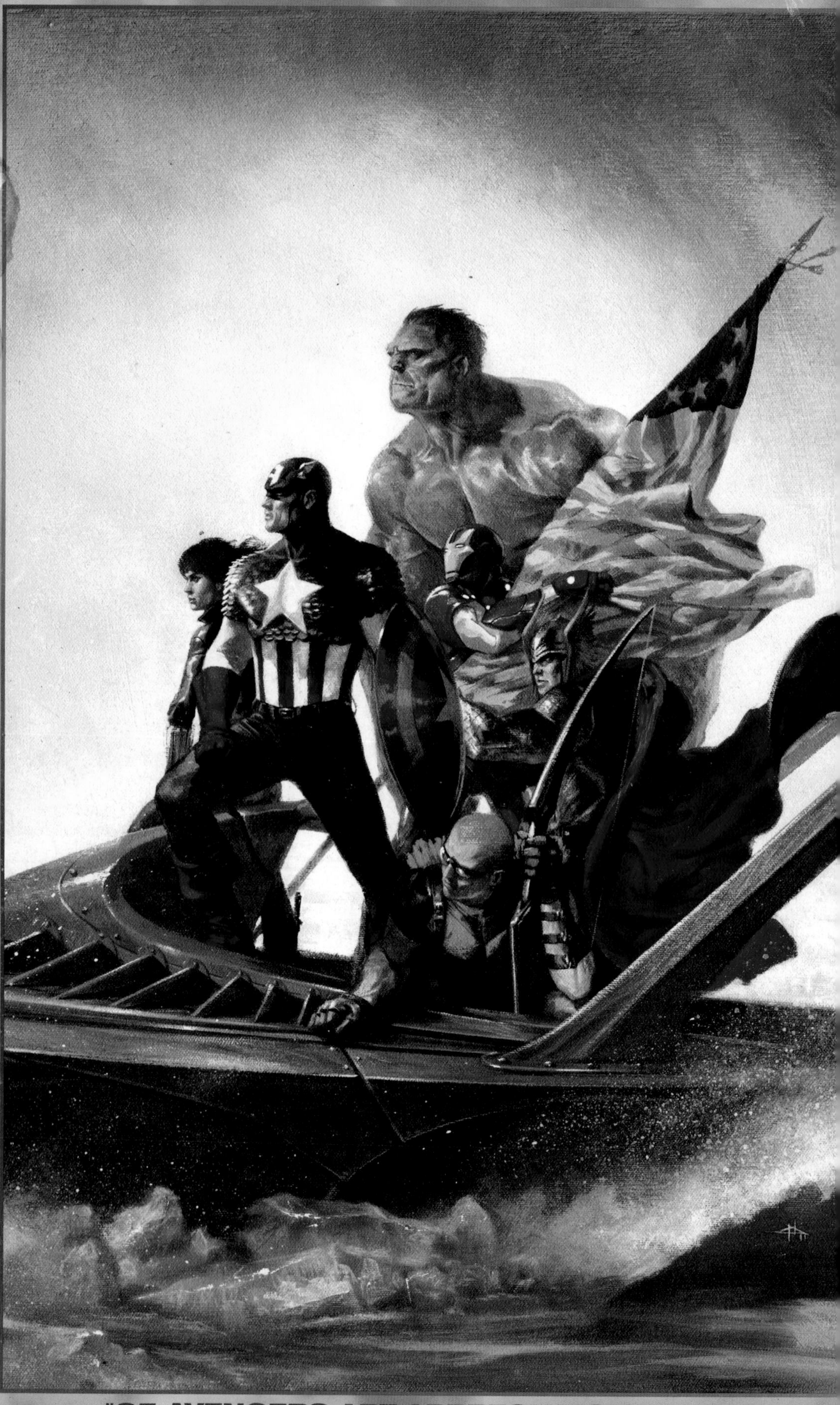

#25 AVENGERS ART APPRECIATION VARIANT
BY GABRIELE DELL'OTTO